Sensor Data Understanding

Marcin Grzegorzek

Bibliographic information published by the Deutsche Nationalbibliothek

The Deutsche Nationalbibliothek lists this publication in the Deutsche Nationalbibliografie; detailed bibliographic data are available on the Internet at http://dnb.d-nb.de .

ISBN 978-3-8325-4633-5

Logos Verlag Berlin GmbH
Comeniushof, Gubener Str. 47,
10243 Berlin
Tel.: +49 (0)30 42 85 10 90
Fax: +49 (0)30 42 85 10 92
INTERNET: http://www.logos-verlag.de

Contents

IV Conclusion 211

Preface

The rapid development in the area of sensor technology has been responsible for a number of societal phenomena. For instance, the increased availability of imaging sensors integrated into digital video cameras has significantly stimulated the UGC (User Generated Content) movement beginning from 2005. Another example is the groundbreaking innovation in wearable technology leading to a societal phenomenon called Quantified Self (QS), a community of people who use the capabilities of technical devices to gain a profound understanding of collected self-related data.

Machine learning algorithms benefit a lot from the availability of such huge volumes of digital data. For example, new technical solutions for challenges caused by the demographic change (ageing society) can be proposed in this way, especially in the context of healthcare systems in industrialised countries. The decision making process is often supported or even fully taken over by machine learning algorithms. We live in a data-driven society and significantly contribute to this concept by voluntarily generating terabytes of data everyday. This societal transformation cannot be stopped anymore. Our objective should be to gain as much benefit from this movement as possible by limiting possible risks connected to it.

The goal of this book is to present selected algorithms for Visual Scene Analysis (VSA, processing UGC) as well as for Human Data Interpretation (HDI, using data produced within the QS movement) and to expose a joint methodological basis between these two scientific directions. While VSA approaches have reached impressive robustness towards human-like interpretation of visual sensor data, HDI methods are still of limited semantic abstraction power. Using selected state-of-the-art examples, this book shows the maturity of approaches towards closing the semantic gap in both areas, VSA and HDI.

Another objective of this book is to sketch a scientific vision of a generic platform for holistic human condition monitoring. Based on the data delivered by sensors integrated in wearables (time series) and, if available, also images, the algorithms will continuously analyse humans' physical, cognitive, emotional and social states/activities. Integrated into a single module for holistic human health monitoring, the software platform will perform a long-term analysis of human data on a very large scale. Intelligent algorithms will automatically detect "interesting events" in these data. Both real-time data analysis and as cumulative assessments will be possible with the platform. The conceptualisation and development of these machine learning algorithms for the recognition of patterns in humans' physiological and behavioural data will happen on different levels of abstraction between the methodology and application.

This book is designated for an interdisciplinary audience who would like to use machine learning techniques to solve problems from the areas of visual scene analysis as well as human data interpretation. Ideally, the book will provide helpful background and guidance to researchers, undergraduate or graduate students, or practitioners who want to incorporate the ideas into their own work. On the one hand, it aims to show the technical feasibility of machine learning techniques towards automatic interpretation of multimodal sensory data. On the other hand, it warns society to carefully monitor the implications of the rapid developments in this area.

I would like to thank all members of the Research Group for Pattern Recognition at the University of Siegen for proofreading this book and providing valuable discussions which helped me to improve it. My special thanks goes to Zeyd Boukhers, Ahmad Delforouzi, Muhammad Hassan Khan, Kristin Klaas, Lukas Köping, Frédéric Li, Przemysław Łagodziński, Kimiaki Shirahama, and Cong Yang. Last but not least, I would like to thank my family for being unfailingly supportive of this effort.

Marcin Grzegorzek

Part I

Introduction

Chapter 1

Fundamental Concept

Sensors are everywhere. By the early 2020s, their number will have already exceeded one trillion [5]. This is driven by falling sensor costs and new fabrication techniques enabling their significant miniaturisation. For example, the startup company mCube (`www.mcubemems.com`) creates motion sensors that are "smaller than a grain of sand" and envisions a world where motion sensors are embedded in "everything that moves".

The rapid development in the area of sensor technology has been responsible for a number of societal phenomena. For instance, the increased availability of imaging sensors integrated into digital video cameras has significantly stimulated the UGC (User Generated Content) movement beginning from 2005[1]. Another example is the groundbreaking innovation in wearable technology leading to a societal phenomenon called Quantified Self (QS), a community of people who use the capabilities of technical devices to gain a profound understanding of collected self-related data.

Huge and continuously increasing volumes of digital sensor data are collected everyday. For example, in June 2016, YouTube users were uploading 400 hours of new video content to the platform per minute[2]. However, the digital sensor data themselves do not provide the users with any added value. They need to be semantically interpreted (understood) in a particular application context to become useful.

The abstraction of digital sensor data towards their semantic understanding using automated algorithms is a challenging scientific problem. The so called semantic gap, the lack of coincidence between automatically extractable data features and human-perceivable semantic meanings [17],

---

[1] A video-sharing platform `www.youtube.com` got launched in February 2005.
[2] `https://www.domo.com/blog/data-never-sleeps-4-0`

must get bridged for this. A person's everyday life requires an immense amount of knowledge about the world. Much of this knowledge is subjective and intuitive, and therefore difficult to articulate in a formal way. Computers need to capture the same knowledge in order to behave in an intelligent way. One of the key challenges in artificial intelligence is how to get this informal knowledge into a computer [6]. In contrast to human experts from a certain application area (e.g., medical doctors), computers do not possess the context knowledge to interpret low-level digital data on a high-level of semantic abstraction (e.g., early diagnosis in medicine) [7].

One of the approaches towards closing the semantic gap aims at integrating knowledge bases called ontologies into the process of low-level data analysis [19]. However, the ontology generation process has been automated up to a certain limited level only which makes this strategy very time consuming. In addition, the integration of the high-level ontology-based reasoning techniques into the low-level data analysis algorithms usually requires the pattern recognition software to be customised towards the context model (application ontology) currently used [2]. This hinders the portability of such solutions across application domains [7].

Currently, the most widely investigated family of approaches aiming to reach high-level interpretations from low-level digital data is called deep learning [4, 6]. Generally, deep learning algorithms allow computers to learn from experience and understand the world in terms of a hierarchy of concepts, with each concept defined in terms of its relation to simpler concepts. By gathering knowledge from experience, this approach avoids the need for human operators to formally specify all of the knowledge that the computer needs. The hierarchy of concepts allows the computer to learn complicated concepts by building them out of simpler ones [7].

In this book, selected state-of-the-art approaches for Visual Scene Analysis (Part II) and for Human Data Interpretation (Part III) all aiming at reaching the highest possible level of semantic interpretation are presented and discussed. The author comprehensively contributed to most of the scientific results described in this book.

This chapter is structured as follows. In Section 1.1, the book is motivated on the application level and from the methodological point of view. Afterwards, the two main applications addressed by this book and in its author's current research, namely Active and Assisted Living (Section 1.2) as well as Digital Medicine (Section 1.3), are introduced. Section 1.4 presents an overall structural concept of the book identifying its author's contributions to the particular chapters.

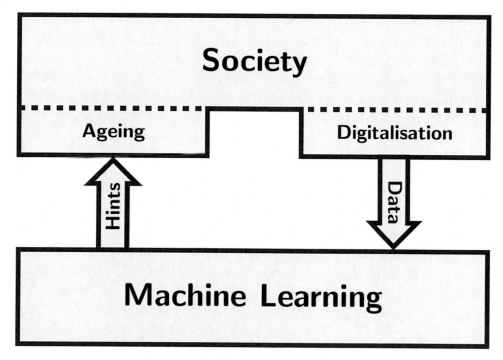

Figure 1.1: The trend towards a digital society results in a huge volume of sensor data generated everyday. These pieces of data improve the performance of machine learning algorithms. In this way, new technical solutions to challenges caused by the demographic change (ageing society) can be proposed.

1.1 Motivation

The selection of applications (Active and Assisted Living as well as Digital Medicine, see Figure 1.4) addressed in this book and in its author's current research is motivated by main phenomena of modern societies. On the one hand, the demographic change leading to society ageing, alongside the shortage of medical staff (especially in rural areas), critically challenges healthcare systems in industrialised countries in their conventional form [7]. On the other hand, the trend towards a digital society (digitalisation) progresses with tremendous speed, so that more and more health-related data is available in digital form. As large volumes of data improve the performance of machine learning algorithms, new technical solutions for problems caused by the demographic change (ageing society) can be proposed (Figure 1.1).

From the methodological point of view, this book presents and reviews selected state-of-the-art algorithms for automatic sensor data understanding. While in the area of image and video analysis (Part II: Visual Scene Analysis) the semantic gap has already been closed up to an impressive grade, the semantic interpretation of human-centred data recorded by sensors embedded in wearable devices (Part II: Human Data Interpretation) has still not reached a satisfactory level [17]. However, the analysis of visual data (2D, 2.5D, or 3D images or videos) and the processing of human-centred sensor data (mostly 1D time series) share the same methodological fundament. The difference is the heterogeneity of data sources. While algorithms for visual scene analysis can usually be built under the assumption of a stable and constant dimensionality of data, in case of human data interpretation the number of sensors available to the system can dynamically change over time. Moreover, the labelling process in the supervised training phase is more objective in case of visual scene analysis (e.g., manual naming of objects in a scene) as for human data interpretation, since human's physiological, emotional, and behavioural states are not always clearly distinguishable. Therefore, the main methodological motivation for this book is to present selected algorithms for Visual Scene Analysis (Part II) and Human Data Interpretation (Part II) and discuss their difference in the semantic interpretation power.

1.2 Active and Assisted Living

The well-established concept of Ambient Assisted Living (AAL) aims at[3]

- extending the time people can live in their preferred environment by increasing their autonomy, self-confidence and mobility;

- supporting the preservation of health and functional capabilities of the elderly;

- promoting a better and healthier lifestyle for individuals at risk;

- enhancing security, preventing social isolation and supporting the preservation of the multifunctional network around the individual;

- supporting carers, families and care organisations;

- increasing the efficiency and productivity of the resources used in the ageing societies.

---

[3]Source: www.aal-europe.eu

In the last years, the term AAL has been extended to Active and Assisted Living to emphasise the importance of physical, cognitive, and social activities for preserving health and functional capabilities of the elderly.

According to the Survey of Health, Ageing and Retirement in Europe (SHARE, www.share-project.org), retirement accelerates the physical, cognitive and mental decline and, therefore, has a negative effect on personal well-being. Staying active and social in retirement are important ingredients for healthy ageing. For seniors who no longer head out to work every day, it is more important than ever to find ways to stay active and to maintain social relationships. And doing so may help seniors ward off a number of health problems. However, finding opportunities for meaningful physical and cognitive activities within interesting social networks becomes increasingly difficult after retirement, especially in rural areas.

The relevance of technical solutions for AAL has continuously been increasing over the last years, especially due to the rapid development in the area of sensor and wearable technology. An example can be seen in Figure 1.2. The users of such sensor-based miniaturised systems are in a closed loop with technology. Human's physiological and behavioural data can be continuously recorded by wearables and automatically analysed by machine learning algorithms to provide the users with real-time guidance as well as recommendations for follow-up activities. In this way, the users can benefit from individualised training programmes optimised in terms of improving their physical, cognitive, mental, emotional and social well-being.

The author of this book has participated in several research projects related to Active and Assisted Living. One of them is summarised below.

In the project **Cognitive Village**[4] [15] funded by the German Federal Ministry of Education and Research and coordinated by Marcin Grzegorzek, technological, economic and social innovations as well as the participatory design approach are integrated into technical assistance systems enabling long-term independent living of elderly and diseased people in their own homes, and even in rural areas where well-developed infrastructure is often missing. Under careful consideration of ethical, legal and social implications as well as the users' real needs, the technical system is collecting digital data about the elderly's daily life provided by sensors voluntarily distributed in their homes as well as by wearables such as smartwatches, intelligent glasses and smartphones. These sensory data is then automat-

---

[4]www.cognitive-village.de

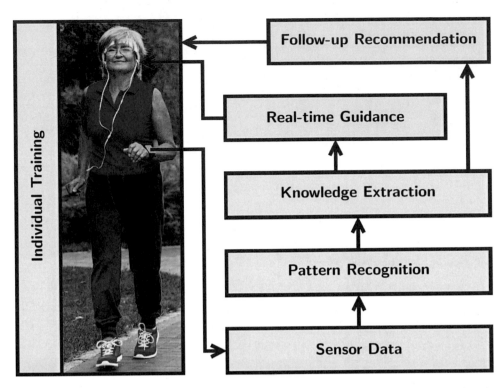

Figure 1.2: Continuous feedback loop between the user and the technology leading to personalised follow-up recommendation and individualised training. Photograph source: www.shutterstock.com.

ically processed, analysed, classified and interpreted by adaptive machine learning algorithms. The objective is to automatically achieve high-level semantic interpretation of activities as well as physical and cognitive states of the elderly for the detection of emergency situations with different criticality grades. Equipping the algorithms with adaptive properties (different users, behaviour changes over time) belongs to the most prominent scientific contributions of Cognitive Village from the machine learning and pattern recognition point of view. In addition, the system is required to cope with the dynamically reconfigurable sensor system delivering the data. The semantic gap in automatic data processing is reduced here by applying probabilistic methods for sensory data fusion, introducing adaptive learning mechanisms, integrating ontological background knowledge as well as probabilistic modelling and automatic detection of extreme events in the data. Deep learning strategies are also used in the Cognitive Village system.

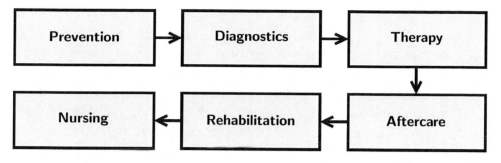

Figure 1.3: Steps of healthcare.

1.3 Digital Medicine

Currently, the patient care is conducted in functionally and geographically isolated medical facilities. It causes fragmentation of medical processes leading to media and technology gaps in the information flow. Missing interoperability of devices and data transfer interfaces is only an exemplary reason for this. A digital and patient-centred care consequently defined along all its steps would improve its medical quality and economic efficiency [7].

Considering the current degree of digitalisation over the healthcare stages depicted in Figure 1.3, the digitalisation has mainly been established in the diagnostics. Especially the modern medical imaging modalities and molecular approaches demonstrate the huge amount of digital data generated in today's healthcare systems for diagnostics. In the remaining healthcare steps, such as prevention or therapy, the degree of digitalisation in the treatment procedures has recently gradually increased [7].

The demographic change leading to society ageing alongside the shortage of medical staff (especially in rural areas) critically challenges healthcare systems in industrialised countries in their conventional form. For this reason, less cost intensive forms of data-driven algorithmically supported treatments will experience an extremely high scientific, societal and economic priority in the near future. Luckily, the digitalisation of our society progresses with a tremendous speed, so that more and more health-related data is available in digital form. For instance, people wear intelligent glasses or/and smartwatches, provide digital data with standardised medical devices (e.g., blood pressure and blood sugar meters following the standard ISO/IEEE 11073) or/and deliver personal behavioural data by their smartphones.

This huge amount of personal data generated every day significantly improves the accuracy of machine learning and pattern recognition algorithms aiming at a holistic assessment of the human health. Better understanding of human physical, mental and cognitive condition makes personalised and preventive interventions possible. However, the ethical, legal and social implications (short ELSI) of this trend must be analysed very carefully. For instance, data-driven precise medical profiles of patients may lead to ethically and legally completely unacceptable pricing models in health insurance.

The health-related digital data voluntarily generated by patients/users on a daily basis is automatically processed, analysed, classified and medically interpreted with support of semi-automatic machine learning and pattern recognition algorithms in a number of projects currently conducted by the author of this book. Two of them are shortly summarised below.

My-AHA[5] (My Active and Healthy Ageing) is an EU-funded project [14] which aims at preventing cognitive and functional decline of older adults, through early risk detection and tailored intervention. A multinational and multidisciplinary consortium is developing an innovative ICT-based platform to detect subtle changes in physical, cognitive, psychological and social domains of older adults that indicate an increased risk of a subsequent vicious cycle of disability and diseases, including dementia, depression, frailty and falls. For this, we develop, apply and investigate machine learning approaches for multimodal data understanding in the context of healthy ageing. Our activities follow the increasing level of semantic abstraction. On the low data classification level we apply and extend multiple existing approaches targeting concrete tasks such as sleep quality estimation, speech emotion analysis, gait analysis, indoor/outdoor localisation, etc. The outcomes of these low-level classifiers are then fused on the middle data analysis level to assess the cognitive, social and physical states of the elderly. Coming onto the high-level of semantic interpretation, the outcomes of the middle layer are fused and jointly analysed towards general multimodal state description of elderly in context of healthy ageing. These multidimensional elderly description profiles deal subsequently as inputs for a generic intervention model that, using concrete parameter values of a particular profile, provides a specific intervention programme optimised for a particular individual. The high heterogeneity of data sources is the main challenge for the pattern recognition software developed in My-AHA.

---

[5]`www.activeageing.unito.it`

In the project **SenseVojta** [8] funded by the German Federal Ministry of Education and Research and conducted in collaboration with the Children's Hospital in Siegen (Kinderklinik Siegen[6]), a sensor-based system for the support of diagnostics, therapy and aftercare following the so called Vojta Principle is developed [10, 11]. The Vojta Principle starts out from what is known as reflex locomotion. While looking for a treatment for children with cerebral palsy, Prof. Vojta observed that these children responded to certain stimuli in certain body positions with recurring motor reactions in the torso and the extremities. The effects of this activation were astonishing: Afterwards, the children with cerebral palsy could first speak more clearly, and after a short time they could stand up and walk more assuredly[7]. In Vojta Therapy, the therapist administers goal-directed pressure to defined zones on the body of a patient who is in a prone, supine or side lying position. In everyone, regardless of age, such stimuli lead automatically and involuntarily, i.e. without actively willed cooperation on the part of the person concerned, to two movement complexes: Reflex creeping in a prone lying position and reflex rolling from a supine and side lying position. Through therapeutic use of reflex locomotion, the involuntary muscle functions necessary for spontaneous movements in everyday life are activated in the patient, particularly in the spine, but also in the arms and legs, the hands and feet, as well as in the face. In this project, we develop a technical solution to support both, professional therapists as well as relatives (e.g., children's parents) performing the therapy. For this, different sensors (e.g., a Kinect camera visually observing the scene as well as wearables measuring the acceleration of extremities) are applied. Data acquired by these sensors is analysed and interpreted by the pattern recognition algorithms conceptualised and implemented in this project. The automatic sensor-based therapy interpretation provides real-time guidance to the therapists/parents. It also cumulatively monitors the therapy progress.

1.4   Outline and Contribution

Overall structural concept of the book relates to research areas investigated by its author in the last years and is depicted in Figure 1.4. The table of contents of this book is aligned to the methodological level (Level: Algo-

---

[6]www.drk-kinderklinik.de
[7]Source: www.vojta.com

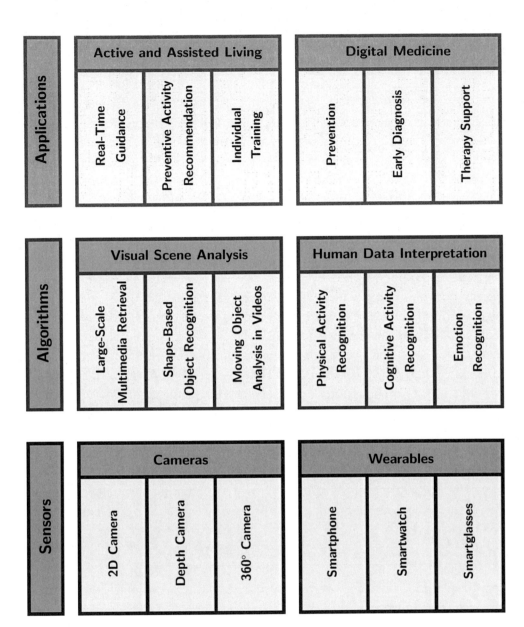

Figure 1.4: Overall concept of the book relates to research areas investigated by its author in the last years. The table of contents of this book is aligned to the methodological level (Level: Algorithms) and, apart from Introduction (Part I) and Conclusion (Part IV), is divided into two parts, Visual Scene Analysis (Part II) and Human Data Interpretation (Part III). Sensor data analysed by the algorithms described in this book are acquired by the mentioned cameras and wearable devices (Level: Sensors). From the application point of view (Level: Applications), Active and Assisted Living as well as Digital Medicine have played a crucial role in the author's research over the last years.

rithms) and, apart from Introduction (Part I) and Conclusion (Part IV), is divided into two parts, Visual Scene Analysis (Part II) and Human Data Interpretation (Part III). Sensor data analysed by the algorithms described in this book are acquired by the mentioned cameras and wearable devices (Level: Sensors). From the application point of view (Level: Applications), Active and Assisted Living as well as Digital Medicine have played a crucial role in the author's research over the last years.

Part II on Visual Scene Analysis is divided into three chapters. In Chapter 2, the scientific area of Large-Scale Multimedia Retrieval (LSMR) is reviewed. It is based on the survey article by Shirahama and Grzegorzek published in 2016 in the Multimedia Tools and Applications journal [17]. Chapter 3 provides an overview of shape-based object recognition. Its contents extend the Pattern Recognition journal article by Yang, Tiebe, Shirahama, and Grzegorzek published in 2016 [20]. In Chapter 4, video interpretation techniques based on the analysis of moving objects are described. The contents of this chapter have their origins in [1] recently accepted for publication in the IEEE Transactions on Circuits and Systems for Video Technology as well as in [3] published in the proceedings of the International Conference on Pattern Recognition 2016, both co-authored by Marcin Grzegorzek.

Part III on Human Data Interpretation also consists of three chapters. Chapter 5 deals with the topic of physical activity recognition using sensors embedded in wearable devices. It is partly based on three articles co-authored by Grzegorzek [9, 12, 18]. In Chapter 6, selected algorithms for cognitive activity recognition are described. Its content extends an article co-authored by Grzegorzek and recently accepted for publication in the Computers in Biology and Medicine journal [13]. Chapter 7 addresses the scientific area of emotion recognition and partly originates from [16] co-authored by Marcin Grzegorzek.

References

[1] Z. Boukhers, K. Shirahama, and M. Grzegorzek. Example-based 3D Trajectory Extraction of Objects from 2D Videos. *IEEE Transactions on Circuits and Systems for Video Technology*, 2017 (accepted for publication).

[2] T. Declerck, M. Granitzer, M. Grzegorzek, M. Romanelli, S. Rüger, and M. Sintek. *Semantic Multimedia*. Springer LNCS 6725, Heidel-

berg, Dordrecht, London, New York, 2011.

[3] A. Delforouzi, A. Tabatabaei, K. Shirahama, and M. Grzegorzek. Unknown Object Tracking in 360-Degree Camera Images. In *International Conference on Pattern Recognition*, pages 1799–1804, Cancun, Mexico, December 2016. IEEE.

[4] Li Deng and Dong Yu. *Deep Learning: Methods and Applications*. 2013.

[5] Joshua Ebner. How sensors will shape big data and the changing economy. *www.dataconomy.com*, January 2015.

[6] Ian Goodfellow, Yoshua Bengio, and Aaron Courville. *Deep Learning*. MIT Press, 2016.

[7] M. Grzegorzek. Medical Data Understanding. In J. Gołuchowski, M. Pańkowska, C. Barry, M. Lang, H. Linger, and C. Schneider, editors, *International Conference on Information Systems Development*, Katowice, Poland, August 2016.

[8] Principal Investigator. *SenseVojta: Sensor-based Diagnosis, Therapy and Aftercare According to the Vojta Principle*. German Federal Ministry of Education and Research (BMBF), 12/2016 – 11/2019.

[9] M. H. Khan, M. S. Farid, and M. Grzegorzek. Gait Recognition Based on Spatiotemporal Features of Human Motion. *Pattern Recognition*, 2017 (accepted for publication).

[10] M. H. Khan, J. Helsper, Z. Boukhers, and M. Grzegorzek. Automatic Recognition of Movement Patterns in the Vojta-Therapy Using RGB-D Data. In *The 23rd IEEE International Conference on Image Processing (ICIP 2016)*, pages 1235–1239, Phoenix, US, September 2016. IEEE.

[11] M. H. Khan, J. Helsper, C. Yang, and M. Grzegorzek. An Automatic Vision-based Monitoring System for Accurate Vojta-Therapy. In *The 15th IEEE/ACIS International Conference on Computer and Information Science (ICIS 2016)*, pages 1–6, Okayama, Japan, June 2016. IEEE.

[12] L. Köping, K. Shirahama, and M. Grzegorzek. A General Framework for Sensor-based Human Activity Recognition. *Computers in Biology and Medicine*, 2017 (accepted for publication).

[13] P. Łagodzinski, K. Shirahama, and M. Grzegorzek. Codebook-based Electrooculography Data Analysis Towards Cognitive Activity Recognition. *Computers in Biology and Medicine*, 2017 (accepted for publication).

[14] Project. *My-AHA: My Active and Healthy Ageing.* Website: www.activeageing.unito.it, European Commission (Horizon 2020), 01/2016 – 12/2019.

[15] Project. *Cognitive Village: Adaptively Learning Technical Support System for Elderly.* Website: www.cognitive-village.de, German Federal Ministry of Education and Research (BMBF), 09/2015 – 08/2018.

[16] K. Shirahama and M. Grzegorzek. Emotion Recognition Based on Physiological Sensor Data Using Codebook Approach. In E. Pietka, P. Badura, J. Kawa, and W. Wieclawek, editors, *5th International Conference on Information Technologies in Biomedicine (ITIB 2016)*, pages 27–39, Kamien Slaski, Poland, June 2016. Springer.

[17] K. Shirahama and M. Grzegorzek. Towards Large-Scale Multimedia Retrieval Enriched by Knowledge about Human Interpretation - Retrospective Survey. *Multimedia Tools and Applications*, 75(1):297–331, January 2016.

[18] K. Shirahama, L. Köping, and M. Grzegorzek. Codebook Approach for Sensor-based Human Activity Recognition. In *ACM International Joint Conference on Pervasive and Ubiquitous Computing*, pages 197–200, Heidelberg, Germany, September 2016. ACM.

[19] S. Staab, A. Scherp, R. Arndt, R. Troncy, M. Grzegorzek, C. Saathoff, S. Schenk, and L. Hardman. Semantic Multimedia. In C. Baroglio, P. A. Bonatti, J. Maluszynski, M. Marchiori, A. Polleres, and S. Schaffert, editors, *Reasoning Web*, pages 125–170, San Servolo, Island, September 2008. Springer LNCS 5224.

[20] C. Yang, O. Tiebe, K. Shirahama, and M. Grzegorzek. Object Matching with Hierarchical Skeletons. *Pattern Recognition*, 55:183–197, July 2016.

Part II

Visual Scene Analysis

Chapter 2

Large-Scale Multimedia Retrieval

Large-Scale Multimedia Retrieval (LSMR) is the task in which a large amount of multimedia data (e.g., image, video and audio) is analysed to efficiently find the ones relevant to a user-provided query. As described in many publications [55, 64, 69, 72], the most challenging issue is how to bridge the semantic gap which is the lack of coincidence between raw data (i.e., pixel values or audio sample values) and semantic meanings that humans perceive from this data. This chapter presents an overview of both traditional and state-of-the-art methods, which play principal roles in overcoming the semantic gap in LSMR.

2.1 Hierarchical Organisation of Semantic Meanings

First of all, by referring to Figure 2.1, let us define semantic meanings targeted by LSMR. Since events are widely-accepted access units to multimedia data, semantic meanings are decomposed based on basic aspects of event descriptions [53, 89]. As shown in Figure 2.1 (a), meanings are organised using three components, *concept*, *event* and *context*. Based on [53, 89], concepts form the participation (or informational) aspect of objects in an event. That is, the event is derived by relating multiple objects. Contexts are the collection of part-of, causal and correlation aspects among events.

More formally, concepts are defined as textual descriptions of mean-

19

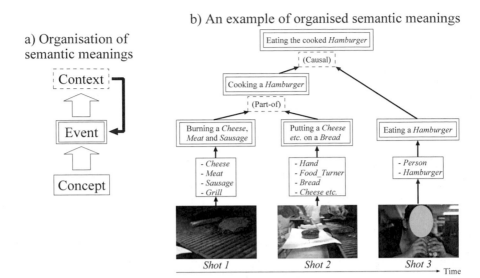

Figure 2.1: An illustration of decomposing meanings based on concepts, events and contexts [55].

ings that can be perceived from images, shots or videos, such as objects like *Person* and *Car*, actions like *Walking* and *Airplane_Flying*, and scenes like *Outdoor* and *Nighttime* [42, 66]. In other words, concepts are the most primitive meanings for multimedia data. Below, concept names are written in italics to distinguish them from the other terms. An event is a higher-level meaning derived from the interaction of objects at a specific situation [26, 63]. In this chapter, it is especially defined by the combination of concepts. For example, in Figure 2.1 (b), *Shot 1* shows *Cheese*, *Meat*, *Sausage* and *Grill*, from which the event "barbecuing" is derived. *Shot 2* displays *Hand*, *Food_Turner*, *Bread*, *Cheese* and so on, where the event "putting *Cheese* etc. on *Bread*" is formed based on movements of these concepts. Furthermore, as depicted by the bold line arrow in Figure 2.1 (a), contexts are used to recursively define higher-level events based on part-of, causal and correlation relations among lower-level ones[1]. In Figure 2.1 (b), based on the part-of relation, the events in *Shot 1* and *2* are combined into the higher-level event "cooking a *Hamburger*". This event and the one in *Shot 3* ("eating a *Hamburger*") are further abstracted into "eating the cooked *Hamburger*". Also, the correlation relation is used to connect two 'weakly-related' events, such as those which occur in sep-

---

[1]In this chapter, contexts only include relations which are obtained from multimedia data themselves, and exclude external data like geo-tags and Web documents.

20

arate locations but at the same time [53]. The final goal of LSMR is the above-mentioned organisation of semantic meanings based on concepts, events and contexts. To make the following discussions simple and clear, an *example* is used to indicate a single unit of multimedia data, such as image, shot, video and audio. When the discrimination among these data formats is not important, examples are used as their abstract name.

However, an event is 'highly-abstracted' in the sense that various objects interact with each other in different situations. In consequence, visual appearances of examples relevant to a certain event can be completely different. In other words, these examples have got a huge variance in the space of low-level features like colour, edge, and motion. One promising solution for this is a *concept-based* approach which projects an example into the space where each dimension represents the detection result of a concept [66]. Owing to recent research progress, several concepts can be robustly detected irrespective of their sizes, directions and deformations in video frames. Thus, compared to the space of low-level features where each dimension just represents the physical value of an example, in the space of concept detection results, each dimension represents the appearance of a human-perceivable meaning. In such a space, the variation of relevant examples to an event becomes smaller and can be modelled more easily. That is, relevant examples that are dissimilar at the level of low-level features become more similar at the level of concepts.

Several publications reported the effectiveness of concept-based approaches. For example, Tešič *et al.* showed that when using the same classifier (SVM), concept detection scores lead to 50-180% higher event retrieval performance than colour and texture features [75]. In addition, Merler *et al.* reported that compared to high-dimensional features (see local features described in the next section), concept detection scores yield the best performance [40]. In particular, the example representation using detection scores for 280 concepts only requires a 15 times smaller data space than high-dimensional features, where data sizes are crucial for the feasibility of LSMR. Furthermore, Mazloom *et al.* demonstrated that concept detection scores offer 3.1-39.4% performance improvement compared to a high-dimensional feature [39].

Figure 2.2 shows an overview of concept-based LSMR. Although Figure 2.2 focuses on the "birthday party" event in videos, it is straightforward to apply the same approach to images or audio signals. First, each video is divided into shots. For this, there exist many accurate shot boundary detection methods. One popular approach is to detect a shot boundary as a significant difference of colour histograms between two consecutive video frames [25]. In the bottom of Figure 2.2, each shot is represented by one video frame, and arranged from front to back based on its shot ID. Then, concept detection is conducted as a binary classification problem. For each concept, a detector is built using training shots annotated with the presence or absence of this concept. After that, the detector is used to associate each shot with a *detection score*, representing a scoring value between 0 and 1 in terms of the presence of the concept. A larger detection score indicates a higher likelihood that the concept being present in a shot.

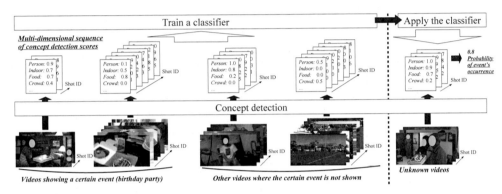

Figure 2.2: An overview of concept-based LSMR where "birthday party" is used as an example event.

Such detection scores are illustrated in the middle of Figure 2.2. For example, the first shot in the leftmost video shows an indoor scene where a person is bringing a birthday cake. Correspondingly, this shot is associated with the large detection scores 0.9, 0.7 and 0.7 for *Person*, *Indoor* and *Food*, respectively. Note that concept detection is uncertain because small (or large) detection scores for a concept may be falsely assigned to shots where it is actually present (or absent). Nonetheless, representative concepts in shots are assumed to be successfully detected, and even if the detection of a concept fails on some shots, its contribution to an event can be appropriately evaluated by statistically analysing many shots. For example, even though the shot exemplified above does not display *Crowd*, a relatively large detection score 0.4 is assigned to this shot. But, by checking the other shots in videos showing the event "birthday party", it can be revealed that *Crowd* is irrelevant to this event. The above concept detection allows us to represent each video as a *multi-dimensional sequence* where each shot defined as a vector of detection scores is temporally ordered, as depicted in the middle of Figure 2.2.

A classifier is built to distinguish videos showing a certain event from the other videos, by comparing multi-dimensional sequences for these videos. The classifier captures intra-/inter-shot concept relations that are specific to the event. For example, corresponding to candle blowing scenes, videos relevant to "birthday party" often contain shots where *Nighttime* and *Explosion_Fire* are detected with high detection scores. In addition, shots displaying *Person* are often followed by shots showing *Singing* or *Dancing*. Finally, the classifier is used to examine whether the event occurs in unknown videos.

In concept-based LSMR, one important issue is how to define a vocabulary of concepts. Such a vocabulary should be sufficiently rich for covering various events. One traditionally popular vocabulary is *Large-Scale Concept Ontology for Multimedia* (LSCOM), which defines a standardised set of $1,000$ concepts in the broadcast news video domain [42]. These concepts are selected based on their 'utility' for classifying content in videos, their 'coverage' for responding to a variety of queries, their 'feasibility' for automatic detection, and the 'availability' (observability) of large-scale training data. It is estimated that if the number of concepts in LSCOM reaches an amount of $3,000$, granting the quality of the new concepts remains similar to the existing ones, the retrieval performance approaches that of the best search engine in text information retrieval [20]. The currently most popular concept vocabulary is *ImageNet* [13, 52]. This is an extension to its predecessor WordNet which is a large lexical ontology where concepts (called synonym sets or synsets) are interlinked based on their meanings [17]. ImageNet aims to assign on average 500 to $1,000$ images to each WordNet concept. In March 2017, $14,197,122$ images are associated with $21,841$ concepts through Amazon's Mechanical Turk, where the assignment of images has been outsourced to Web users[2]. The developers of ImageNet plan to assign 50 million images to $80,000$ concepts in the near future. In what follows, concept-based LSMR will be explained by mainly focusing on two main processes, concept detection in Section 2.2 and event retrieval in Section 2.3.

---

[2]http://image-net.org/

2.2 Concept Detection

Concept detection (including object detection, scene recognition, image and video classification etc.) has been investigated for a long time. It can be formulated as a binary classification problem in machine learning, where for each concept a detector is trained to distinguish examples showing it from the others. This requires two types of training examples, *positive examples* and *negative examples*. The former and latter are examples that are annotated with the concept's presence and absence, respectively. By referring to these training examples, the detector examines *test examples* where neither the concept's presence nor absence is known. In accordance with this machine learning setting, Section 2.2.1 presents the basic framework by mainly focusing on representations of examples (i.e., features), and then Section 2.2.2 provides the state-of-the-art methods that extract useful representations by analysing a large amount of examples.

2.2.1 Global versus Local Features

Classical methods cannot achieve accurate concept detection. One main reason is the weakness of *global features* which are extracted from the whole region of an example. In other words, they only express overall characteristics of an example. As an example of global features, Figure 2.3 shows a colour feature indicating the distribution of colours included in an image. This kind of overall representation loses a lot of information. For example, from the colour feature in Figure 2.3, appearances of the car, road and vegetation cannot be deduced any more. In addition, the overall characteristics of the example can easily change depending on the camera techniques and shooting environments. For instance, the colour distribution of the image in Figure 2.3 changes substantially if it is taken in a brighter or darker lighting condition.

To overcome the weakness of global features, Schmid and Mohr proposed to represent an example as a collection of *local features*, each of which is extracted from a local region of the example [54]. The top right of Figure 2.3 illustrates local features extracted from local regions circled in yellow. In addition, [36] developed a local feature called *Scale-Invariant Feature Transform* (SIFT) which represents the shape in a local region, reasonably invariant with respect to changes in illumination, rotation, scaling and viewpoint. By extracting a large number of such local features from an example, it can be ensured that at least some of them represent

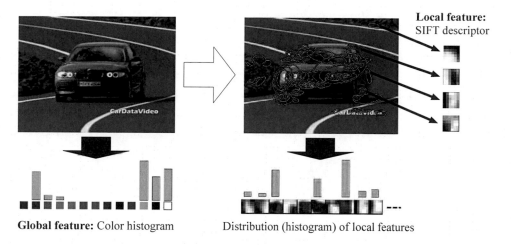

Local feature: SIFT descriptor

Global feature: Color histogram   Distribution (histogram) of local features

Figure 2.3: A comparison between a global feature and a local feature [56].

characteristic regions of a concept. More specifically, even if the car in Figure 2.3 is partially masked by other objects, local features that characterise a wheel, window or headlight are extracted from the visible part of the car. Sande *et al.* developed extended SIFT features that are defined in different colour spaces and have unique invariance properties for lighting conditions [81]. Furthermore, local features are defined around trajectories, each of which is obtained by tracking a sampled point in a video [86]. The resulting local features represent the displacement of a point, the derivative of that displacement, and edges around a trajectory. Also, *Speeded-UP Robust Features* (SURF) are similar to SIFT features, but can be efficiently computed based on the integral image structure which quickly identifies the sum of pixel values in any image region [3].

Based on local features, Csurka *et al.* developed a simple and effective example representation called *Bag of Visual Words* (BoVW), where each example is represented as the collection of characteristic local features, called *visual words* [10]. In BoVW, millions of local features are first grouped into clusters where each cluster centre is a visual word representing a characteristic local region. Then, each local feature extracted from an example is assigned to the most similar visual word. As a result, as seen from the bottom right of Figure 2.3, the example is represented as a vector (histogram) where each dimension represents the frequency of a visual word. This way, the example is summarised into a single vector where the detailed information is maintained by visual words (local features) that are robust with respect to varied visual appearances. The effectiveness of

25

BoVW has been validated by many researchers [10, 27, 59, 81, 96].

Many extensions of BoVW have been proposed, such as soft assignment which extracts a smoothed histogram by assigning each local feature to multiple visual words based on kernel density estimation [81], sparse coding which represents the distribution of a large number of base functions used to sparsely approximate local features [91, 92], Gaussian Mixture Model (GMM) supervector which estimates the distribution of local features using a GMM [22], Fisher vector encoding which considers the first and second order differences between the distribution of local features and the reference distribution [49], and Vector of Locally Aggregated Descriptors (VLAD) which concatenates vectors each representing the accumulated difference of a visual word to the assigned local features [1, 24].

Another reason for the unsatisfactory performance of classical concept detection is the insufficiency of training examples. Although local features are useful for managing diverse visual appearances of a concept, instances with significantly different appearances are included in the same concept category. For example, the concept *Car* includes saloon cars, buses, trucks and so on. Regarding this, a classifier can conduct accurate detection on test examples where instances of a concept are similar to those in training examples. However, detection is not accurate on test examples where instances have significantly different characteristics from those in training examples. Thus, a large number of training examples are required to address the diversity attributed to the difference in instance types of an object. In general, the detection performance is proportional to the logarithm of the number of positive examples, although each concept has its own complexity of recognition [43]. This means that 10 times more positive examples improve the performance by 10%. Considering this importance of the number of training examples, researchers have developed Web-based collaborative annotation systems where annotation of large-scale multimedia data is distributed to many users on the Web [2, 83]. That is, these users collaboratively annotate a large number of examples as positive or negative. In an extreme case, 80 million training images yield accurate recognition performance [77].

However, regular users on the Web are unlikely to volunteer to annotate when no benefit or no reason is given. In consequence, only researchers participate in annotation, which makes it difficult to collect large-scale annotation. Von Ahn and Dabbish proposed a *Games With A Purpose* (GWAP) approach where users play a game, and as a side effect, a computationally difficult task is solved [84, 85]. More concretely, users play a fun game without knowing that they conduct image annotation. Owing to the motivation that users want to have fun, as of July 2008, 200, 000 users contributed to assigning more than 50 million labels to images on the Web [85]. Another approach that motivates users is *crowdsourcing* that outsources problems performed by designated human (employee) to users on the Web [50]. In the field of multimedia annotation, one of the most famous crowdsourcing systems is Amazon's Mechanical Turk where anyone can post small tasks and specify prices paid for completing them [28]. ImageNet, which is the currently most popular large-scale concept vocabulary (see the previous section), has been created via Mechanical Turk [13, 52].

A detector for a concept is built based on BoVW-based features and large-scale training examples. In most cases, the detector is built as a *Support Vector Machine* (SVM) [79], which constructs a classification boundary based on the 'margin maximisation' principle so that it is placed in the middle between positive and negative examples. This 'moderate' boundary which is biased toward neither positive nor negative examples is suitable for BoVW. Specifically, many visual words (e.g., thousands of visual words) are required to maintain the discrimination power of BoVW. That is, an example is represented as a high-dimensional vector. This renders the nearest neighbour classifier ineffective because of many irrelevant dimensions to similarity calculation [6]. In contrast, the margin maximisation makes the generalisation error of an SVM independent of the number of dimensions, if this number is sufficiently large [79]. Actually, SVMs have been successfully applied to BoVW with thousands of dimensions [10, 81, 27, 59].

Below, two important issues for accurate concept detection are discussed. The first is how to sample local features. In general, local feature extraction consists of two modules, *region detector* and *region descriptor* [96]. The former detects regions useful for characterising objects, and the latter represents each of the detected regions as a vector. For example, SIFT features are typically extracted using Harris-Laplace (or Harris-affine) detector to identify regions where pixel values largely change in multiple directions. Such regions are regarded as useful for characterising local shapes of objects, like corners of buildings, vehicles and human eyes. Then, each detected region is described as a 128-dimensional vector representing the distribution of edge orientations. However, a concept is shown in significantly different regions, and in videos, it does not necessarily appear in all video frames. Considering this 'uncertainty' of concept appearances, it is necessary to extract the BoVW representation of an example by exhaus-

27

tively sampling local features in both the spatial and temporal dimensions. Actually, the performance is improved as the number of sampled local features increases [47]. In addition, Snoek *et al.* compared two methods [67]. One extracts features only from one video frame in each shot (one shot contains more than 60 frames), and the other extracts features every 15 frames. They found out that the latter exceeds the former by 7.5 to 38.8%. The second issue is an expensive computational cost to process a large number of training examples and exhaustively sampled local features. So far, many methods for reducing these computational costs have been developed based on special hardware like computer cluster [90] and General-Purpose computing on Graphics Processing Units (GPGPU) [82], or based on algorithm sophistication with sub-problem decomposition [15], tree structures [22] and matrix operations [61].

2.2.2 Feature Learning

Global and local features described in the previous section are 'hand-crafted' or 'human-crafted' in the sense that their representations are manually specified in advance [4]. For instance, a SIFT feature is described as a 128-dimensional vector where each dimension represents the frequency of a certain edge orientation in a local region. However, such a hand-crafted feature is insufficient for representing diverse concept appearances. This is because all of such appearances cannot be assumed in advance and cannot be appropriately represented by the feature. Apart from this, the human brain recognises concepts in a hierarchical fashion where simple cells are gradually combined into more abstract complex cells [29]. This hierarchical brain functionality is recently implemented as *deep learning* that constructs a feature hierarchy with higher-level features formed by the composition of lower-level features [4, 5]. Such a feature hierarchy is represented as a multi-layer neural network. In every layer, each of the artificial neurons composes a more abstract feature based on outputs of neurons in the previous layer.

Figure 2.4 shows a conceptual comparison between a traditional machine learning approach using a hand-crafted feature and a deep learning approach. The former in Figure 2.4 (a) uses a 'shallow architecture' consisting of two layers, where the first layer transforms an example into a feature represented by a high-dimensional vector, and in second layer aggregates values of this feature into a detection result of a concept. On the other hand, the deep learning in Figure 2.4 (b) first projects an example into the most primitive features at the bottom layer, and then these features are projected into more abstract ones at the second layer. This abstraction of features is iterated to obtain a detection result of the concept. For example, features in the bottom and second layers correspond to typical edges and their combinations, respectively. Moreover, features at in upper layer represent parts of a car, and the ones in the top layer indicate the whole car. Like this, the workflow from processing pixels to recognising a concept is unified into a deep architecture, which is extracted from large-scale data.

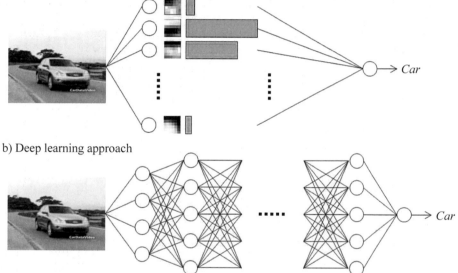

Figure 2.4: A conceptual comparison between traditional machine learning and deep learning approaches.

Deep learning mainly offers the following three advantages (see [5] for more detail): The first is its discrimination power compared to the shallow one in the traditional machine learning approach. The latter requires $O(N)$ parameters to distinguish $O(N)$ examples, while the former can represent up to $O(2^N)$ examples using only $O(N)$ parameters [5]. Intuitively, a huge first layer (i.e., very high-dimensional feature vector) is required for the traditional approach to discriminate diverse examples. In contrast, the discrimination power of the deep architecture is exponentially increased based on the combination of features in two consecutive layers. The second advantage is the invariance property where more abstract features are generally invariant to subtle changes in visual appearances. The last one is the explanatory factor that the learnt feature hierarchy can capture valuable patterns or structures underlying raw images or videos. Finally, a classifier for detecting a concept is created by using the learnt hierarchy as initialisation of a multi-layer neural network, or building a supervised classifier by constructing the feature vector of each example based on the hierarchy (this is called *transfer learning* [38]).

One of the most fundamental deep learning models called AlexNet is implemented as an eight-layer Convolutional Neural Network (CNN) which iteratively conducts convolution or pooling of outputs by neurons in the previous layer [30]. Convolution works as feature extraction using filters each represented by weights of a neuron. On the other hand, pooling summarises outputs of neighbouring neurons to extract more abstract features. The parameter optimisation is conducted by stochastic gradient descent which updates each weight of a neuron by backpropagating the derivative of training errors in terms of this weight. In ILSVRC 2012 which is a worldwide competition on large-scale image classification [11], AlexNet with the error rate of 15.3% significantly outperformed the others (the second best error rate was 26.1%). Also, Le *et al.* developed a nine-layer stacked sparse autoencoder to train concept detectors from unlabelled images [32]. Each layer consists of three sub-layers, filtering, pooling and normalisation, which respectively offer feature extraction from small regions of the previous layer, the invariance of features (neighbouring neurons' outputs) to local deformation of visual appearances, and the range adjustment of features. The stacked sparse autoencoder is optimised layer-by-layer so that sparse features constructed in a layer can be accurately converted back into the ones in the previous layer. By training such a stacked autoencoder using 10 million unlabelled images with $16,000$ cores, it was shown that the highest-level neurons characterise concepts like *Face*, *Cat_Face* and *Human_Body*. Moreover, compared to state-of-the-art methods, the multi-layer classifier using the stack autoencoder as the initialisation yields 15% and 70% performance improvement for $10,000$ and $22,000$ concept detection tasks, respectively. Inspired by the above-mentioned research, many improved deep learning models have been proposed such as VGGNet which is a very deep CNN with consisting of 16 (or 19) layers with small filter fields (3×3) [62], GoogLeNet which is a 22-layer CNN where multiple convolutions are performed in parallel [71], and ResNet which is a 152-layer CNN where neuron outputs in a layer are forwarded to a layer which is more distant than the one-level higher layer [21].

2.3 Event Retrieval

There are two scenarios of event retrieval. In the first scenario, a machine learning setting similar to concept detection is adopted by regarding concept detection scores for each examples as its feature vector. To formulate this, examples are re-defined as follows: Positive examples indicate the ones showing a certain event, while all the other examples are signified as negative. Based on training examples consisting of these positive and negative examples, a classifier is built to examine the occurrence of the event in unknown test examples. The second scenario is called *zero-shot learning* that builds a classifier for an event with no training example. In other words, the classifier is trained by considering how the event is semantically configured by concepts [31, 19]. For example, a classifier for the event "a person is playing guitar outdoors" is constructed so as to assign high weights to detection scores for the concepts *Person*, *Outdoors* and *Playing_Guitar*, because these concepts are obviously important for the event.

The following discussion mainly focuses on the first scenario where a user provides a small number of positive examples for an event. It should be noted that although a huge diversity of examples can be negative, it is difficult or unrealistic for the user to provide such negative examples. On the other hand, negative examples are necessary for accurately shaping regions of examples relevant to the event [33, 60]. With respect to this, Natsev *et al.* assumed that only a small number of examples in the database are relevant to an event, and all the others are irrelevant [44]. Based on this, they proposed an approach which selects negative examples as randomly sampled examples because almost all of them should be irrelevant to the query. This approach works well and has been validated in many high performance retrieval systems [46, 65]. Keeping this preparation of training examples, existing event retrieval methods are summarised by classifying them into two categories. The first described in Section 2.3.1 focuses on events within images/shots, and the second in Section 2.3.2 targets events over video shot sequences.

2.3.1   Event Retrieval within Images/Shots

Given positive examples for an event, methods in this category construct a classifier that fuses concept detection scores for a test example (image or shot) into a single *relevance score*. This score indicates the relevance of the test example to the event. Existing methods are roughly classified into four categories, *linear combination*, *discriminative*, *similarity-based* or *probabilistic*. Linear combination builds a classifier that computes the relevance score of a test example by weighting detection scores for multiple concepts. One popular approach to build such a classifier is to analyse concept detection scores in positive examples. If the average detection score for a concept in positive examples is large, this concept is regarded as related to the query and associated with a large weight [45, 88]. Discriminative methods construct a discriminative classifier (typically, SVM) using positive and negative examples for an event [45, 46]. The relevance score of a test example is obtained as the classifier's output. Similarity-based methods compute the relevance score of a test example as the similarity between positive examples and the test example in terms of concept detection scores. The method in [34] uses the cosine similarity and a modified entropy as similarity measures. Probabilistic methods estimate a probabilistic distribution of concepts using detection scores in positive examples, and use it to compute the relevance score of a test example. In [51], the relevance score of a test image is computed as the similarity between the multinomial distribution of concepts estimated from positive examples and the one estimated from the test image.

In the zero-shot learning scenario, one popular approach to classifier construction is 'text-based weighting' where a concept is associated with a large weight if its name is lexically similar to a term in the text description of the query [45, 88]. The lexical similarity between a concept name and a term can be measured by employing a lexical ontology like WordNet [17], or recently by utilising their vector representations (word2vec [41]) obtained by a neural network, which is trained on a large amount of text data [94]. Another approach is to construct an embedding space between visual features and text descriptions for training examples [19]. Given a test example, its text description is estimated by projecting its visual features into the embedding representation, which is then further projected into a text description. Finally, the similarity between this description and the text description of an event is computed.

2.3.2 Event Retrieval over Shot Sequences

This section only focuses on the usual machine learning setting to detect an event over video shot sequences. One big problem is the difficulty of annotating the relevance of each shot. The reasons are two-fold: First, it is labour-intensive to annotate shots contained in each video. Second, videos are known as *continuous media* where sequences of media quanta (i.e., video frames and audio samples) convey semantic meanings when continuously played over time [18]. Due to this temporal continuity, any segment of a video can become a meaningful unit [73]. Specifically, humans tend to relate each shot in a video to surrounding ones. Let us consider a video where the event "birthday party" is shown. One person may think that the event occurs in a shot where a birthday cake is brought to a table, followed by a shot showing a candle blowing scene. But, another person may perceive that the surrounding shots displaying participants' chatting are also a part of the birthday party. This kind of shot relation makes it ambiguous to determine the boundary of an event. Thus, objective annotation is only possible at the video level in terms of whether each video contains an event or not. Hence, a classifier needs to be built under this *weakly supervised setting* where even if a training video is annotated as relevant to the meaning, it includes many irrelevant shots.

The simplest approach to build a classifier under the weakly supervised setting[3] is to create a 'video-level vector' using by *max-pooling* [9, 35] or *average-pooling* [76], which computes each dimension value as the maximum or average concept detection score over shots in a video. However, such video-level vectors are clearly too coarse, because max-pooling may over-estimate detection scores for irrelevant concepts to an event, and average-pooling may under-estimate the ones for relevant concepts.

Shirahama *et al.* developed a more sophisticated method using a Hidden Conditional Random Field (HCRF) [57]. It is a probabilistic discriminative classifier with a set of hidden states. These states are used as the intermediate layer to discriminate between relevant and irrelevant shots to an event. Specifically, each shot in a video is assigned to a hidden state by considering its concept detection scores and transitions among hidden states. Then, hidden states and transitions are optimised so as to max-

---

[3]Event detection under weakly supervised setting is being explored in TRECVID Multimedia Event Detection task [63]. Although some other methods (e.g., [23, 74, 80]) can treat weakly supervised setting, they use low-level features, so are excluded from the discussion.

imise the discrimination between positive and negative videos. It is shown that the optimised hidden states and transitions successfully capture concepts and their temporal relations, that are specific to the event. Sun and Nevatia proposed a method which extracts temporal concept transitions in an event using Fisher kernel encoding [70]. Using all training videos, they first build an HMM which works as a prior distribution, representing concept transitions in the general case. Then, the video-level vector of a video is created by computing the difference between the actual transitions of concept detection scores in the video, and the transitions predicted by the HMM. Thereby, vectors of positive videos for an event represent characteristic concept transitions by suppressing trivial transitions that are observed in many negative videos. Finally, Lu and Grauman developed a metric which can quantify the context between two events, by finding concepts that appear in the first event and strongly influence the second one [37]. Such influences are measured by performing a random walk on the bipartite graph, which consists of event and concept nodes. A concept is regarded as influential if its ignorance leads to a dramatic decrease of the probability of transition between two event nodes. In [37], the metric was used to create summaries consisting of events associated with semantically consistent contexts.

2.4   Conclusion and Future Trends

This chapter presented a survey of traditional and state-of-the-art LSMR methods by mainly focusing on concept detection and event retrieval processes. Regarding the former, thanks to the preparation of large-scale datasets like ImageNet [13, 52] and the development of deep learning approaches in Section 2.2.2, many concepts can be detected with acceptable accuracies. One open issue for concept detection is how to successfully extend deep learning approaches that have been successful for the image (i.e., spatial) domain to the video (i.e., temporal) domain. Although several methods use 3D convolutional neural network [78] or Long Short Term Memory (LSTM) [68], there is still significant room for improvement. Compared to concept detection, event retrieval needs much more research attention for both performance improvement and method innovation, as discussed below.

2.4.1 Reasoning

Existing event retrieval approaches lack *reasoning* to precisely infer events (higher-level semantic meanings) based on ontological properties and relations of concepts. Even though some works consider hierarchical relations among concepts, they only use is-a (generalisation/specialisation) connections among concepts [12, 98]. Reasoning based on concept properties and relations is necessary because concept detection itself has the following two limitations: First, concepts are too general to identify examples that users want to retrieve. Secondly, most of the existing methods use concepts in isolation. For example, various events are displayed in examples where the concepts *Person*, *Hand* and *Ball* are present. In other words, examples that users really want to see cannot be identified by independently examining presences of *Person*, *Hand* and *Ball*. Instead, if it is observed that the *Hand* of a *Person* is moving and the *Ball* is separating from the *Person*, the event "throwing a ball" can be derived.

Due to the poor performance of past concept detection methods, the above kind of reasoning has received little research attention. However, considering their recent improvements, it seems to be the right time for the reasoning to be widely addressed in LSRM. For this, [8] developed an interesting approach which optimally specialises detected concepts and their relations, so that they are the most probable and ontologically-consistent. This approach, which formulates reasoning as an optimisation problem based on constraints defined by the ontology, can be considered as a promising future direction of LSMR.

2.4.2 Uncertainties in Concept Detection

Reasoning requires overcoming the crucial problem of how to manage 'uncertainties' in concept detection. There are still many concepts that cannot be detected with high accuracies. In addition, real-world examples are 'unconstrained' in the sense that they can be taken by arbitrary camera techniques and in arbitrary shooting environments [26]. Hence, even in the future, it cannot be expected to detect concepts with 100% of accuracy. If one relies on uncertain concept detection results, detection errors for some concepts damage the whole reasoning process.

Shirahama *et al.* have developed a pioneering method which can handle uncertainties based on *Dempster-Shafer Theory* (DST) [58]. DST is a generalisation of Bayesian theory where a probability is not assigned to a variable, but instead to a subset of variables [14]. Given a set of concepts C, and S a subset of C, a 'mass function' $m(S)$ is defined over an example to indicate the probability that one concept in S is present in the example. For instance, $m(\{Person, Car\})$ represents the probability that either *Person* or *Car* could be present in an example. In the extreme case, $m(C)$ represents the probability that every concept could be present; that is, it is unknown which concept is present. Using such a mass function, DST can represent uncertainties in concept detection much more powerfully than Bayesian theory, because the latter can only represent uncertainties by assigning 0.5 to the probability of a concept's presence. However, the derivation of a mass function is quite intractable, because it is very subjective or impossible to prepare training examples by annotating them from the perspective that one of a set of concepts could be present. Thus, based on the set-theoretic operation in DST, it is proved that a probabilistic classifier using a mass function can be transformed into the one using a 'plausibility', which is an upper bound probability that a concept could possibly be present in an example. By modelling these plausibilities based on the distribution of positive and negative examples for each concept, a classifier is constructed in the framework of maximum likelihood estimation. It is reported that this classifier yields about 19% performance improvement compared to a classifier which uses concept detection scores without considering uncertainties. One useful future direction might be to incorporate a reasoning mechanism into the above-mentioned classifier, where concept properties and relations are used as constraints in maximum likelihood estimation.

2.4.3 Adaptive Learning

It is often difficult for a user to precisely express his/her interesting event, because of the poor lexical vocabulary. For example, when the user wants to search for an event involving a specific model of "Porsche", it often happens that he/she does not know the model name. Only specifying the keyword "Porsche" leads to retrieved examples showing different models. This kind of discrepancy between the user's search intent and the event description (query) specified by him/her is called the *intention gap* [93]. Thus, *adaptive learning* is necessary for the user to interactively specialise an initially ambiguous description into an appropriate one. One of the most popular adaptive learning approaches is *Relevance Feedback* (RF) that asks a user to provide feedback regarding the relevance or irrelevance of currently retrieved examples [97]. These newly labelled examples are used to refine the current classifier. RF is closely related to *active learning* to select the most informative examples for improving the performance of a classifier, and asks the user to label them [87]. Such RF (or active learning) methods enable us to adaptively obtain satisfying event retrieval results with reduced manual effort.

Below, an adaptive learning approach for concept detection is firstly presented, and its extension to event retrieval is discussed at the end of this section. The traditional RF relies on the very restrictive communication between a classifier and a user, where the user only informs the classifier whether an example is relevant to a certain semantic meaning or not. In the real world, the communication between a teacher and a learner is a lot more complex. In particular, if the learner makes a mistake, the teacher will explain it to him/her. Based on this idea, [48] developed an *Attribute-based Feedback* (AF) which realises the complex communication between a user and a classifier. Here, *attributes* are semantically meaningful descriptions, such as parts (e.g., "propeller"), shapes (e.g., "round"), textures (e.g., "stripe"), rough scene categories (e.g., "natural"), and non-verbal properties (e.g., "properties that dogs have but cats do not") [16, 31]. Similar to concept detection, a detector for each attribute is built to identify its presence in an example. As a result, the example is represented as a vector where each dimension represents the output of the detector for one attribute. For example, in Figure 2.5, the example (a) is associated with the large output value 0.6 for the attribute "natural", because trees and the grass are displayed in a large region. Note that, since attributes represent lower-level semantic meanings than concepts, automatic detection of the former is relatively easier than that of the latter [95].

AF uses attributes as a language between a classifier and a user to implement their complex communication [48]. Specifically, if an example that the classifier regards as relevant to a concept's presence is judged to be irrelevant by a user, he/she can explain the reason for this misclassification. Let us consider Figure 2.5 where examples are represented as points in the multi-dimensional space defined by detector outputs for different attributes. For simple visualisation, only two dimensions are shown in Figure 2.5 where the horizontal dimension represents detector outputs for the attribute "natural". Assume that for the concept *Streets*, a classifier (SVM) with the boundary depicted by the dashed line is built using three positive and four negative examples, which are marked by blue circles and

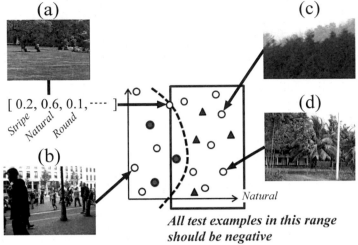

- Concept: Streets
- Feedback: The test example (a) is too natural as a street scene

(a)

[0.2, 0.6, 0.1, ····]

Stripe   Natural   Round

(b)

(c)

(d)

Natural

All test examples in this range should be negative

Figure 2.5: Attribute feedback overview

red triangles, respectively. Test examples are represented by white circles. One popular RF approach (uncertainty sampling [87]) asks the user to give feedback to the test example (a) that is the closest to the classification boundary. Under this setting, the user can not only annotate the test example (a) as negative in terms of the concept's presence, but also explain "this example is too natural for *Streets*". This implies that test examples which have higher detector outputs for the attribute "natural" than the test example (a), should also be negative. In Figure 2.5, these test examples like (c) and (d) are located in the red rectangle. This way, based on the attribute explained in a reason, the annotation for one example can be propagated to other examples, so that the performance of a classifier can be effectively improved. Furthermore, attributes, which are used as features of the classifier, can be refined based on user feedback [7]. In Figure 2.5, the above exemplified explanation has another implication that the detector for the attribute "natural" should output lower values for positive examples for *Streets* than the one for the test example (a). Using this as a constraint, the detector is refined so that the positive example in the red rectangle is associated with a lower value than the one for the test example (a). This way, both of the classifier and attribute detectors are refined by AF.

The AF described above only targets the efficient refinement of concept

38

classifiers based on attributes. But, AF can be flexibly used for various levels of semantic meanings. Here, classifiers for a certain level of meanings are refined by regarding one lower level of meanings as attributes. In particular, AF seems useful for event retrieval where concepts are considered as attributes, and accurate classifiers for events can be built with reduced manual annotation effort. Furthermore, by viewing events as attributes, AF may succeed in effectively extracting their causal relations.

References

[1] R. Arandjelovic and A. Zisserman. All about VLAD. In *Proceedings of the 2013 IEEE Conference on Computer Vision and Pattern Recognition (CVPR 2013)*, pages 1578–1585, Washington, DC, USA, June 2013. IEEE Computer Society.

[2] S. Ayache and G. Quénot. Video corpus annotation using active learning. In *Proceedings of the 30th European Conference on IR Research (ECIR 2008)*, pages 187–198, Berlin, Heidelberg, April 2008. Springer Berlin Heidelberg.

[3] H. Bay, T. Tuytelaars, and L. Gool. SURF: Speeded up robust features. In *Proceedings of the Ninth European Conference on Computer Vision (ECCV 2006)*, pages 404–417, Berlin, Heidelberg, May 2006. Springer Berlin Heidelberg.

[4] Y. Bengio. Learning deep architectures for AI. *Foundations and Trends in Machine Learning*, 2(1):1–127, January 2009.

[5] Y. Bengio, A. Courville, and P. Vincent. Representation learning: A review and new perspectives. *IEEE Transactions on Pattern Analysis and Machine Intelligence*, 35(8):1798–1828, August 2013.

[6] K. S. Beyer, J. Goldstein, R. Ramakrishnan, and U. Shaft. When is "nearest neighbor" meaningful? In *Proceedings of the 7th International Conference on Database Theory (ICDT 1999)*, pages 217–235, London, UK, UK, January 1999. Springer-Verlag.

[7] A. Biswas and D. Parikh. Simultaneous active learning of classifiers & attributes via relative feedback. In *Proceedings of the 2013 IEEE Conference on Computer Vision and Pattern Recognition (CVPR 2013)*,

pages 644–651, Washington, DC, USA, June 2013. IEEE Computer Society.

[8] N. Chen, Q.-Y. Zhou, and V. Prasanna. Understanding web images by object relation network. In *Proceedings of the 21st International Conference on World Wide Web (WWW 2012)*, pages 291–300, New York, NY, USA, April 2012. ACM.

[9] Cheng H. *et al.* SRI-Sarnoff AURORA system at TRECVID 2012: Multimedia event detection and recounting. In *Proceedings of TREC Video Retrieval Evaluation (TRECVID) 2012 Workshop (TRECVID 2012)*, Gaithersburg, MD, USA, November 2012. National Institute of Standards and Technology (NIST).

[10] G. Csurka, C. Bray, C. Dance, and L. Fan. Visual categorization with bags of keypoints. In *Proceedings of ECCV 2004 Statistical Learning in Computer Vision (SLCV 2004)*, pages 1–22, Berlin, Heidelberg, May 2004. Springer Berlin Heidelberg.

[11] J. Deng, A. Berg, S. Satheesh, H. Su, A. Khosla, and F.-F. Li. Imagenet large scale visual recognition challenge 2012 (ilsvrc 2012). http://image-net.org/challenges/LSVRC/2012/index#workshop.

[12] J. Deng, A. C. Berg, and F.-F. Li. Hierarchical semantic indexing for large scale image retrieval. In *Proceedings of the 2011 IEEE Conference on Computer Vision and Pattern Recognition (CVPR 2011)*, pages 785–792, Washington, DC, USA, June 2011. IEEE Computer Society.

[13] J. Deng, W. Dong, R. Socher, L.-J. Li, K. Li, and F.-F. Li. ImageNet: A large-scale hierarchical image database. In *Proceedings of the 2009 IEEE Conference on Computer Vision and Pattern Recognition (CVPR 2009)*, pages 248–255, Washington, DC, USA, June 2009. IEEE Computer Society.

[14] T. Denoeux. Maximum likelihood estimation from uncertain data in the belief function framework. *IEEE Transactions on Knowledge and Data Engineering*, 25(1):119–130, January 2013.

[15] R.-E. Fan, P.-H. Chen, and C.-J. Lin. Working set selection using second order information for training support vector machines. *Journal of Machine Learning Research*, 6:1889–1918, December 2005.

[16] A. Farhadi, I. Endres, D. Hoiem, and D. Forsyth. Describing objects by their attributes. In *Proceedings of the 2009 IEEE Conference on Computer Vision and Pattern Recognition (CVPR 2009)*, pages 1778–1785, Washington, DC, USA, June 2009. IEEE Computer Society.

[17] C. Fellbaum. *WordNet: An Electronic Lexical Database*. MIT Press, Cambridge, MA, USA, 1998.

[18] D. J. Gemmell, H. M. Vin, D. D. Kandlur, P. V. Rangan, and L. A. Rowe. Multimedia storage servers: A tutorial. *IEEE Computer*, 28(5):40–49, May 1995.

[19] A. Habibian, T. Mensink, and C. G. M. Snoek. Videostory embeddings recognize events when examples are scarce. *CoRR*, abs/1511.02492, 2015.

[20] A. Hauptmann, R. Yan, W.-H. Lin, M. Christel, and H. Wactlar. Can high-level concepts fill the semantic gap in video retrieval? A case study with broadcast news. *IEEE Transactions on Multimedia*, 9(5):958–966, August 2007.

[21] K. He, X. Zhang, S. Ren, and J. Sun. Deep residual learning for image recognition. In *Proceedings of the 2016 IEEE Conference on Computer Vision and Pattern Recognition (CVPR 2016)*, pages 770–778, Washington, DC, USA, June 2016. IEEE Computer Society.

[22] N. Inoue and K. Shinoda. A fast and accurate video semantic-indexing system using fast MAP adaptation and GMM supervectors. *IEEE Transactions on Multimedia*, 14(4):1196–1205, August 2012.

[23] N. Inoue, T. Wada, Y. Kamishima, K. Shinoda, and S. Sato. TokyoTech+Canon at TRECVID 2011. In *Proceedings of TREC Video Retrieval Evaluation (TRECVID) 2011 Workshop (TRECVID 2011)*, Gaithersburg, MD, USA, November 2011. National Institute of Standards and Technology (NIST).

[24] H. Jégou, F. Perronnin, M. Douze, J. Sánchez, P. Perez, and C. Schmid. Aggregating local image descriptors into compact codes. *IEEE Transactions on Pattern Analysis and Machine Intelligence*, 34(9):1704–1716, September 2012.

[25] K. C. Jay. *Video Content Analysis Using Multimodal Information: For Movie Content Extraction, Indexing and Representation.* Kluwer Academic Publishers, Norwell, MA, USA, 2003.

[26] Y.-G. Jiang, S. Bhattacharya, S.-F. Chang, and M. Shah. High-level event recognition in unconstrained videos. *International Journal of Multimedia Information Retrieval*, 2(2):73–101, June 2013.

[27] Y.-G. Jiang, J. Yang, C.-W. Ngo, and A. G. Hauptmann. Representations of keypoint-based semantic concept detection: A comprehensive study. *IEEE Transactions on Multimedia*, 12(1):42–53, January 2010.

[28] A. Kittur, E. H. Chi, and B. Suh. Crowdsourcing user studies with mechanical turk. In *Proceedings of the SIGCHI Conference on Human Factors in Computing Systems (CHI 2008)*, pages 453–456, New York, NY, USA, April 2008. ACM.

[29] N. Krüger, P. Janssen, S. Kalkan, M. Lappe, A. Leonardis, J. Piater, A. J. Rodríguez-Sánchez, and L. Wiskott. Deep hierarchies in the primate visual cortex: What can we learn for computer vision? *IEEE Transactions on Pattern Analysis and Machine Intelligence*, 35(8):1847–1871, August 2013.

[30] A. Krizhevsky, I. Sutskever, and G. Hinton. ImageNet classification with deep convolutional neural networks. In F. Pereira, C. J. C. Burges, L. Bottou, and K. Q. Weinberger, editors, *Advances in Neural Information Processing Systems (NIPS) 25*, pages 1106–1114. Curran Associates, Inc., 2012.

[31] C. H. Lampert, H. Nickisch, and S. Harmeling. Learning to detect unseen object classes by between-class attribute transfer. In *Proceedings of the 2009 IEEE Conference on Computer Vision and Pattern Recognition (CVPR 2009)*, pages 951–958, Washington, DC, USA, June 2009. IEEE Computer Society.

[32] Q. Le, M. Ranzato, R. Monga, M. Devin, K. Chen, G. Corrado, J. Dean, and A. Ng. Building high-level features using large scale unsupervised learning. In *Proceedings of the 29th International Conference on Machine Learning (ICML 2012)*, New York, NY, USA, June 2012. ACM.

[33] X. Li and C. G. M. Snoek. Visual categorization with negative examples for free. In *Proceedings of the 17th ACM International Conference on Multimedia (MM 2009)*, pages 661–664, New York, NY, USA, October 2009. ACM.

[34] Xirong Li, Dong Wang, Jianmin Li, and Bo Zhang. Video search in concept subspace: A text-like paradigm. In *Proceedings of the 6th ACM International Conference on Image and Video Retrieval (CIVR 2007)*, pages 603–610, New York, NY, USA, July 2007. ACM.

[35] J. Liu, S. McCloskey, and Y. Liu. Local expert forest of score fusion for video event classification. In *Proceedings of the 12th European Conference on Computer Vision (ECCV 2012)*, pages 397–410, Berlin, Heidelberg, October 2012. Springer Berlin Heidelberg.

[36] D. G. Lowe. Object recognition from local scale-invariant features. In *Proceedings of the International Conference on Computer Vision (ICCV 1999)*, pages 1150–1157, Washington, DC, USA, September 1999. IEEE Computer Society.

[37] Z. Lu and K. Grauman. Story-driven summarization for egocentric video. In *Proceedings of the 2013 IEEE Conference on Computer Vision and Pattern Recognition (CVPR 2013)*, pages 2714–2721, Washington, DC, USA, June 2013. IEEE Computer Society.

[38] Y. Matsumoto, T. Shinozaki, K. Shirahama, M. Grzegorzek, and K. Uehara. Kobe university, nict and university of siegen on the trecvid 2016 avs task. In *Proceedings of TREC Video Retrieval Evaluation (TRECVID) 2016 Workshop (TRECVID 2016)*, Gaithersburg, MD, USA, November 2016. National Institute of Standards and Technology (NIST).

[39] M. Mazloom, A. Habibian, and C. G. M. Snoek. Querying for video events by semantic signatures from few examples. In *Proceedings of the 21st ACM International Conference on Multimedia (MM 2013)*, pages 609–612, New York, NY, USA, October 2013. ACM.

[40] M. Merler, B. Huang, L. Xie, G. Hua, and A. Natsev. Semantic model vectors for complex video event recognition. *IEEE Transactions on Multimedia*, 14(1):88–101, February 2012.

[41] T. Mikolov, I. Sutskever, K. Chen, G. S. Corrado, and J. Dean. Distributed representations of words and phrases and their compositionality. In C. J. C. Burges, L. Bottou, M. Welling, Z. Ghahramani, and K. Q. Weinberger, editors, *Advances in Neural Information Processing Systems (NIPS) 26*, pages 3111–3119. Curran Associates, Inc., 2013.

[42] M. Naphade, J.R. Smith, J. Tesic, S.-F. Chang, W. Hsu, L. Kennedy, A. Hauptmann, and J. Curtis. Large-scale concept ontology for multimedia. *IEEE Multimedia*, 13(3):86–91, July-September 2006.

[43] M. R. Naphade and J. R. Smith. On the detection of semantic concepts at TRECVID. In *Proceedings of the 12th Annual ACM International Conference on Multimedia (MM 2004)*, pages 660–667, New York, NY, USA, October 2004. ACM.

[44] A. P. Natsev, M. R. Naphade, and J. Tešić. Learning the semantics of multimedia queries and concepts from a small number of examples. In *Proceedings of the 13th Annual ACM International Conference on Multimedia (MM 2005)*, pages 598–607, New York, NY, USA, November 2005. ACM.

[45] Apostol (Paul) Natsev, Alexander Haubold, Jelena Tešić, Lexing Xie, and Rong Yan. Semantic concept-based query expansion and reranking for multimedia retrieval. In *Proceedings of the 15th ACM International Conference on Multimedia (MM 2007)*, pages 991–1000, New York, NY, USA, September 2007. ACM.

[46] C. Ngo, Y.-G. Jiang, X.-Y. Wei, W. Zhao, Y. Liu, J. Wang, S. Zhu, and S.-F. Chang. VIREO/DVM at TRECVID 2009: High-level feature extraction, automatic video search and content-based copy detection. In *Proceedings of TREC Video Retrieval Evaluation (TRECVID) 2009 Workshop (TRECVID 2009)*, pages 415–432, Gaithersburg, MD, USA, November 2009. National Institute of Standards and Technology (NIST).

[47] E. Nowak, F. Jurie, and B. Triggs. Sampling strategies for bag-of-features image classification. In *Proc. of the Ninth European Conference on Computer Vision (ECCV 2006)*, pages 490–503, Berlin, Heidelberg, May 2006. Springer Berlin Heidelberg.

[48] A. Parkash and D. Parikh. Attributes for classifier feedback. In *Proceedings of the 12th European Conference on Computer Vision (ECCV 2012)*, pages 354–368, Berlin, Heidelberg, October 2012. Springer Berlin Heidelberg.

[49] F. Perronnin and C. Dance. Fisher kernels on visual vocabularies for image categorization. In *Proceedings of the 2007 IEEE Conference on Computer Vision and Pattern Recognition (CVPR 2007)*, pages 1–8, Washington, DC, USA, June 2007. IEEE Computer Society.

[50] A. J. Quinn and B. B. Bederson. Human computation: A survey and taxonomy of a growing field. In *Proceedings of the SIGCHI Conference on Human Factors in Computing Systems (CHI 2011)*, pages 1403–1412, New York, NY, USA, May 2011. ACM.

[51] N. Rasiwasia, P.J. Moreno, and N. Vasconcelos. Bridging the gap: Query by semantic example. *IEEE Transactions on Multimedia*, 9(5):923–938, August 2007.

[52] O. Russakovsky, J. Deng, H. Su, J. Krause, S. Satheesh, S. Ma, Z. Huang, A. Karpathy, A. Khosla, M. Bernstein, A. C. Berg, and F.-F. Li. ImageNet large scale visual recognition challenge. *International Journal of Computer Vision*, 115(3):211–252, December 2015.

[53] A. Scherp and V. Mezaris. Survey on modeling and indexing events in multimedia. *Multimedia Tools and Applications*, 70(1):7–23, May 2014.

[54] C. Schmid and R. Mohr. Local grayvalue invariants for image retrieval. *IEEE Transactions on Pattern Analysis and Machine Intelligence*, 19(5):530–535, May 1997.

[55] K. Shirahama and M. Grzegorzek. Towards Large-Scale Multimedia Retrieval Enriched by Knowledge about Human Interpretation - Retrospective Survey. *Multimedia Tools and Applications*, 75(1):297–331, January 2016.

[56] K. Shirahama, M. Grzegorzek, and B. Indurkhya. Human-Machine Cooperation in Large-Scale Multimedia Retrieval: A Survey. *Journal of Problem Solving*, 8(1):36–63, 2015.

[57] K. Shirahama, M. Grzegorzek, and K. Uehara. Weakly supervised detection of video events using hidden conditional random fields. *International Journal of Multimedia Information Retrieval*, 4(1):17–32, March 2015.

[58] K. Shirahama, K. Kumabuchi, M. Grzegorzek, and K. Uehara. Video retrieval based on uncertain concept detection using dempster-shafer theory. In A. K. Baughman, J. Gao, J.-Y. Pan, and V. Petrushin, editors, *Multimedia Data Mining and Analytics: Disruptive Innovation*, pages 269–294. Springer International Publishing, 2015.

[59] K. Shirahama, Y. Matsuoka, and K. Uehara. Event retrieval in video archives using rough set theory and partially supervised learning. *Multimedia Tools and Applications*, 57(1):145–173, March 2012.

[60] K. Shirahama, Y. Matsuoka, and K. Uehara. Hybrid negative example selection using visual and conceptual features. *Multimedia Tools and Applications*, 71(3):967–989, August 2014.

[61] K. Shirahama and K. Uehara. Kobe university and Muroran institute of technology at TRECVID 2012 semantic indexing task. In *Proceedings of TREC Video Retrieval Evaluation (TRECVID) 2012 Workshop (TRECVID 2012)*, pages 239–247, Gaithersburg, MD, USA, November 2012. National Institute of Standards and Technology (NIST).

[62] K. Simonyan and A. Zisserman. Very deep convolutional networks for large-scale image recognition. *CoRR*, abs/1409.1556, 2014.

[63] A. F. Smeaton, P. Over, and W. Kraaij. Evaluation campaigns and TRECVid. In *Proceedings of the 8th ACM International Workshop on Multimedia Information Retrieval (MIR 2006)*, pages 321–330, New York, NY, USA, October 2006. ACM.

[64] A.W.M. Smeulders, M. Worring, S. Santini, A. Gupta, and R. Jain. Content-based image retrieval at the end of the early years. *IEEE Transactions on Pattern Analysis and Machine Intelligence*, 22(12):1349–1380, December 2000.

[65] C. *et al.* Snoek. The MediaMill TRECVID 2009 semantic video search engine. In *Proceedings of TREC Video Retrieval Evaluation (TRECVID) 2009 Workshop (TRECVID 2009)*, pages 226–238,

Gaithersburg, MD, USA, November 2009. National Institute of Standards and Technology (NIST).

[66] C. G. M. Snoek and M. Worring. Concept-based video retrieval. *Foundations and Trends in Information Retrieval*, 2(4):215–322, April 2009.

[67] C. G. M Snoek, M. Worring, J.-M. Geusebroek, D. Koelma, and F.J. Seinstra. On the surplus value of semantic video analysis beyond the key frame. In *Proceedings of the 2005 IEEE International Conference on Multimedia and Expo (ICME 2005)*, pages 386–389, Washington, DC, USA, July 2005. IEEE Computer Society.

[68] N. Srivastava, E. Mansimov, and R. Salakhutdinov. Unsupervised learning of video representations using lstms. In *Proceedings of the 32Nd International Conference on International Conference on Machine Learning (ICML 2015)*, pages 843–852. JMLR.org, July 2015.

[69] S. Staab, A. Scherp, R. Arndt, R. Troncy, M. Grzegorzek, C. Saathoff, S. Schenk, and L. Hardman. Semantic Multimedia. In C. Baroglio, P. A. Bonatti, J. Maluszynski, M. Marchiori, A. Polleres, and S. Schaffert, editors, *Reasoning Web*, chapter 4, pages 125–170. Springer LNCS 5224, San Servolo, Island, September 2008.

[70] C. Sun and R. Nevatia. ACTIVE: Activity concept transitions in video event classification. In *Proceedings of the 2013 IEEE International Conference on Computer Vision (ICCV 2013)*, pages 913–920, Washington, DC, USA, December 2013. IEEE Computer Society.

[71] C. Szegedy, W. Liu, Y. Jia, P. Sermanet, S. Reed, D. Anguelov, D. Erhan, V. Vanhoucke, and A. Rabinovich. Going deeper with convolutions. In *Proceedings of the 2015 IEEE Conference on Computer Vision and Pattern Recognition (CVPR 2015)*, pages 1–9, Washington, DC, USA, June 2015. IEEE Computer Society.

[72] R. Tadeusiewicz. Intelligent web mining for semantically adequate images. In *Proceedings of the Fifth Atlantic Web Intelligence Conference (AWIC 2007)*, pages 3–10, Berlin, Heidelberg, June 2007. Springer Berlin Heidelberg.

[73] K. Tanaka, Y. Ariki, and K. Uehara. Organization and retrieval of video data (special issue on new generation database technologies).

IEICE Transactions on Information and Systems, 82(1):34–44, January 1999.

[74] K. Tang, F.-F. Li, and D. Koller. Learning latent temporal structure for complex event detection. In *Proceedings of the 2012 IEEE Conference on Computer Vision and Pattern Recognition (CVPR 2012)*, pages 1250–1257, Washington, DC, USA, June 2012. IEEE Computer Society.

[75] J. Tešič, A. P. Natsev, and J. R. Smith. Cluster-based data modeling for semantic video search. In *Proceedings of the 6th ACM International Conference on Image and Video Retrieval (CIVR 2007)*, pages 595–602, New York, NY, USA, July 2007. ACM.

[76] A. Tim, H. O. Song, and T. Darrell. Detection bank: An object detection based video representation for multimedia event recognition. In *Proceedings of the 20th ACM International Conference on Multimedia (MM 2012)*, pages 1065–1068, New York, NY, USA, October 2012. ACM.

[77] A. Torralba, R. Fergus, and W.T. Freeman. 80 million tiny images: A large data set for nonparametric object and scene recognition. *IEEE Transactions on Pattern Analysis and Machine Intelligence*, 30(11):1958–1970, November 2008.

[78] D. Tran, L. Bourdev, R. Fergus, L. Torresani, and M. Paluri. Learning spatiotemporal features with 3d convolutional networks. In *Proceedings of the 2015 IEEE International Conference on Computer Vision (ICCV 2015)*, pages 4489–4497, Washington, DC, USA, December 2015. IEEE Computer Society.

[79] Vapnik V. *Statistical Learning Theory*. Wiley-Interscience, Hoboken, NJ, USA, 1998.

[80] Ar. Vahdat, K. Cannons, G. Mori, S. Oh, and I. Kim. Compositional models for video event detection: A multiple kernel learning latent variable approach. In *Proceedings of the 2013 IEEE International Conference on Computer Vision (ICCV 2013)*, pages 1185–1192, Washington, DC, USA, December 2013. IEEE Computer Society.

[81] K. E. A. van de Sande, T. Gevers, and C. G. M. Snoek. Evaluating color descriptors for object and scene recognition. *IEEE Transactions on Pattern Analysis and Machine Intelligence*, 32(9):1582–1596, September 2010.

[82] K. E. A. van de Sande, T. Gevers, and C. G. M. Snoek. Empowering visual categorization with the GPU. *IEEE Transactions on Multimedia*, 13(1):60–70, February 2011.

[83] T. Volkmer, J. R. Smith, and A. P. Natsev. A web-based system for collaborative annotation of large image and video collections: an evaluation and user study. In *Proceedings of the 13th Annual ACM International Conference on Multimedia (MM 2005)*, pages 892–901, New York, NY, USA, November 2005. ACM.

[84] L. von Ahn and L. Dabbish. Labeling images with a computer game. In *Proceedings of the SIGCHI Conference on Human Factors in Computing Systems (CHI 2004)*, pages 319–326, New York, NY, USA, April 2004. ACM.

[85] L. von Ahn and L. Dabbish. Designing games with a purpose. *Communications of the ACM*, 51(8):58–67, August 2008.

[86] H. Wang, A. Klaser, C. Schmid, and C.-L. Liu. Action recognition by dense trajectories. In *Proceedings of the 2011 IEEE Conference on Computer Vision and Pattern Recognition (CVPR 2011)*, pages 3169–3176, Washington, DC, USA, June 2011. IEEE Computer Society.

[87] M. Wang and X.-S. Hua. Active learning in multimedia annotation and retrieval: A survey. *ACM Transactions on Intelligent Systems and Technology*, 2(2):10:1–10:21, February 2011.

[88] X.-Y. Wei, Y.-G. Jiang, and C.-W. Ngo. Concept-driven multi-modality fusion for video search. *IEEE Transactions on Circuits and Systems for Video Technology*, 21(1):62–73, January 2011.

[89] U. Westermann and R. Jain. Toward a common event model for multimedia applications. *IEEE Multimedia*, 14(1):19–29, January-March 2007.

[90] R. Yan, M.-O. Fleury, M. Merler, A. Natsev, and J. R. Smith. Large-scale multimedia semantic concept modeling using robust subspace

bagging and mapreduce. In *Proceedings of the First ACM Workshop on Large-scale Multimedia Retrieval and Mining (LS-MMRM 2009)*, pages 35–42, New York, NY, USA, October 2009. ACM.

[91] J. Yang, K. Yu, Y. Gong, and T. Huang. Linear spatial pyramid matching using sparse coding for image classification. In *Proceedings of the 2009 IEEE Conference on Computer Vision and Pattern Recognition (CVPR 2009)*, pages 1794–1801, Washington, DC, USA, June 2009. IEEE Computer Society.

[92] K. Yu, T. Zhang, and Y. Gong. Nonlinear learning using local coordinate coding. In Y. Bengio, D. Schuurmans, J. Lafferty, C. K. I. Williams, and A. Culotta, editors, *Advances in Neural Information Processing Systems (NIPS) 22*, pages 2223–2231. Curran Associates Inc., 2009.

[93] Z.-J. Zha, L. Yang, T. Mei, M. Wang, Z. Wang, T.-S. Chua, and X.-S. Hua. Visual query suggestion: Towards capturing user intent in internet image search. *ACM Transactions on Multimedia Computing, Communications, and Applications*, 6(3):13:1–13:19, August 2010.

[94] H. Zhang, Y.-J. Lu, M. de Boer, F. ter Haar, Z. Qiu, K. Schutte, W. Kraaij, and C.-W. Ngo. Vireo-tno @ trecvid 2015: Multimedia event detection. In *Proceedings of TREC Video Retrieval Evaluation (TRECVID) 2015 Workshop (TRECVID 2015)*, Gaithersburg, MD, USA, November 2015. National Institute of Standards and Technology (NIST).

[95] H. Zhang, Z.-J. Zha, Y. Yang, S. Yan, Y. Gao, and T.-S. Chua. Attribute-augmented semantic hierarchy: Towards bridging semantic gap and intention gap in image retrieval. In *Proceedings of the 21st ACM International Conference on Multimedia (MM 2013)*, pages 33–42, New York, NY, USA, October 2013. ACM.

[96] J. Zhang, M. Marszalek, S. Lazebnik, and C. Schmid. Local features and kernels for classification of texture and object categories: A comprehensive study. *International Journal of Computer Vision*, 73(2):213–238, June 2007.

[97] X.S. Zhou and T.S. Huang. Relevance feedback in image retrieval: A comprehensive review. *Multimedia Systems*, 8(6):536–544, April 2003.

[98] S. Zhu, X.-Y. Wei, and C.-W. Ngo. Error recovered hierarchical classification. In *Proceedings of the 21st ACM International Conference on Multimedia (MM 2013)*, pages 697–700, New York, NY, USA, October 2013. ACM.

Chapter 3

Shape-Based Object Recognition

This chapter addresses approaches for shape representation and matching, including own contributions. Section 3.1 states the problem of shape-based object recognition and motivates its practical importance. Strategies for shape representation with coarse- and fine-grained features are proposed and discussed in Section 3.2. In Section 3.3, matching algorithms for the aforementioned shape descriptors are introduced. Experiments and results are presented in Section 3.4. Finally, conclusions are drawn and further possible research directions are listed in Section 3.5.

3.1 Problem Statement and Motivation

Shape is a very important object property being perceptually unique due to the fact that it is both complex and structured. Shapes are perceived veridically and are the only perceptual attributes of objects that allow unambiguous classification [54]. Estimating similarities of object shapes belongs to the most common unconscious human activities. Humans process shapes using a huge knowledge database of prior experiences and taking into account the surrounding environment. For instance, a horse and a cat become, for humans, less similar to each other, if a dog suddenly appears in the scene and chases away a stork. Moreover, humans unconsciously consider both the outer contour and the topology of an object for categorisation. However, it is really difficult to imitate the amazing human shape interpretation and abstraction capabilities with computer-based algorithms [75].

Shape-based object representation (Section 3.2) requires effective and perceptually significant features based on either boundary or region information. However, there are three main challenges. The first one is how to extract efficient descriptors that are invariant to shape rotation, translation and scaling. The second one is how to extract shape descriptors that are robust to noise and distortions. The third challenge is how to generate descriptors with low computational complexity. In Section 3.2, two main strategies to face these challenges are presented. Firstly, simple geometry descriptors for capturing coarse-grained shape features are described. Secondly, rich descriptors modelling fine-grained shape details are presented.

Shape matching (Section 3.3) aims to calculate the overall similarity (or dissimilarity) between two object shapes based on their descriptors. For coarse-grained shape descriptors, the matching between shapes is usually conducted using state-of-the-art vector similarity/dissimilarity functions. In contrast, fine-grained shape descriptors often have complex structures and the matching process usually optimises the assignment of shape parts. Several matching algorithms for coarse- and fine-grained shape features are described in Section 3.3.

3.2   Shape Representation

Shape-based object representation requires perceptually significant features extracted from object boundary information. It is sufficient to generate coarse-grained shape descriptors modelling global shape properties for some applications (e.g., [26, 74]). For others, fine-grained shape descriptors capturing detailed shape information are necessary.

3.2.1   Survey of Related Methods

A detailed review of coarse-grained shape representation techniques is given in [2, 85]. According to [80], common coarse-grained shape descriptors include the area, the circularity (perimeter^2/area), the eccentricity (length of major axis/length of minor axis), the major axis orientation, the bending energy, etc. Other descriptors including convexity, ratio of principle axis, circular variance and elliptic variance have been proposed by Peura *et al.* [53]. These descriptors can only discriminate shapes with large-scale differences. B-Splines [16, 27, 72] are also used for shape representation. Chain codes [3, 81], a widely known shape representation technique, are not reliable for object matching [3] due to discretisation errors with respect to rotation and scale [32].

Compared to the representation methods listed above, signature-based shape descriptors have a higher ability to discriminate coarse-grained differences. A shape signature represents a shape by a one dimensional function derived from boundary points [85]. Many signature-based shape descriptors exist [71, 84], including centroidal profile, complex coordinates, centroid distance, tangent angle, cumulative angle, curvature and chord-length, etc. Besides the high matching cost, shape signatures are sensitive to noise, and slight changes in the boundary can cause large errors in matching [84].

Fine-grained shape descriptors are classified into two types: contour- and region-based methods. A detailed discussion and review of those methods can be found in [79].

One of the most common contour-based shape representation techniques is called Shape Context [10]. Its basic idea is to pick a certain number of points on the shape contour and describe each of them using the properties of its connections to remaining points. Sharon et al. [61] proposed the figure print of a shape. It is generated by a series of conformal maps, starting from mapping the object to a unit circle in the complex plane, then from the boundary of the object to the exterior of the circle, so that the final boundary is a diffeomorphism from the unit circle to itself. In contrast to these approaches, Maney et al. [47] used integral invariants to describe shapes with similar invariant properties as their differential counterparts. An advantage of such a structural invariant approach is the ability to handle occlusions and possibility of partial matching in shapes. With this motivation, several invariant-based shape representation methods have been proposed [28, 78, 32]. There are four types of commonly used invariants: (1) algebraic invariants [67], (2) geometric invariants [62], (3) differential invariants [13], and (4) integral invariants [28, 32]. A broad review of those types of invariants used for shape representation is given in [13].

Another category of shape description methods integrates local and global contour properties in a hierarchical way. McNeill et al. [50] introduced a hierarchical procrustes method for shape matching based on shape contour segmentation. The hierarchical representation avoids the problems associated with pure global or local descriptors. Xu et al. [73] established the contour flexibility technique to extract both global and local features that depicts the deformable potential at contour points. Felzenszwalb *et al.* presented in [24] the shape tree algorithm which segments a curve into two halves in the middle, and the two halves are further segmented into respective halves. Raftopoulos *et al.* [55] proposed a method based on global-local transformation to represent shape curvature being robust to noise. Bai *et al.* [7] introduced the shape vocabulary representation using bag-of-words, where the shape contours are segmented into fragments and represented as words of shape contours in different scales. Although most of those descriptors are invariant to shape rotation, translation and scaling, they need to sample many contour points to precisely represent the shape characteristics. The main reason is that since those methods do not know which contour point is useful for matching, they need to use a large number of contour points to achieve accurate correspondences and alignments. Thus, all of the descriptors mentioned above incur high computational complexity.

Region-based shape descriptors take advantage of the information from the inside of a shape. One of the most commonly used methods is based on skeletonisation. Skeleton is an important shape descriptor for deformable object matching since it integrates both geometrical and topological features of an object. Skeleton-based descriptors usually lead to a better performance than contour-based shape descriptors in the presence of partial occlusion and articulation of parts [59]. This is because skeletons have a notion of both the interior and the exterior of the shape, and are useful for finding the intuitive correspondence of deformable shapes. In order to generate proper skeletons for object matching, several skeletonisation methods have been developed [19, 25, 36, 49]. One typical approach is the Max-Disk Model [15] which continuously collects the centre points of maximal tangent disks that touch the object boundary in two or more locations. However, the skeleton obtained by this approach is sensitive to small changes and noises in the object boundary [52, 63]. The reason is that a small protrusion on the boundary may result in a large skeleton branch. To solve this problem, Cong *et al.* [77] proposed an algorithm to represent a shape using hierarchical skeletons. A hierarchical skeleton is a collection of skeletons representing a shape at different granularity levels.

Recently, researchers have begun to combine both contour- and region-based shape features for robust shape matching and classification. Bai *et al.* [8] proposed to integrate shape contour and skeleton for object classification. This method can also be extended to incorporate other shape features like Shape Context (SC) [10] and Inner Distance (ID) [42], etc.

Shen *et al.* [64] proposed to recognise shapes by a new shape descriptor which captures the features of a contour fragment associated with skeletal information. Benefiting from the association, this descriptor provides the complementary geometric information from both contour and skeleton parts, including the spatial distribution and the thickness change along the shape part.

3.2.2 Coarse-grained Shape Representation

In this section, an intuitive coarse-grained shape descriptor with low computation complexity is proposed. The biggest motivation of this descriptor is that for some shapes, partition points are difficult to be generated. For instance, the Discrete Curve Evolution (DCE) [6] cannot be applied on a circle since all contour points could be vertices. Therefore, the shape descriptor proposed in this section is directly calculated based on shape regions. Prior to feature extraction, the orientation of each shape is adjusted by rotating it to the angle so that the straight line connecting its two maximally distant contour points becomes vertical and the majority of contour points lie on the left side of this line (see Figure 3.1). If the

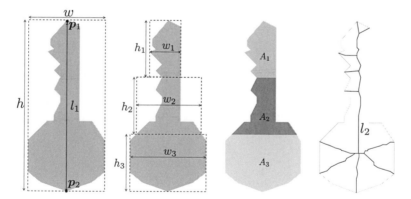

Figure 3.1: Shape bounding box and equally high sub-boxes ($h_1 = h_2 = h_3$) used for feature extraction. A_1, A_2 and A_3 are the areas of the top, middle, and bottom sub-objects, respectively.

number of contour points on both sides of the line defined by p_1 and p_2 is the same, the orientation is adjusted so that the straight line connecting its two maximally distant contour points becomes vertical and the majority of contour points lie on the upper $h/2$ side. If the object has a star-like or circle-like shape, one straight line connecting its two maximally distant contour points is selected and the shape is rotated so that the straight line becomes vertical.

After rotation, an object shape is described by a 10-dimensional feature vector. For this, the bounding box of the whole shape as well as the three equally high sub-boxes are used for feature generation (Figure 3.1). For feature generation, the first f_1' and the last feature f_{10}' express the length of a shape contour and the length of a shape skeleton l_2, respectively. Here, the shape skeleton is generated by the fast thinning algorithm presented in [86] without any pre- and post-processing steps. The remaining features are computed as follows:

$$
\begin{aligned}
f_2' &= \tfrac{h}{w}; \quad f_3' = \tfrac{h_1}{w_1}; \quad f_4' = \tfrac{h_2}{w_2}; \qquad\qquad f_5' = \tfrac{h_3}{w_3}; \\
f_6' &= \tfrac{A_3}{A_1}; \quad f_7' = \tfrac{A_2}{A_1}; \quad f_8' = A_1 + A_2 + A_3; \quad f_9' = l_1
\end{aligned}
\tag{3.1}
$$

Subsequently, two feature normalisation steps are performed. First, in order to ensure scale invariance, the non-ratio elements (f_1', f_8', f_9' and f_{10}') of the feature vector are divided by a half of the bounding box perimeter. Second, all the feature values are linearly scaled to the range $(0, 1]$ with the following equation:

$$
f_i = \frac{f_i' - \min\{f_1', \cdots, f_{10}'\} + 1}{\max\{f_1', \cdots, f_{10}'\} - \min\{f_1', \cdots, f_{10}'\} + 1}
\tag{3.2}
$$

In order to avoid $f_i = 0$ and a zero denominator, a value 1 is added to both, the numerator and the denominator. This scaling procedure is needed for the Support Vector Machine (SVM) [68] applied in the classification tasks. It avoids attributes in greater numeric ranges dominating the small ones. Another reason for the scaling is to avoid numerical difficulties during the calculation. Because kernel values usually depend on the inner products of feature vectors (e.g., the linear kernel and the polynomial kernel), large attribute values might cause numerical problems. After the normalisation, a shape can be represented by a feature vector with 10 normalised feature values:

$$
\boldsymbol{f} = (f_1, f_2, \ldots, f_i, \ldots, f_{10})^{\mathrm{T}}
\tag{3.3}
$$

3.2.3 Fine-grained Shape Representation

Considering all contour points for determining the similarity between object shapes causes high computational costs. Moreover, most of the contour points do not possess any relevance for the description of the shape characteristics. For this reason, the method described in this section represents a shape with only a small number of interesting points. Each interesting point is defined as a contour point that represents a rigid region of a shape. More specifically, shapes are usually composed of different regions (Figure 3.2 (a)) with some regions being likely to be deformed. In contrast,

(a) Shape regions   (b) Interesting points

Figure 3.2: Shape regions and interesting points.

other regions are resilient against shape deformations like the bird's head, bone ends or the handle of a hammer in Figure 3.2. Such regions are regarded as rigid. As interesting points are mainly detected within rigid regions, they are robust to shape deformation (Figure 3.2 (b)).

In this section, a procedure to select interesting points (Paragraph: Interesting Points) and a method to describe those points by feature vectors (Paragraph: Point Context) are presented.

Interesting Points: In this paragraph, the procedure of selecting interesting points $p_{i=1,...,N}$ from a given shape is shortly summarised. It is based on the assumption that distinctive contour parts like the legs or the tail of an elephant are characterised by a high curvature in comparison to the overall shape trend [77]. The procedure itself consists of the following steps. First, a polygonisation process is performed to suppress contour noise without removing significant shape parts. For this, the well-known *Douglas-Peucker* technique [21] is recursively applied to the object's contour. As a result, the contour is converted into a polygon. Second, the so called reference point of the object shape is localised. It is a point inside of the shape having the highest distance to the contour. Third, the distance between each single contour point and its closest reference point is computed. By ordering these values, a sequence is generated where interesting points characterised by high curvatures are detected as peaks. Figure 3.3 shows results of interesting points selection for exemplary shapes.

Point Context: In [45, 46], the so called point context descriptor is proposed representing each interesting point $p_{i=1,2,...,N}$ based on its geo-

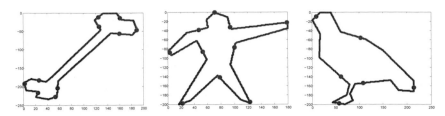

Figure 3.3: Interesting points of a bone, a bird and a person.

metrical and topological location. It is calculated using vectors originating from p_i to all other sample points $q_{i=1,2,...,M}$ on a shape contour in the clockwise order. For p_i, two vectors are computed, one representing the distance of p_i to each of $q_{j=1,2,...,M}$, and the second representing the orientation of the vector from p_i to each $q_{j=1,2,...,M}$. The distance from p_i to q_j is defined as follows:

$$\mathcal{D}_{i,j} = \log(1 + \|p_i - q_j\|^2) \quad . \tag{3.4}$$

The orientation $\Theta_{i,j}$ is defined as the orientation of the vector $p_i - q_j$. In this way, a single interesting point p_i is represented by two M-dimensional vectors $\mathcal{D}_{i,\star}$ and $\Theta_{i,\star}$.

The proposed point descriptor is different from the method described in [10]. Firstly, it only considers interesting points for feature vector computation instead of uniformly or randomly selecting sample points. This strategy can reduce the mismatches and computational complexity conspicuously. Secondly, the point descriptor described above is translation and scaling invariant since the distance between point contexts is computed after normalising $\mathcal{D}_{i,j}$ and $\Theta_{i,j}$. In addition, the point context features are generated by the Euclidean distance and the four quadrant inverse tangent methods, i.e., their values remain the same even if a shape is rotated. Thus, the proposed descriptor is also rotation invariant. On the contrary, the approach in [10] is not intrinsically rotation invariant because each point is characterised by the tangent angle which is ineffective in case of points for which no reliable tangent can be computed.

Shape Representation: Finally, given an arbitrary shape, its contour can be represented by coordinates as well as the distance and orientation vectors for all interesting points:

$$\{p_i, \mathcal{D}_{i,\star}, \Theta_{i,\star}\} \quad ; \quad i = 1, \ldots, N \quad . \tag{3.5}$$

60

Here, the rotation invariance property of Eq. 3.5 is briefly discussed. Theoretically, for a single interesting point, the proposed point context descriptor is rotation invariant since it employs methods like Euclidean distance and four quadrant inverse tangent stabilising the point context features even if the shape is rotated. However, considering a shape with multiple interesting points, the proposed global descriptor (Eq. 3.5) is not completely invariant to rotation since the order of interesting points may change if it is rotated. This problem can be easily solved by some shape preprocessing methods [76].

3.3   Shape Matching

In this section, several shape matching methods using the descriptors presented in Section 3.2 are introduced. Before going further into this discussion, it is important to clarify the meaning and the aim of shape matching. In some publications [5, 10, 47], shape matching indicates a process of putting into correspondence different parts of two given shapes [47]. For instance, establishing point correspondence among contours or skeletons, searching corresponding sub-regions between shapes, etc. Based on the correspondences between points or regions, a similarity (or dissimilarity) value can be calculated to compare shapes. However, for some descriptors, the correspondence-based shape matching cannot be properly applied due to the feature structure [18, 75] and time complexity constraints [45, 46]. In such cases, a shape similarity (or dissimilarity) is calculated by vector distance methods [11, 17, 57, 82] or feature statistics [18, 46]. No matter how the shape similarity (or dissimilarity) is calculated, the ultimate goal is to compare objects based on their contours. With these observations, shape matching in this section means a process of calculating similarity (or dissimilarity) between two given shapes based on their descriptors.

3.3.1   Survey of Related Methods

For coarse-grained features, shape matching is performed by calculating similarities (or dissimilarities) between shapes without investigating correspondences between points or regions. The most commonly applied methods in this context include Euclidean distance [17], correlation [82], HI [57], χ^2-statistics [57] and Hellinger [11], etc. These algorithms treat shape descriptors as global feature vectors and calculate similarities or dissimilarities based on appropriate vector functions. One drawback of those methods is that they assume each feature space dimension to have the same relevance in terms of distinguishing two given shapes which is not always reasonable. In some cases, discriminative properties of a feature space need to be analysed in detail by methods like Fisher Linear Discriminant Analysis [58]. If the influence of each feature can be flexibly weighted for a particular shape dataset, the discriminative power of the shape descriptor can be improved.

For fine-grained features, shapes are usually matched by searching correspondences on points or other elements of two given shapes. Comprehensive surveys of shape matching techniques with respect to correspondence can be found in [51, 70]. In contrast to coarse-grained shape matching methods, correspondence-based shape matching measures the similarity between shapes using element-to-element matching. Shape matching for fine-grained shape features depends on the type of descriptor used [48]. For contour-based descriptors, a matching cost is calculated by searching correspondences between shape contour points [12]. Hausdorff distance [30] calculates the distance of two point sets by both the maximum and the minimum distance between point pairs. Hence, this method is sensitive to noise and slight variations. Belongie *et al.* proposed a correspondence-based shape matching method using shape contexts [10] with the comparison of two shapes done by matching their point histograms. For region-based features, shape matching techniques involve feature analysis based on graph matching [56]. Bai *et al.* proposed a skeleton-based shape matching approach which uses the Hungarian algorithm to find the best correspondence of skeleton endpoints in terms of their geodesic paths [5]. However, all these matching methods may suffer from the initial alignment problem due to boundary noise or shape symmetry. As shown in Figure 3.4, there are many mismatched points (marked in blue) in both the skeleton-based method [5] and the shape context-based algorithm [10]. One possible way to overcome this problem is to disregard point correspondences detected with a similarity value below a certain threshold [1, 34, 57].

In addition to the methods mentioned above, several matching strategies [41, 83] have been proposed that consider geometric relations among multiple points. Leordeanu *et al.* proposed a spectral technique for matching problems using pairwise constraints [41] where the correspondence between two pairs of points is established. This strategy suffers from the similarity of lines defined by every pair of points. Zass *et al.* proposed to

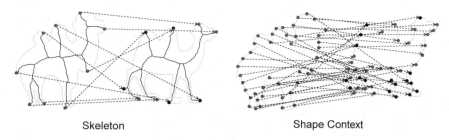

Skeleton   Shape Context

Figure 3.4: Point (green dots) correspondences between two camels determined using the skeleton-based matching [5] and the shape context-based matching approach [10].

match points using hyper-graphs [83] which are going beyond the pairwise strategy. Specifically, each point set is modelled by a hyper-graph where the relations between points are represented by hyper-edges. A match between the point sets is then modelled as a hyper-graph matching problem. Due to the theoretical advance and empirical success, hyper-graph matching has attracted increasing attention and many algorithms within this category have been introduced [14, 20, 40, 44].

3.3.2 Shape Matching using Coarse-grained Features

This section introduces the shape matching and classification methods based on the shape feature vector f defined in Section 3.2.2. Assume $f^\star$ and $f^\diamond$ are feature vectors representing two object shapes:

$$\begin{aligned}
f^\star &= (f_1^\star, f_2^\star, \cdots, f_n^\star, \cdots, f_{10}^\star)^{\mathrm{T}} \\
f^\diamond &= (f_1^\diamond, f_2^\diamond, \cdots, f_k^\diamond, \cdots, f_{10}^\diamond)^{\mathrm{T}}
\end{aligned} \qquad (3.6)$$

Now, a function for calculating the dissimilarity value between the shapes represented by $f^\star$ and by $f^\diamond$ is introduced:

$$d'(f^\star, f^\diamond) = \frac{1}{10} \sum_{m=1}^{10} \frac{\sigma_m |f_m^\star - f_m^\diamond|}{|f_m^\star + f_m^\diamond|} \quad , \qquad (3.7)$$

where σ_m is the weight for each feature to be determined in a separate optimisation process. Due to this optimisation, σ_m adapts the proposed feature space to a particular dataset. Moreover, it helps the proposed feature to avoid the overfitting problem by applying a proper σ_m to different features. The proposed dissimilarity measure has been inspired by the Chi-Square kernel [31], which comes from the Chi-Square distribution. Since the proposed shape descriptor contains a bag of features that are discretely distributed, the Chi-Square kernel can effectively model the overlap among them. The values of the dissimilarity function (Eq. 3.7) belong to the range $d(\boldsymbol{f}^{\star}, \boldsymbol{f}^{\diamond}) \in [0, 1]$ which enables their easy conversion to similarity values:

$$s(\boldsymbol{f}^{\star}, \boldsymbol{f}^{\diamond}) = 1 - d'(\boldsymbol{f}^{\star}, \boldsymbol{f}^{\diamond}) \quad . \tag{3.8}$$

3.3.3   Shape Matching using Fine-grained Features

Based on the properties of the shape descriptor discussed in Section 3.2.3, the aim is to consider the geometric relations among multiple interesting points using high-order graph matching, which is an approach to match two graphs by extracting the correspondences of multiple nodes [69]. This approach is adopted by considering nodes as interesting points described by point contexts. As shown in Figure 3.5 (a), singleton point matching is a well-known assignment problem where the interesting point is matched with one point in another shape. The pairwise matching (Figure 3.5 (b)) finds consistent correspondences between two pairs of interesting points by taking into consideration both how well their descriptors match and how similar their pairwise geometric relations are. The third-order matching (see Figure 3.5 (c)) determines the correspondence of point triples between the shapes to be compared. More specifically, a triple of interesting points in one shape is matched with a triple in another shape.

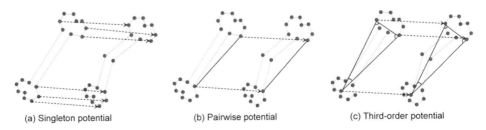

(a) Singleton potential   (b) Pairwise potential   (c) Third-order potential

Figure 3.5: Singleton, pairwise, and third-order matching.

Let $\boldsymbol{p}_{1,i} \in P_1$ and $\boldsymbol{p}_{2,j} \in P_2$ denote interesting points (and their sets) corresponding to the shapes D_1 and D_2, respectively. A set of point correspondences between P_1 and P_2 is denoted by $P = P_1 \times P_2$. Now,

	1st	2nd	3rd	4th	5th	6th	7th	8th	9th	10th
No Optimisation	700	647	600	567	521	488	447	426	405	342
Opt. by [9]	640	584	552	501	463	424	398	381	303	145
Own Opt. [76]	**700**	**657**	**615**	**591**	**553**	**518**	**475**	**467**	**420**	**363**

Table 3.1: Retrieval results on the MPEG7 dataset for different parameter optimisation techniques.

the following binary correspondence indicator is defined:

$$x_{i,j} = \begin{cases} 1 & ; \quad \text{if } \boldsymbol{p}_{1,i} \text{ corresponds to } \boldsymbol{p}_{2,j} \\ 0 & ; \quad \text{otherwise} \end{cases} . \qquad (3.9)$$

In this definition, a basic constraint is that each point from P_1 is mapped to at most one point in P_2, while for each point from P_2 there is at most one corresponding point in P_1. The general approach to determine the final point correspondence is to find an optimum distribution of $x_{i,j}$ for all elements of P so that the matching costs (singlet, pairwise, or triplet) are at a minimum [77].

3.4 Experiments and Results

In this section, experiments and results for shape-based object retrieval are described. Techniques based on coarse-grained features are evaluated in Section 3.4.1. Section 3.4.2 presents retrieval results for shapes represented by fine-grained features.

3.4.1 Shape Retrieval using Coarse-grained Features

Object retrieval algorithms based on the coarse-grained shape features are evaluated using the MPEG7 [37] dataset (Figure 3.6). MPEG7 consists of 1400 shapes representing 70 object classes (20 per class). 10 shapes from each category (altogether 700 shapes) are randomly selected for supervised parameter optimisation [76]. The remaining 700 shapes are employed for testing. Table 3.1 shows retrieval results achieved for this dataset with different optimisation options. More specifically, the numbers of correct shapes returned by the retrieval process on the first 10 positions are given,

Figure 3.6: Sample shapes from the MPEG7 [37] database.

whereas the retrieval process is conducted 700 times (once for each of the 700 testing shapes).

In addition, the retrieval result is validated using the so-called bull's eye score. To compute it, every shape in the database is compared to all other shapes, and the number of shapes from the same class among the 20 most similar shapes is reported. The bull's eye retrieval rate is the ratio of the total number of shapes from the same class to the highest possible number ($20 \times 70 = 1400$ for 700 testing shapes). The own matching algorithm applied together with the optimisation technique introduced in [76] achieves a bull's eye score of 94%.

The second experiment is conducted on the MPEG400 dataset since shapes in this dataset have much larger intra-class variations. The object retrieval results are compared to the contour-based method introduced in [75]. The experiments are performed twice, once with and once without parameter optimisation. As one can see in Table 3.2, the own algorithm described in this book outperforms the contour-based approach

MPEG400	1st	2nd	3rd	4th	5th	6th	7th	8th	9th	10th
Contour-based [75]	375	348	333	325	317	311	300	295	276	275
Own (No Opt.)	**381**	**355**	**341**	**320**	**322**	**316**	**304**	**295**	**269**	**260**
Own (Opt.)	**381**	**370**	**365**	**354**	**337**	**342**	**328**	**315**	**300**	**301**

Table 3.2: Object retrieval on the MPEG400 dataset. The second and the third row show the results for the own matching algorithm, without and with supervised parameter optimisation, respectively.

published in [75]. Moreover, supervised parameter optimisation improves the performance significantly.

3.4.2 Shape Retrieval using Fine-grained Features

In this section, the own approaches for interesting point detection (Section 3.2.3), point context description (Section 3.2.3), and high-order matching (Section 3.3.3) are experimentally compared to related state-of-the-art methods.

Interesting Point Detector: The interesting point detector described in Section 3.2.3 is evaluated using the Kimia216 dataset [60] in a shape retrieval scenario. The similarity value between each shape and its query is calculated using the interesting point matching algorithm explained in Section 3.3.3. For the isolated evaluation of the interesting point detection method, the same point descriptors as well as the same matching strategies are used for all compared algorithms. A quantitative evaluation of the own approach in comparison to related state-of-the-art methods is given in Table 3.3.

Point Context Descriptor: The experimental evaluation of the point context descriptor defined in Section 3.2.3 is performed in a shape retrieval scenario using the MPEG400 dataset consisting of 400 objects categorised in 20 classes. Its performance is compared to two related description techniques, namely Shape Context (SC) [10] and Point Context and Contour Segments (PCCS) [23]. For an isolated assessment of the description power only, the same sets of interesting points as well the same matching method (Hungarian algorithm) are applied in all three cases. Detailed

67

SC	1st	2nd	3rd	4th	5th	6th	7th	8th	9th	10th
IP1	216	210	195	184	181	172	161	146	148	128
IP2	216	205	195	190	187	179	180	170	171	161
IP3	**216**	**212**	**206**	**197**	**191**	**190**	**186**	**186**	**183**	**171**

PC	1st	2nd	3rd	4th	5th	6th	7th	8th	9th	10th
IP1	216	211	205	196	192	191	186	178	177	175
IP2	216	210	205	203	194	188	179	170	160	155
IP3	**216**	**212**	**211**	**211**	**205**	**200**	**201**	**195**	**193**	**195**

Table 3.3: Evaluation of interesting point detectors on the Kimia216 dataset [60]. SC: Shape Context [10] descriptor; PC: Point Context [77] descriptor; IP1: Interesting point detection using DCE [38]; IP2: Interesting point detection using visual curvature [43]; IP3: Interesting point detection performed with the own approach.

retrieval results are reported in Table 3.4.

High-Order Matching: The own approach for high-order matching (Section 3.3.3) is evaluated on two datasets: Kimia99 [60] and Tetrapod120. Kimia99 is composed of 9 classes, each one containing 11 shapes. Tetrapod120 includes 120 visually similar tetrapod animals categorised in six classes (camel, cattle, deer, dog, elephant, and horse). Example shapes of both datasets are depicted in Figure 3.7. The performance comparison between the own method and related state-of-the-art techniques like Inner Distance (ID) [42], Shape Context (SC) [10], and Path Similarity Skeleton Graph Matching PSSGM [5] based on both datasets (Kimia99 and Tetrapod120) is given in Table 3.5.

3.5   Conclusion and Future Trends

The last half century has seen the development of many biological or physical theories that have explicitly or implicitly involved object shapes and other spatial entities in the real world. Simultaneously, mathematicians

MPEG400	1st	2nd	3rd	4th	5th	6th	7th	8th	9th	10th
SC [10]	370	343	310	302	277	272	265	264	239	240
PCCS [23]	377	351	336	331	317	302	287	282	273	262
PC	**391**	**377**	**372**	**364**	**356**	**343**	**338**	**319**	**304**	**276**

Table 3.4: Experimental comparison of the Point Context (PC) descriptor introduced in Section 3.2.3 to SC [10] and PCCS [23] using the MPEG400 dataset.

Figure 3.7: Rows 1 and 2: Sample shapes from the Kimia99 [60] dataset. Rows 3 - 5: Tetrapod120 examples.

and other researchers have studied the properties of object shapes and have been stimulated by many application areas where object shapes are useful [66]. Moreover, computer scientists and engineers have developed numerous algorithms using object shapes. In this chapter, state-of-the-art methodology for shape representation and matching including own contributions is presented and experimentally evaluated.

For shape representation (Section 3.2), there is always a trade-off between accuracy and efficiency. On the one hand, shape should be described as accurately as possible. On the other hand, a shape descriptor should be compact to simplify indexing and retrieval. Keeping this in mind, two shape descriptors are introduced in Section 3.2. The first one captures coarse-grained shape features with low computational complexity so that it can be

Kimia99	1st	2nd	3rd	4th	5th	6th	7th	8th	9th	10th
Inner Distance [42]	99	97	92	89	85	85	76	75	63	53
Shape Context [10]	99	97	91	88	84	83	76	76	68	62
PSSGM [5]	99	99	99	99	96	97	95	93	89	73
Own Method	**99**	**99**	**96**	**92**	**88**	**84**	**80**	**78**	**73**	**60**

Tetrapod120	1st	2nd	3rd	4th	5th	6th	7th	8th	9th	10th
Inner Distance [42]	120	118	106	101	90	83	77	69	70	56
Shape Context [10]	100	80	70	53	53	51	40	28	27	27
PSSGM [5]	120	109	101	98	81	78	68	66	65	59
Own Method	**120**	**115**	**111**	**105**	**105**	**103**	**98**	**93**	**94**	**87**

Table 3.5: Experimental comparison of the own method to ID [42], SC [10], and PSSGM [5] on Kimia99 and Tetrapod120 datasets.

fused with some rich descriptors [5, 10] to improve its description power. The second one models fine-grained shape properties. Experiments illustrate that the coarse-grained features have a promising description power (Section 3.4.1) and improve their matching accuracy after fusion with rich descriptors. In Section 3.4.2, high robustness of fine-grained features is experimentally proven.

For shape matching, the algorithms are designed based on the type and structure of shape descriptors they use. Specifically, for the coarse-grained descriptor, shape matching is applied by calculating the distances between shape feature vectors. In order to improve the matching accuracy and flexibility of the coarse-grained descriptor, a supervised optimisation strategy is applied to control the discrimination power of each dimension in the feature space. For the fine-grained descriptor, shape matching is more complex since it contains rich feature structures. In addition to the inherent matching strategy, i.e., one-to-one interesting point matching, the idea of high-order graph matching is also considered to improve the matching accuracy of interesting points. For this, several potential functions are specifically designed. The experiments in Section 3.4 show the impressive robustness of the proposed methods in an object retrieval scenario.

In the future, two directions will be considered to extend the research on shape-based object retrieval. In the first one, the deep learning method [39] will be used for shape generation and recognition. With a deep learning framework [33], the shape generation and recognition could be realised in a more accurate way. For the second direction, a 2D-to-3D skeleton matching algorithm will be designed for non-rigid 2D-to-3D object matching. The last decade has witnessed a tremendous growth in 3D sensing and printing technologies. The availability of large 3D object datasets makes it necessary to explore and search in 3D shape collections. As ordinary users are not skilled to model 3D shapes as a query, one typical way is to use 2D-to-3D shape retrieval approaches such as sketch-based shape retrieval [22]. However, the underlying problem of multimodal similarity between a 3D object and its 2D representation is challenging, especially in case of non-rigid shapes [35]. As skeleton models integrate both geometrical and topological features of 2D and 3D objects, it is reasonable to consider it for non-rigid object matching. Particularly, 2D skeletons can be generated from object shapes [6] or natural images [65]. For 3D object collections, their skeletons can be formed depending on different 3D models like meshes [4], point clouds [29], etc. With the 2D-to-3D skeleton matching, both 2D object shapes and nature images can be easily used as the query for 3D object retrieval.

References

[1] Ravindra K. Ahuja, Thomas L. Magnanti, and James B. Orlin. *Network Flows: Theory, Algorithms, and Applications*. Prentice-Hall, Inc., 1993.

[2] A. Amanatiadis, V. G. Kaburlasos, A. Gasteratos, and S. E. Papadakis. Evaluation of shape descriptors for shape-based image retrieval. *IET Image Processing*, 5(5):493–499, 2011.

[3] Fabián Arrebola and Francisco Sandoval. Corner detection and curve segmentation by multiresolution chain-code linking. *Pattern Recognition*, 38(10):1596–1614, 2005.

[4] Oscar Kin-Chung Au, Chiew-Lan Tai, Hung-Kuo Chu, Daniel Cohen-Or, and Tong-Yee Lee. Skeleton extraction by mesh contraction. *ACM Transactions on Graphics*, 27(3):1–10, 2008.

[5] X. Bai and L.J. Latecki. Path similarity skeleton graph matching. *IEEE Transactions on Pattern Analysis and Machine Intelligence*, 30(7):1282–1292, 2008.

[6] X. Bai, L.J. Latecki, and Wen yu Liu. Skeleton pruning by contour partitioning with discrete curve evolution. *IEEE Transactions on Pattern Analysis and Machine Intelligence*, 29(3):449–462, 2007.

[7] X. Bai, C. Rao, and X. Wang. Shape vocabulary: A robust and efficient shape representation for shape matching. *IEEE Transactions on Image Processing*, 23(9):3935–3949, 2014.

[8] Xiang Bai, Wenyu Liu, and Zhuowen Tu. Integrating contour and skeleton for shape classification. In *IEEE International Conference on Computer Vision Workshops*, pages 360–367, 2009.

[9] Xiang Bai, Xingwei Yang, L.J. Latecki, Wenyu Liu, and Zhuowen Tu. Learning context-sensitive shape similarity by graph transduction. *IEEE Transactions on Pattern Analysis and Machine Intelligence*, 32(5):861–874, 2010.

[10] S. Belongie, J. Malik, and J. Puzicha. Shape matching and object recognition using shape contexts. *PAMI*, 24(4):509–522, 2002.

[11] A. Bhattacharyya. On a measure of divergence between two multinomial populations. *The Indian Journal of Statistics*, 7(4):401–406, 1946.

[12] Alexander M. Bronstein, Michael M. Bronstein, Alfred M. Bruckstein, and Ron Kimmel. Analysis of two-dimensional non-rigid shapes. *International Journal of Computer Vision*, 78(1):67–88, 2008.

[13] WeiGuo Cao, Ping Hu, YuJie Liu, Ming Gong, and Hua Li. Gaussian-curvature-derived invariants for isometry. *Science China Information Sciences*, 56(9):1–12, 2012.

[14] Ming-Ching Chang and Benjamin B. Kimia. Measuring 3d shape similarity by graph-based matching of the medial scaffolds. *Computer Vision and Image Understanding*, 115(5):707–720, 2011.

[15] W. Choi, K. Lam, and W. Siu. Extraction of the euclidean skeleton based on a connectivity criterion. *Pattern Recognition*, 36(3):721–729, 2003.

[16] F. S. Cohen and Jin-Yinn Wang. Part i: Modeling image curves using invariant 3-d object curve models-a path to 3-d recognition and shape estimation from image contours. *IEEE Transactions on Pattern Analysis and Machine Intelligence*, 16(1):1–12, 1994.

[17] Per-Erik Danielsson. Euclidean distance mapping. *Computer Graphics and image processing*, 14(3):227–248, 1980.

[18] Jarbas Joaci de Mesquita Sa Junior and Andre Ricardo Backes. Shape classification using line segment statistics. *Information Sciences*, 305:349–356, 2015.

[19] P. Dimitrov, James N. Damon, and K. Siddiqi. Flux invariants for shape. In *IEEE Conference on Computer Vision and Pattern Recognition*, pages 835–841, 2003.

[20] O. Duchenne, F. Bach, In-So Kweon, and J. Ponce. A tensor-based algorithm for high-order graph matching. *IEEE Transactions on Pattern Analysis and Machine Intelligence*, 33(12):2383–2395, 2011.

[21] Konrad Ebisch. A correction to the douglas-peucker line generalization algorithm. *Computers & Geosciences*, 28(8):995–997, 2002.

[22] Mathias Eitz, Ronald Richter, Tamy Boubekeur, Kristian Hildebrand, and Marc Alexa. Sketch-based shape retrieval. *ACM Transactions on Graphics*, 31(4):1–10, 2012.

[23] Christian Feinen, Cong Yang, Oliver Tiebe, and Marcin Grzegorzek. Shape matching using point context and contour segments. In *Asian Conference on Computer Vision (ACCV 2014)*, pages 95–110. Springer LNSC, November 2014.

[24] P. F. Felzenszwalb and J.D. Schwartz. Hierarchical matching of deformable shapes. In *IEEE Conference on Computer Vision and Pattern Recognition*, pages 1–8, 2007.

[25] L. Gorelick, M. Galun, E. Sharon, R. Basri, and A Brandt. Shape representation and classification using the poisson equation. *IEEE Transactions on Pattern Analysis and Machine Intelligence*, 28(12):1991–2005, 2006.

[26] M. Grzegorzek, C. Li, J. Raskatow, D. Paulus, and N. Vassilieva. Texture-based text detection in digital images with wavelet features and support vector machines. In *International Conference on Computer Recognition Systems*, pages 857–866, 2013.

[27] Yu-Hua Gu and Tardi Tjahjadi. Coarse-to-fine planar object identification using invariant curve features and b-spline modeling. *Pattern Recognition*, 33(9):1411–1422, 2000.

[28] Byung-Woo Hong and Stefano Soatto. Shape matching using multi-scale integral invariants. *IEEE Transactions on Pattern Analysis and Machine Intelligence*, 37(1):151–160, 2015.

[29] Hui Huang, Shihao Wu, Daniel Cohen-Or, Minglun Gong, Hao Zhang, Guiqing Li, and Baoquan Chen. L1-medial skeleton of point cloud. *ACM Transactions on Graphics*, 32(4):1–8, 2013.

[30] Daniel P Huttenlocher, Gregory A Klanderman, and William J Rucklidge. Comparing images using the hausdorff distance. *IEEE Transactions on Pattern Analysis and Machine Intelligence*, 15(9):850–863, 1993.

[31] Miljenko Huzak. *International Encyclopedia of Statistical Science*, chapter Chi-Square Distribution, pages 245–246. 2011.

[32] Faraz Janan and Michael Brady. Shape description and matching using integral invariants on eccentricity transformed images. *International Journal of Computer Vision*, 113(2):92–112, 2014.

[33] Yangqing Jia, Evan Shelhamer, Jeff Donahue, Sergey Karayev, Jonathan Long, Ross Girshick, Sergio Guadarrama, and Trevor Darrell. Caffe: Convolutional architecture for fast feature embedding. In *ACM International Conference on Multimedia*, pages 675–678, 2014.

[34] Harold W. Kuhn. The hungarian method for the assignment problem. *Naval Research Logistics Quarterly*, 2:83–97, 1955.

[35] Z. Lahner, E. Rodola, F. R. Schmidt, M. M. Bronstein, and D. Cremers. Efficient globally optimal 2d-to-3d deformable shape matching. In *IEEE Conference on Computer Vision and Pattern Recognition*, page to appear, 2016.

[36] L. Lam, S.-W. Lee, and C.Y. Suen. Thinning methodologies-a comprehensive survey. *IEEE Transactions on Pattern Analysis and Machine Intelligence*, 14(9):869–885, 1992.

[37] L. J. Latecki, R. Lakamper, and T. Eckhardt. Shape descriptors for non-rigid shapes with a single closed contour. In *IEEE Conference on Computer Vision and Pattern Recognition*, pages 424–429, 2000.

[38] Longin Jan Latecki and Rolf Lakämper. Convexity rule for shape decomposition based on discrete contour evolution. *Computer Vision and Image Understanding*, 73(3):441–454, 1999.

[39] Yann LeCun, Yoshua Bengio, and Geoffrey Hinton. Deep learning. *Nature*, 521(7553):436–444, 2015.

[40] Jungmin Lee, Minsu Cho, and Kyoung Mu Lee. Hyper-graph matching via reweighted random walks. In *IEEE Conference on Computer Vision and Pattern Recognition*, pages 1633–1640, 2011.

[41] M. Leordeanu and M. Hebert. A spectral technique for correspondence problems using pairwise constraints. In *IEEE International Conference on Computer Vision*, volume 2, pages 1482–1489. 2005.

[42] H. Ling and D.W. Jacobs. Shape classification using the inner-distance. *IEEE Transactions on Pattern Analysis and Machine Intelligence*, 29(2):286–299, 2007.

[43] HaiRong Liu, L.J. Latecki, Wenyu Liu, and Xiang Bai. Visual curvature. In *IEEE Conference on Computer Vision and Pattern Recognition*, pages 1–8, 2007.

[44] Hairong Liu, Longin Jan Latecki, and Shuicheng Yan. Robust clustering as ensembles of affinity relations. In *Advances in neural information processing systems*, pages 1414–1422, 2010.

[45] ChengEn Lu, L.J. Latecki, N. Adluru, Xingwei Yang, and Haibin Ling. Shape guided contour grouping with particle filters. In *IEEE International Conference on Computer Vision*, pages 2288–2295, 2009.

[46] Tianyang Ma and L.J. Latecki. From partial shape matching through local deformation to robust global shape similarity for object detection. In *IEEE Conference on Computer Vision and Pattern Recognition*, pages 1441–1448, 2011.

[47] S. Manay, D. Cremers, Byung-Woo Hong, A. J. Yezzi, and S. Soatto. Integral invariants for shape matching. *IEEE Transactions on Pattern Analysis and Machine Intelligence*, 28(10):1602–1618, 2006.

[48] K. V. Mardia and I. L. Dryden. Shape distributions for landmark data. *Advances in Applied Probability*, 21(4):742–755, 1989.

[49] N. Mayya and V. T. Rajan. Voronoi diagrams of polygons: A framework for shape representation. In *IEEE Conference on Computer Vision and Pattern Recognition*, pages 638–643, 1994.

[50] G. McNeill and S. Vijayakumar. Hierarchical procrustes matching for shape retrieval. In *IEEE Conference on Computer Vision and Pattern Recognition*, pages 885–894, 2006.

[51] K. Mikolajczyk and C. Schmid. A performance evaluation of local descriptors. *IEEE Transactions on Pattern Analysis and Machine Intelligence*, 27(10):1615–1630, 2005.

[52] R.L. Ogniewicz and O. Kbler. Hierarchic voronoi skeletons. *Pattern Recognition*, 28(3):343–359, 1995.

[53] M. Peura and J. Iivarinen. Efficiency of simple shape descriptors. In *Third International Workshop on Visual Form*, pages 443–451, 1997.

[54] Z. Pizlo. *3D Shape - Its Unique Place in Visual Perception*. MIT Press, 2010.

[55] Konstantinos A. Raftopoulos and Stefanos D. Kollias. The global local transformation for noise resistant shape representation. *Computer Vision and Image Understanding*, 115(8):1170–1186, 2011.

[56] Martin Reuter, Franz-Erich Wolter, and Niklas Peinecke. Laplace-spectra as fingerprints for shape matching. In *Proceedings of the 2005 ACM symposium on Solid and physical modeling*, pages 101–106, 2005.

[57] Yossi Rubner, Carlo Tomasi, and Leonidas J. Guibas. The earth mover's distance as a metric for image retrieval. *International Journal of Computer Vision*, 40(2):99–121, 2000.

[58] Bernhard Scholkopft and Klaus-Robert Mullert. Fisher discriminant analysis with kernels. *Neural networks for signal processing IX*, 1(1):1, 1999.

[59] T. B. Sebastian and Benjamin B. Kimia. Curves vs. skeletons in object recognition. *Signal Processing*, 85(2):247–263, 2005.

[60] Thomas B. Sebastian, Philip N. Klein, and Benjamin B. Kimia. Recognition of shapes by editing their shock graphs. *IEEE Transactions on Pattern Analysis and Machine Intelligence*, 26(5):550–571, 2004.

[61] Eitan Sharon and David Mumford. 2d-shape analysis using conformal mapping. *International Journal of Computer Vision*, 70(1):55–75, 2006.

[62] A. Shashua and N. Navab. Relative affine structure: canonical model for 3d from 2d geometry and applications. *IEEE Transactions on Pattern Analysis and Machine Intelligence*, 18(9):873–883, 1996.

[63] B. H. Shekar and Bharathi Pilar. Shape representation and classification through pattern spectrum and local binary pattern a decision level fusion approach. In *International Conference on Signal and Image Processing*, pages 218–224, 2014.

[64] Wei Shen, Yuan Jiang, Wenjing Gao, Dan Zeng, and Xinggang Wang. Shape recognition by bag of skeleton-associated contour parts. *Pattern Recognition Letters*, 2016.

[65] Wei Shen, Kai Zhao, Yuan Jiang, Yan Wang, Zhijiang Zhang, and Xiang Bai. Object skeleton extraction in natural images by fusing scale-associated deep side outputs. In *IEEE Conference on Computer Vision and Pattern Recognition*, page to appear, 2016.

[66] Kaleem Siddiqi and Stephen Pizer. *Medial representations: mathematics, algorithms and applications*, volume 37. Springer Science & Business Media, 2008.

[67] David McG. Squire and Terry M. Caelli. Invariance signatures: Characterizing contours by their departures from invariance. *Computer Vision and Image Understanding*, 77(3):284–316, 2000.

[68] Johan AK Suykens and Joos Vandewalle. Least squares support vector machine classifiers. *Neural processing letters*, 9(3):293–300, 1999.

[69] Lorenzo Torresani, Vladimir Kolmogorov, and Carsten Rother. Feature correspondence via graph matching: Models and global optimization. In *European Conference on Computer Vision*, pages 596–609. 2008.

[70] Oliver Van Kaick, Hao Zhang, Ghassan Hamarneh, and Daniel Cohen-Or. A survey on shape correspondence. 30(6):1681–1707, 2011.

[71] Peter J. Van Otterloo. *A Contour-oriented Approach to Shape Analysis*. Prentice Hall International Ltd., Hertfordshire, UK, 1991.

[72] Yue Wang and Eam Khwang Teoh. A novel 2d shape matching algorithm based on b-spline modeling. In *International Conference on Image Processing*, volume 1, pages 409–412, 2004.

[73] C. Xu, J. Liu, and X. Tang. 2d shape matching by contour flexibility. *IEEE Transactions on Pattern Analysis and Machine Intelligence*, 31(1):180–186, 2009.

[74] Cong Yang, Chen Li, Oliver Tiebe, Kimiaki Shirahama, and Marcin Grzegorzek. Shape-based classification of environmental microorganisms. In *International Conference on Pattern Recognition (ICPR 2014)*, pages 3374–3379. IEEE Computer Society, August 2014.

[75] Cong Yang, Oliver Tiebe, Pit Pietsch, Christian Feinen, Udo Kelter, and Marcin Grzegorzek. Shape-based object retrieval by contour segment matching. In *International Conference on Image Processing (ICIP 2014)*, pages 2202–2206. IEEE Computer Society, August 2014.

[76] Cong Yang, Oliver Tiebe, Pit Pietsch, Christian Feinen, Udo Kelter, and Marcin Grzegorzek. Shape-based object retrieval and classification with supervised optimisation. In *International Conference on Pattern Recognition Applications and Methods (ICPRAM 2015)*, pages 204–211. Springer, January 2015.

[77] Cong Yang, Oliver Tiebe, Kimiaki Shirahama, and Marcin Grzegorzek. Object matching with hierarchical skeletons. *Pattern Recognition*, 55:183–197, 2016.

[78] Jianyu Yang, Hongxing Wang, Junsong Yuan, Youfu Li, and Jianyang Liu. Invariant multi-scale descriptor for shape representation, matching and retrieval. *Computer Vision and Image Understanding*, 145:43–58, 2016.

[79] M. Yang, K. K. Idiyo, and R. Joseph. A survey of shape feature extraction techniques. *Pattern Recognition*, pages 43–90, 2008.

[80] Ian T. Young, Joseph E. Walker, and Jack E. Bowie. An analysis technique for biological shape. i. *Information and Control*, 25(4):357–370, 1974.

[81] Bo Yu, Lei Guo, Tianyun Zhao, and Xiaoliang Qian. A curve matching algorithm based on freeman chain code. In *IEEE International Conference on Intelligent Computing and Intelligent Systems*, pages 669–672, 2010.

[82] G.U. Yule and M.G. Kendall. Partial correlation. In *An Introduction to the Theory of Statistic*, page 1968. 258-270.

[83] R. Zass and A. Shashua. Probabilistic graph and hypergraph matching. In *IEEE Conference on Computer Vision and Pattern Recognition*, pages 1–8, 2008.

[84] Dengsheng Zhang and Guojun Lu. A comparative study of fourier descriptors for shape representation and retrieval. In *Asian Conference on Computer Vision*, pages 646–651, 2002.

[85] Dengsheng Zhang and Guojun Lu. Review of shape representation and description techniques. *Pattern Recognition*, 37(1):1–19, 2004.

[86] TY Zhang and Ching Y. Suen. A fast parallel algorithm for thinning digital patterns. *Communications of the ACM*, 27(3):236–239, 1984.

Chapter 4

Moving Object Analysis for Video Interpretation

Extracting and analysing object trajectories from videos is a basic problem in computer vision and has important applications in event understanding, robot localisation, video surveillance, etc. 2D and 3D trajectories of objects represent high-level semantic features, which can be used to automatically understand object activities in different kinds of videos [2].

In this chapter, selected methods for video interpretation based on the analysis of moving objects are described. Section 4.1 provides an overview of existing approaches in the area of object tracking in 2D, divided into methods working with rectangular and omnidirectional video data, respectively. In Section 4.2, algorithms for extracting 3D object trajectories from 2D videos are introduced. Finally, conclusions are drawn and further possible research directions are mentioned in Section 4.3.

4.1 Object Tracking in 2D Video

This section is structured as follows. Section 4.1.1 surveys state-of-the-art approaches for object tracking, both in rectangular and polar video. Section 4.1.2 presents a popular and robust approach in this category called Tracking-Learning-Detection [15]. In Section 4.1.3, the topic of object tracking in omnidirectional video data is addressed. An experimental evaluation of selected algorithms is presented and discussed in Section 4.1.4.

	Wang et al. [33]	Wen et al. [30]	He et al. [12]	Ma et al. [18]	Mazzu et al. [20]	Milan et al. [22]	Milan et al. [21]	Xiao et al. [31]	Zhang et al. [35]	Karthikeyan et al. [16]	Chen et al. [4]	Scotti et al. [25]	Rameau et al. [24]	Xiong et al. [32]	Markovic et al. [19]
Polar Object Tracking											X	X	X	X	X
Multiple Target Tracking	X	X	X			X	X			X	X	X			
Outdoor Application	X	X	X		X	X	X	X	X		X		X		
Real-time Tracking	X				X						X				
Moving Camera	X	X	X	X	X	X	X	X	X						X
Occlusion Handling	X	X	X	X		X	X	X	X			X	X	X	
	Rectangular Video										**Polar Video**				

Table 4.1: Distribution of object tracking properties over related methods.

4.1.1 Survey of Related Approaches

This section lists and shortly summarises most related approaches for object tracking, starting with those using rectangular video followed by algorithms working with polar video data. Table 4.1 shows the distribution of common object tracking properties over these methods.

Object Tracking in Rectangular Video

In [33], tracking of different kinds of interacting objects is formulated as a network-flow mixed integer program. This is made possible by tracking all objects simultaneously using intertwined flow variables and expressing the fact that one object can appear or disappear at locations where another is in terms of linear flow constraints. The proposed method is able to track invisible objects whose only evidence is the presence of other objects that contain them. Furthermore, the tracklet-based implementation yields real-time tracking performance. The performance of the approach is demonstrated on scenes involving cars and pedestrians, bags being carried and dropped by people, and balls being passed from one player to the next in team sports. In particular, it is shown that by estimating jointly and globally the trajectories of different types of objects, the presence of the ones which were not initially detected based solely on image evidence can be inferred from the detections of the others.

In [30], an algorithm is proposed that formulates the multi-object tracking task as one to exploit hierarchical dense structures on an undirected hypergraph constructed based on tracklet affinity. The dense structures indicate a group of vertices that are inter-connected with a set of hyperedges with high affinity values. The appearance and motion similarities among multiple tracklets across the spatio-temporal domain are considered globally by exploiting high-order similarities rather than pairwise ones, thereby facilitating the distinguishability of spatially close targets with similar appearance. In addition, the hierarchical design of the optimisation process helps the proposed tracking algorithm handle long-term occlusions robustly.

In multi-object tracking, it is critical to explore the data associations by exploiting the temporal information from a sequence of frames rather than the information from the adjacent two frames. Since straightforwardly obtaining data associations from multi-frames is an NP-hard multidimensional assignment (MDA) problem, most existing methods solve this MDA problem by either developing complicated approximate algorithms, or simplifying MDA as a 2D assignment problem based upon the information extracted only from adjacent frames. In [12], it is shown that the relation between associations of two observations is the equivalence relation in the data association problem, based on the spatial-temporal constraint that the trajectories of different objects must be disjoint. Therefore, the MDA problem can be equivalently divided into independent subproblems by equivalence partitioning. In contrast to existing works for solving the MDA problem, the authors of [12] developed a connected component model (CCM) by exploiting the constraints of the data association and the equivalence relation on the constraints. Based upon CCM, the global solution of the MDA problem for multi-object tracking can be efficiently obtained by optimising a sequence of independent data association subproblems.

Feature pooling in a majority of sparse coding based tracking algorithms computes final feature vectors only by low-order statistics or extreme responses of sparse codes. The high-order statistics and the correlations between responses to different dictionary items are neglected. In [18], a more generalised feature pooling method for visual tracking is presented which utilises the probabilistic function to model the statistical distribution of sparse codes. Since immediate matching between two distributions usually requires high computational costs, the Fisher vector to derive a more compact and discriminative representation for sparse codes of the visual target is introduced. The approach encodes target patches by local coordinate coding, utilises Gaussian mixture model to compute Fisher vectors, and finally trains semi-supervised linear kernel classifiers for visual tracking. In order to handle the drifting problem during the tracking process, these classifiers are updated online with current tracking results.

Under a tracking framework, the definition of the target state is the basic step for automatic understanding of dynamic scenes. More specifically, far object tracking raises challenges related to the potentially abrupt size changes of the targets as they approach the sensor. If not handled, size changes can introduce heavy issues in data association and position estimation. This is why adaptability and self-awareness of a tracking module are desirable features. The paradigm of cognitive dynamic systems (CDSs) can provide a framework under which a continuously learning cognitive module can be designed. In particular, CDS theory describes a basic vocabulary of components that can be used as the founding blocks of a module capable of learning behavioural rules from continuous active interactions with the environment. This quality is fundamental to deal with dynamic situations. In [20], a general CDS-based approach to tracking is proposed. It is shown that such a CDS-inspired design can lead to the self-adaptability of a Bayesian tracker in fusing heterogeneous object features, overcoming size change issues.

The task of tracking multiple targets is often addressed with the so-called tracking-by-detection paradigm, where the first step is to obtain a set of target hypotheses for each frame independently. Tracking can then be regarded as solving two separate, but tightly coupled problems. The first is to carry out data association, i.e., to determine the origin of each of the available observations. The second problem is to reconstruct the actual trajectories that describe the spatio-temporal motion pattern of each individual target. The former is inherently a discrete problem, while the latter should intuitively be modelled in continuous space. Having to deal with an unknown number of targets, complex dependencies, and physical constraints, both are challenging tasks on their own and thus most previous work focuses on one of these subproblems. In [22], a multi-target tracking approach is presented that explicitly models both tasks as minimisation of a unified discrete-continuous energy function. Trajectory properties are captured through global label costs, a recent concept from multi-model fitting, which is introduced to tracking. Specifically, label costs describe physical properties of individual tracks, e.g., linear and angular dynamics, or entry and exit points. Further, the paper introduces pairwise label costs to describe mutual interactions between targets in order to avoid collisions. By choosing appropriate forms for the individual energy components, powerful discrete optimisation techniques can be leveraged to address data association, while the shapes of individual trajectories are updated by gradient-based continuous energy minimisation.

Many recent advances in multiple target tracking aim at finding a (nearly) optimal set of trajectories within a temporal window. To handle the large space of possible trajectory hypotheses, it is typically reduced to a finite set by some form of data-driven or regular discretisation. In [21], an alternative formulation of multitarget tracking as minimisation of a continuous energy is proposed. Contrary to recent approaches, [21] focuses on designing an energy that corresponds to a more complete representation of the problem, rather than one that is amenable to global optimisation. Besides the image evidence, the energy function takes into account physical constraints, such as target dynamics, mutual exclusion, and track persistence. In addition, partial image evidence is handled with explicit occlusion reasoning, and different targets are disambiguated with an appearance model. To nevertheless find strong local minima of the proposed nonconvex energy, a suitable optimisation scheme that alternates between continuous conjugate gradient descent and discrete transdimensional jump moves is constructed. These moves, which are executed so that they always reduce the energy, allow the search to escape weak minima and explore a much larger portion of the search space of varying dimensionality.

[31] presents a method for single target tracking of arbitrary objects in challenging video sequences. Targets are modelled at three different levels of granularity (pixel level, parts-based level and bounding box level), which are cross-constrained to enable robust model relearning. The main contribution of this paper is an adaptive clustered decision tree method

which dynamically selects the minimum combination of features necessary to sufficiently represent each target part at each frame, thereby providing robustness with computational efficiency. The adaptive clustered decision tree is implemented in two separate parts of the tracking algorithm: firstly to enable robust matching at the partsbased level between successive frames; and secondly to select the best superpixels for learning new parts of the target.

Semantic object segmentation in video is an important step for large-scale multimedia analysis. In many cases, however, semantic objects are only tagged at video-level, making them difficult to be located and segmented. To address this problem, in [35] an approach to segment semantic objects in weakly labelled video via object detection is proposed. In this approach, a novel video segmentation-by-detection framework is introduced, which first incorporates object and region detectors pre-trained on still images to generate a set of detection and segmentation proposals. Based on the noisy proposals, several object tracks are then initialised by solving a joint binary optimisation problem with min-cost flow. As such tracks actually provide rough configurations of semantic objects, the object segmentation is refined while preserving the spatiotemporal consistency by inferring the shape likelihoods of pixels from the statistical information of tracks.

Visual attention is a crucial indicator of the relative importance of objects in visual scenes to human viewers. In [16], an algorithm to extract objects which attract visual attention from videos is proposed. As human attention is naturally biased towards high level semantic objects in visual scenes, this information can be valuable to extract salient objects. The proposed algorithm extracts dominant visual tracks using eye tracking data from multiple subjects on a video sequence by a combination of mean-shift clustering and Hungarian algorithm. These visual tracks guide a generic object search algorithm to get candidate object locations and extents in every frame. Further, [16] proposes a novel multiple object extraction algorithm by constructing a spatio-temporal mixed graph over object candidates. Bounding box based object extraction inference is performed using binary linear integer programming on a cost function defined over the graph. Finally, the object boundaries are refined using grabcut segmentation.

86

Object Tracking in Polar Video

Dual-camera systems have been widely used in surveillance because of the ability to explore the wide field of view (FOV) of the omnidirectional camera and the wide zoom range of the PTZ camera. Most existing algorithms require a priori knowledge of the omnidirectional camera's projection model to solve the nonlinear spatial correspondences between the two cameras. To overcome this limitation, in [4], two methods are proposed: geometry and homography calibration, where polynomials with automated model selection are used to approximate the camera projection model and spatial mapping, respectively. The proposed methods not only improve the mapping accuracy by reducing its dependence on the knowledge of the projection model but also feature reduced computations and improved flexibility in adjusting to varying system configurations. Although the fusion of multiple cameras has attracted increasing attention, most existing algorithms assume comparable FOV and resolution levels among multiple cameras. Different FOV and resolution levels of the omnidirectional and PTZ cameras result in another critical issue in practical tracking applications. The omnidirectional camera is capable of multiple object tracking while the PTZ camera is able to track one individual target at a time to maintain the required resolution. It becomes necessary for the PTZ camera to distribute its observation time among multiple objects and visit them in sequence. Therefore, this paper addresses a novel scheme where an optimal visiting sequence of the PTZ camera is obtained so that in a given period of time the PTZ camera automatically visits multiple detected motions in a target-hopping manner.

In [25], a novel integrated multicamera video-sensor (panoramic catadioptric vision tracker plus - PCVT+) is proposed for surveillance systems. In the proposed setup an omni-directional imaging device is used in conjunction with a pan, tilt, zoom (PTZ) camera leading to an innovative kind of sensor that is able to automatically track any moving object within the guarded area at a higher zoom level. In particular, the catadioptric sensor is firstly calibrated and used in order to track every single object that is moving within its 360-degree field of view. Omni-directional image portions are eventually rectified and pan, tilt and zoom parameters of the moving camera are automatically adjusted by the image processing system in order to track detected objects. A cooperative strategy was developed for the selection of the object to be tracked by the PTZ sensor in the case of multiple targets.

A technique for applying visual tracking algorithms to omnidirectional image sequences is presented in [24]. The method is based on a spherical image representation which allows taking into account the distortions and nonlinear resolution of omnidirectional images.

Using stereo disparity or depth information to detect and track moving objects has received increasing attention in recent years. However, this approach suffers from some difficulties, such as synchronisation between two cameras and doubling of the image-data size. Besides, traditional stereo-imaging systems have a limited field of view (FOV), which means that they need to rotate the cameras when an object moves out of view. In [32], the authors present a depth-space partitioning algorithm for performing object tracking using single-camera omni-stereo imaging system. The proposed method uses a catadioptric omni directional stereo-imaging system to capture omni-stereo image pairs. This imaging system has 360-degree FOV, avoiding the need for rotating cameras when tracking a moving object. In order to estimate omni-stereo disparity, the authors present a depth-space partitioning strategy. It partitions, three-dimensional depth space with a series of co-axial cylinders models the disparity estimation as a pixel-labelling problem and establishes an energy minimisation function for solving this problem using graph cuts optimisation. Based on the omni-stereo disparity-estimation results, the authors detect and track-moving objects based on omni-stereo disparity motion vector, which is the difference between two consecutive disparity maps.

Equipping mobile robots with an omnidirectional camera is very advantageous in numerous applications as all information about the surrounding scene is stored in a single image frame. [19] is concerned with detection, tracking and following of a moving object with an omnidirectional camera. The camera calibration and image formation is based on the spherical unified projection model thus yielding a representation of the omnidirectional image on the unit sphere. Detection of moving objects is performed by calculating a sparse optical flow in the image and then lifting the flow vectors on the unit sphere where they are discriminated as dynamic or static by analytically calculating the distance of the terminal vector point to a great circle arc. The flow vectors are then clustered and the centre of gravity is calculated to form the sensor measurement. Furthermore, the tracking is posed as a Bayesian estimation problem on the unit sphere and the solution based on the von Mises-Fisher distribution is utilised. Visual servoing is performed for the object following task where the control law calculation is based on the projection of a point on the unit sphere.

4.1.2 Tracking-Learning-Detection

A very popular and robust approach for object tracking in rectangular video is presented in [15]. It is called Tracking-Learning-Detection (TLD). TLD is a framework designed for long-term tracking of an unknown object in a video stream.

The authors of [15] start the motivation of their own approach stating the fact that most of the existing long-term tracking algorithms apply either tracking or detection and do not combine these two strategies. Tracking algorithms estimate the object motion. Trackers require only initialisation, are fast and produce smooth trajectories. On the other hand, they accumulate errors during run-time (drift) and typically fail if the object disappears from the camera view. Research in tracking aims at developing increasingly robust trackers that track "longer". The post-failure behaviour is not directly addressed. Detection-based algorithms estimate the object location in every frame independently. Detectors do not drift and do not fail if the object disappears from the camera view. However, they require an offline training stage and therefore cannot be applied to unknown objects.

The main idea of [15] is to let tracking and detection algorithms work together. Moreover, it also incorporates a learning module observing the performance of both, tracker and detector, and learning from this observation. The components of the framework are characterised as follows:

Tracker estimates the object's motion between consecutive frames under the assumption that the frame-to-frame motion is limited and the object is visible. The tracker is likely to fail and never recover if the object moves out of the camera view.

Detector treats every frame as independent and performs full scanning of the image to localise all appearances that have been observed and learned in the past. As any other detector, the detector makes two types of errors: false positives and false negatives.

Learning observes performance of both, tracker and detector, estimates the detector's errors and generates training examples to avoid these errors in the future. The learning component assumes that both the tracker and the detector can fail. By the virtue of the learning, the detector generalises to more object appearances and discriminates against background.

Figure 4.1: An example of an omnidirectional camera image.

In the next section (Section 4.1.3) an approach is presented that extends TLD towards object tracking in polar video.

4.1.3 Tracking in Omnidirectional Video

An omnidirectional camera (from "omni", meaning all) is a camera with a 360-degree field of view in the horizontal plane, or with a visual field that covers (approximately) the entire sphere (example image in in Figure 4.1). While it is not limited to a single viewpoint and can observe a large area, it distorts the objects in the scene. For this reason, existing methods for object tracking in 2D rectangular video cannot be applied for these data without appropriate modifications. Below, the MTLD [7], an accordingly modified version of the TLD summarised in Section 4.1.2, is described. The general MTLD processing pipeline is depicted in Figure 4.2. Its modifications compared to TLD are as follows:

Image Rectification: First, a rectification transformation is applied converting polar images into rectangular ones (see example in Figure 4.3).

Classifier Modification: By the image rectification, in-plane rotation is mostly removed. However, in some cases, the desired object is not detected robustly due to the out-of-plane rotation problem. To resolve this issue, the nearest neighbour classifier performing this detection is modified in such a way to accept more variance in the

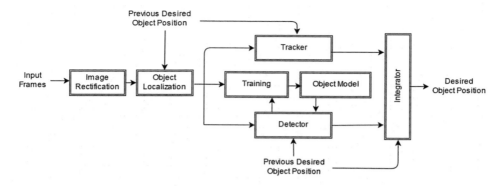

Figure 4.2: Block diagram of the MTLD method.

Figure 4.3: Image from Figure 4.1 after rectification.

appearance of the candidate objects. This strategy improves the detection performance of the desired objects. However, it also increases the number of false positives. To tackle this problem, objects with a high replacement in consecutive frames are ignored. The block diagram of the MTLD detector is depicted in Figure 4.4.

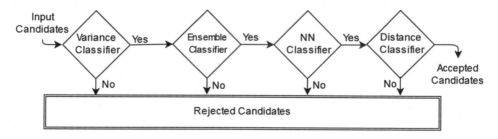

Figure 4.4: Block diagram of the modified object detector.

Search Area Restriction: The MTLD approach attempts to decrease the computational cost of the TLD method. For this reason, the

91

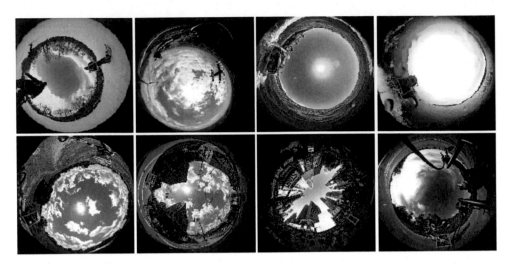

Figure 4.5: Example polar images from the video dataset used for experiments.

object searching area in MTLD is restricted to a region around the object location in the previous frame. Due to the wide field of view in 360-degree images, even when the camera is moving, the object location in successive frames does not change significantly. Thus, the limitation of the searching area does not negatively influence the tracking performance.

Detection Strategy Modification: TLD uses the tracker output to train the detector. However, it has been observed that it does not play an important role in updating the detector output. To improve the detection performance, the currently detected object is included in the positive example set rather than the tracker output. Usually, the object size varies in a very limited way between two successive frames of a polar video. MTLD assumes the size difference to be lower than 25% which additionally optimises the algorithm.

4.1.4 Experiments and Results

To comparatively evaluate the TLD (Section 4.1.2) and the MTLD method (Section 4.1.3), a set of 9 different video samples with diverse frame numbers and various objects has been used. Example images of this dataset are presented in Figure 4.5. The objects meant to be tracked include cars, motorcycles, pedestrians, human head, human body and aeroplane.

Video Topic	Frames	TLD		MTLD	
		Recall	Precision	Recall	Precision
Snorkelling	683	0.038	1.000	0.840	0.870
Snowboard	248	0.516	0.516	0.670	0.670
Airplane	761	0.760	0.760	0.760	0.740
Park	58	0.650	1.000	1.000	1.000
Pedestrians	129	0.640	0.640	0.860	0.860
Motorcycles	83	1.000	1.000	1.000	1.000
Car Racing	330	1.000	1.000	1.000	1.000
TPittsburgh	294	0.920	1.000	1.000	1.000
Motocross	250	1.000	1.000	1.000	1.000
Average		0.624	0.875	0.860	0.861

Table 4.2: Evaluation results in terms of recall and precision.

They feature both in-plane and out-of-plane rotations. Initial experiments showed that TLD cannot track objects in 360-degree images due to the lack of the rectification step. For this reason, all frames have first been rectified and then passed to the TLD and the MTLD method for processing.

The experimental results of the MTLD in comparison to the TLD are presented in Table 4.2. As one can see, MTLD outperforms TLD significantly. While the average precision has remained similar in both cases (87.5% for TLD; 86.1% to MTLD), the average recall has been improved from 62.4% to 86.0%

4.2   3D Trajectory Extraction from 2D Video

Capturing spatio-temporal relations among objects in the 3D space is crucial for the semantic analysis of activities and events in videos. Starting with a description of the Reversible Jump Markov Chain Monte Carlo (RJ-MCMC) particle filtering [17] (Section 4.2.1), this section presents a probabilistic method extracting 3D trajectories of objects from 2D videos captured from a monocular moving camera [2, 3] in Section 4.2.1, describes its application to human behaviour analysis in crowded surveillance video [1] in Section 4.2.2, and, finally, discusses the evaluation results achieved for it in Section 4.2.3.

Compared to other approaches, the method explained in this section can extract 3D trajectories in a much less restrictive way than comparable approaches known from the literature. Based on example object appearances, it estimates the focal length of the camera and computes the depth of detected objects. Contrary to other 3D trajectory extraction methods, the algorithm presented in this section is able to process videos taken from both, a stable camera and a non-calibrated moving camera without any restrictions. For this, the Reversible Jump Markov Chain Monte Carlo (RJ-MCMC) particle filtering [17] has been modified to be more suitable for camera odometry without relying on geometrical feature points (details in Section 4.2.1).

4.2.1 RJ-MCMC Particle Filtering

Practically, objects such as people or cars move freely in the space. Due to the variety of their appearances and occlusions, the extraction of their 3D trajectories is a challenging task. For this, most existing approaches use 3D sensors (e.g., lidar - light detection and ranging, stereo camera, depth cameras). For instance, Choi et al. [5] propose a method, which robustly extracts 3D object trajectories using 3D cameras.

However, this section addresses a much more challenging task for extracting 3D object trajectories from 2D video data. For this, an example-based approach is adopted in order to estimate objects' depths based on a large-scale training dataset, where each example appearance of an object is associated with the corresponding size. Given an object bounding box, the approach retrieves the most similar candidates from the training dataset, where the mean size of all candidates is assigned to the query object. The query object is then projected to the real world given its size in the image plane, its estimated size in the real world and the camera matrix.

Another challenging problem is the enormous number of objects in the scene, where the simultaneous estimation of several objects makes the state dimension huge and variable. Therefore, the method proposed by Khan et al. [17] called "Reversible Jump Markov Chain Monte Carlo (RJ-MCMC) particle filtering" is applied here, where the difference to classical particle filtering methods lies in its capability to generate a small number of hypotheses to estimate the entire probability distribution. In addition, the Markov Random Field (MRF) is applied to control the interaction of objects.

The problem of extracting 3D trajectories of objects is formulated as finding the most probable configuration, by estimating the maximum a posteriori (MAP) solution of $P(\Delta_t|\Psi_{0,..,t})$, given all observations $\Psi_{0,..,t}$. Here, Δ_t represents the configuration to be estimated, which consists of 3D positions of existing objects at time t. For every particle j, one hypothesis (update, add, delete, stay or leave) is generated and evaluated afterwards given the visual observation Ψ_t and the previous configuration Δ_{t-1}. The MAP solution of the posterior distribution can be formulated as follows:

$$P(\Delta_t|\Psi_{0,..,t}) \propto$$
$$\underbrace{P(\Psi_t|\Delta_t)}_{a} \int \underbrace{P(\Delta_t|\Delta_{t-1})}_{b} \underbrace{P(\Delta_{t-1}|\Psi_{0,..,t-1})}_{c} d\Delta_{t-1} \quad . \qquad (4.1)$$

In Equation 4.1, the first term (a) represents the observation likelihood expressing the measurement model of the compatibility of a hypothetical configuration Δ_t given the observation Ψ_t. The second term (b) is the transition model controlling the smoothness of object movements and their interactions given their previous movements at $t-1$. Finally, the third term (c) represents the posterior probability at time $t-1$, which is assumed to be available at the initial time. Below, detailed explanations about the observation model, the transition model and the sampling process are given.

Observation Model

In order to find the best configuration for the visual observation, each hypothesis is evaluated by the projection of all objects onto the image plane with respect to the current camera parameters of their last known appearances. The observation model can be then expressed as the product of all measurements:

$$P(\Psi_t|\Delta_t) = \prod_i P(\Psi_t|\varphi_{\Phi_t}(\Delta_t^i)) \quad , \qquad (4.2)$$

where $P(\Psi_t|\varphi_{\Phi_t}(\Delta_t^i))$ denote the measurement of the hypothesis corresponding to the i-th object Δ_t^i in Δ_t. All objects are assumed to be located on the ground plane, and their detection is performed in accordance with

Figure 4.6: An illustration of object observation computation based on point matching.

the algorithm proposed by Felzenszwalb *et al.* [9]. Subsequently, the leave and update hypotheses are assessed based on matching similarity between its last valid appearance and its current projection onto the image plane w.r.t camera parameters Φ_t. For this VLFeat [29] that can achieve fast and accurate point matching between two images is employed. More precisely, for an update hypothesis of the object at time t, its bounding box BOX_1 projection from the real world onto the image plane $(\varphi_{\Phi_t}(\Delta_t^i))$ w.r.t Φ_t is used. BOX_1 is then resized to the same size as the output bounding box of the corresponding object given by the detector in the initial frame (BOX_2). Figure 4.6 illustrates the matching process between BOX_1 and BOX_2. Its key-points are marked as $(+)$ and $(\circ)$, respectively, where the best match is related to the highest number of matched points and the smallest average of pixel displacements. The observation likelihood of Δ^i at t is given by the similarity $S_t^{\Delta^i}$ as follows:

$$P(\Psi_t|\varphi_{\Phi_t}(\Delta_t^i)) = S_t^{\Delta^i} = \frac{\ell}{\rho \times (\mu + 1)} \quad , \tag{4.3}$$

where ρ and μ denote the diagonal length of ROI_1 and the average of pixel displacement field, respectively, and ℓ is the number of matched points between BOX_1 and BOX_2. To obtain BOX_1, the object hypothesis is projected from the real world to the image plane using the projection function φ_{Φ_t} given the translation vector T_t and the rotation matrix R_t at time t. Moreover, $\varphi_{\Phi_t}^{-1}$ is the inverse projection function, which is used to project a newly detected object from the image plane to the camera coordinate system.

Transition Model

Since objects are assumed to move fluently in the space, the second term of Equation 4.1 controls the transition smoothness between configurations. However, objects usually try to avoid collisions which perturbs the evenness in their movement. Hence, objects affect each other in their movement, whereas fast objects impact the area in front of them, contrary to the slow ones influencing the area around them [26]. Therefore, the independence and the interaction models (described in paragraphs below) are considered to represent object transition as follows:

$$P(\Delta_t|\Delta_{t-1}) = P_{\text{independence}}(\Delta_t|\Delta_{t-1}) \, P_{\text{interaction}}(\Delta_t|\Delta_{t-1}) \quad . \tag{4.4}$$

Independence Model: In this model, objects are supposed to move smoothly with a rational change. Given the position at $t-1$ and the current velocity $v_t^i = v_{t-1}^i - v_{t-2}^i$, the independence model of the i-th object's 3D position Δ_t^i at t is controlled by a simple normal distribution with its maximum value at $\Delta_{t-1}^i + v_t^i$:

$$P_{\text{independence}}(\Delta_t^i|\Delta_{t-1}^i) = \mathcal{N}\left(\Delta_{t-1}^i + v_t^i, 1\right) \quad . \tag{4.5}$$

Interaction Model: In real scenarios, objects either move together in groups or separately. This can be characterised by the distance between them and their velocities. Using Markov Random Field (MRF), two modes (group and repulsion) are defined, which control the relation between two objects Δ_t^{i1} and Δ_t^{i2} (this relation can change over time). Therefore, a hidden variable σ is employed in order to switch between modes, where the probability of repulsion and relation is computed at every frame based on the previous mode. The interaction model can be represented as follows:

$$P_{\text{interaction}}(\Delta_t|\Delta_{t-1}) = \prod_{i_1<i_2} \omega(\Delta_t^{i_1}, \Delta_t^{i_2}; \sigma_t^{\Delta^{i_1},\Delta^{i_2}}) \quad , \tag{4.6}$$

where $\sigma_t^{\Delta^{i_1},\Delta^{i_2}}$ is a binary variable (1: repulsion; 2: group) determined as the most probable mode for the time t, while $\omega(\Delta_t^{i_1}, \Delta_t^{i_2}; \sigma_t^{\Delta^{i_1},\Delta^{i_2}})$ is the probability mode of $\Delta_t^{i_1}$ and $\Delta_t^{i_2}$ based on $\sigma_t^{\Delta^{i_1},\Delta^{i_2}}$.

Sampling

In order to approximate the best configuration, N hypotheses are randomly generated at each time t starting from an arbitrary configuration $\Delta_t^{j=0}$.

A hypothesis is accepted if it is better than the previous one; otherwise, it is rejected. The jump from one hypothesis to another is applied only to one randomly selected object, whereas the jump is accepted only if the acceptance ratio $A \geq 1$. Following the Metropolis-Hastings algorithm, the acceptance ratio of the jump from j-th hypothesis to $j + 1$-th one is computed as follows:

$$A = \frac{P(\Psi_t|\Theta_t^{j+1})}{P(\Psi_t|\Theta_t^j)} \frac{P(\Theta_t^{j+1}|\Psi_{0,..,t-1})}{P(\Theta_t^j|\Psi_{0,..,t-1})} \frac{Q(\Theta_t^j;\Theta_t^{j+1})}{Q(\Theta_t^{j+1};\Theta_t^j)} \quad . \quad (4.7)$$

Each model in the set is reversible to another or to itself, e.g., the actions *Add* and *Delete* (described in the paragraphs below) counteract each other.

Add: This jump allows to add a new object Δ^{new} which did not exist neither at $t-1$ nor in the previous jump $t(j-1)$. For this, an arbitrary position and category (w.r.t the size of objects in that category) are assigned to the newly added object, ensuring that its projection falls exactly within the image boundary. The corresponding bounding box is evaluated using the object detector [9], where the proposal distribution $Q_A(\Delta_t^{j+1};\Delta_t^j)$ takes the detection confidence (0: non detected, 1: certainly detected). In addition, the detected bounding box is compared to existing objects in order to not overtake the identity of one of them.

Delete: As the reversible jump for *Add*, delete jump is applied in order to deny a formerly added object at $t(< j)$, if it is sufficiently similar to one of the objects that existed at $t-1$ but not at the time of its addition. The proposal distribution $Q_D(\Delta_t^{j+1};\Delta_t^j)$ is then the maximum similarity between the newly added object and the last valid appearances of the remaining objects.

Stay: This model inserts a randomly selected object from the set $\epsilon_t^{S(j)}$, consisting objects that are no longer in Δ_t^j but existed at $t-1$. The proposal distribution samples a new position from that in its last existence at t:

$$Q_S(\Delta_t^{j+1};\Delta_t^j) = \begin{cases} \frac{1}{|\epsilon_t^{S(j)}|} P(\Psi_t|\varphi_{\Phi_t}(\Delta_t^{i(j+1)})) & \text{if} \quad i \in \epsilon_t^{S(j)} \\ 0 & \text{otherwise} \end{cases} \quad . \quad (4.8)$$

Leave: As a reversible jump of stay, this model removes a randomly selected object from $\epsilon_t^{L(j)}$, which is the set of objects that exist in Θ_t^j and existed in Θ_{t-1}. The proposal is then:

$$
Q_L(\Delta_t^{j+1}; \Delta_t^j) = \begin{cases} \frac{1}{|\epsilon_t^{L(j)}|} & \text{if} \quad i \in \epsilon_t^{L(j)} \\ 0 & \text{otherwise} \end{cases} . \tag{4.9}
$$

Update: This jump proposes a new position of a randomly selected object from $\epsilon_t^{L(j)}$. The proposal distribution is modelled by a simple normal distribution, where the mean is the current position $\Delta_t^{i,j}$ of the i-th object: $Q_U(\Delta_t^{i,j+1}; \Delta_t^{i,j}) = \mathcal{N}(\Delta_t^{i,j+1}, 1)$. Note that the update jump is reversed by another update jump.

4.2.2 Convoy Detection in Crowded Video

Both 3D and 2D trajectories can be used to automatically detect group activities, which might be important to analyse crowded surveillance videos. This detection can be done by considering a group pattern as a set of moving feature points [26]. Stationary groups represented as a batch of feature points can also be analysed [34]. The analysis of people's trajectories independently of each other is very difficult in crowded environments due to complexity and scalability problems. For this reason, the algorithm presented in this section performs the analysis of *convoys*, considering two or more pedestrians moving or standing together as one pattern.

The difficulty of detecting convoys lies in the high pedestrian density, where patterns change their intra properties (e.g., relative positions of pedestrians in one group) and inter properties (e.g., a group can cross another group) over time. Therefore, a two-phase algorithm is proposed consisting of a density clustering phase and an intersection phase, where the former is unaffected to the intra properties of pedestrians. In other words, even if the relative positions of pedestrians in a group change, it allows them to stay in the same group as long as they are densely connected. Meanwhile, inter properties are handled by intersecting pedestrian groups iteratively, where if the same pedestrians continuously form a group over a frame sequence, they are regarded as a convoy.

The idea of extracting convoy patterns from trajectories is similar to the work proposed in [13, 14], but a new pattern called *noncontinuous convoy* is proposed.

Noncontinuous Convoy: Jeung et al. [13] proposed a convoy as a group of objects which are *density-connected* with each other during a consecutive period of time. Here, *density-connected* is a measurable way to spatially determine whether people stay together or not. However, convoys with such density-connected objects are not as capable as expected in real-life circumstances because of the very rigid constraint of consecutiveness. For example, two pedestrians who are walking together may not be density-connected for a few seconds for some reasons. Furthermore, pedestrian detection may be unstable, or two pedestrians may become separated by an obstacle, etc. Therefore, they are not considered as density-connected, so it is not possible to represent the trajectories of pedestrians walking together properly.

Thus, a new convoy pattern called *noncontinuous convoy* is proposed. It is defined by relaxing the constraint of consecutiveness. For the previous example, as long as cluster members (pedestrians) do not walk separately for a long time, the convoy formed by them does not terminate, that is, it persists until they get back together. To quantify the tolerable length of separation, a parameter called *elasticity* (λ) is adopted, where it is the minimal ratio of the number of density-connected frames to the life time of a noncontinuous convoy. Arguably, a convoy is equivalent to a noncontinuous convoy with the elasticity equal to 1 ($\lambda = 1.0$), while a noncontinuous convoy with $\lambda = 0.5$ means that convoy members are density-connected in over a half of its life time.

Clustering and Intersection: The proposed two-phase algorithm consists of a clustering phase and an intersection phase to extract convoys from trajectories. For intuition, Figure 4.7 represents an example case of 4 pedestrians. At the beginning, candidates are found as clusters of pedestrians who are spatially close to each other at all times [8]. In the course of time, candidates are separated due to the intersection with candidates from the previous frame. Candidates preserving their status for longer than a certain time threshold are considered as convoys. Note that a convoy involves at least two persons and its minimum duration is set to 2 frames.

Candidate Expiring Mechanism: Additionally, a candidate expiring mechanism is proposed in order to detect noncontinuous convoys. The key idea is to avoid flushing the candidate set so that convoys with sizes smaller than the threshold are not removed immediately. Specifically, besides the existing duration attribute (t_{duration}), the timestamp of creation

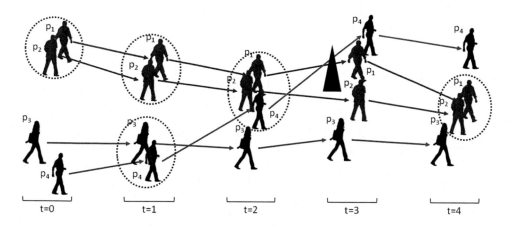

Figure 4.7: An illustration of convoy detection.

(t_{creation}) is assigned to each candidate in order to count the life time of a noncontinuous convoy. Thus, the number of frames that have passed since a particular candidate was created by calculating the difference between the current time (t_{now}) and the time of creation is available. Meanwhile, the unmodified duration is the number of frames where they are density-connected. Thus, we can remove a candidate if it satisfies the following condition:

$$\frac{t_{\text{duration}}}{t_{\text{now}} - t_{\text{creation}}} \leq \lambda \tag{4.10}$$

The clustering and intersection algorithm with the candidate expiring mechanism performs a density-based clustering algorithm DBSCAN [8] for all the pedestrians in the coming frame. The output of DBSCAN are clusters of density-connected pedestrians. Then, for initialisation, if there are no candidates, the current clusters are added to the candidate set R and continue to process the next frame. Then the algorithm refines convoy candidates by intersecting them with the new clusters. An intersection result that exceeds the assumed size threshold is stored as a new candidate. Then, the new clusters are added to R, which is updated for the next frame. Subsequently, the algorithm begins to evaluate the candidates by elasticity. If a candidate exceeds the duration threshold, it is considered as a convoy. Meanwhile, a candidate is discarded, if it does not satisfy the elasticity criteria.

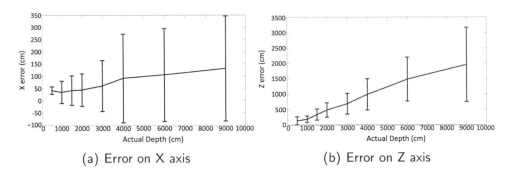

(a) Error on X axis   (b) Error on Z axis

Figure 4.8: Object depth estimation errors on the X and the Z axis.

4.2.3 Experiments and Results

For the evaluation of 3D trajectory extraction, the tracking set of Kitti [11] benchmark consisting of 21 different sequences is used. This dataset provides a sequence of associated bounding boxes representing object trajectories on the image plane. For the ground truth of 3D trajectories, the left and the right images of each sequence are employed to compute the depths of the corresponding tracked objects. The sequential 3D positions of the object are subsequently computed given their positions on the image plane and their depths. The sequences in this dataset are not associated with the ground truth of the camera odometry. Therefore, the evaluation of the 3D object trajectory extraction is performed in terms of the relation between each object and the camera for every timestamp t. For this, the lack of the ground truth is compensated by transforming all obtained trajectories to the corresponding camera position. Here, the camera coordinate system is used, considering the principal point as a centre.

In order to demonstrate the effectiveness of the proposed method in extracting 3D object trajectories, sequential positions of the objects are evaluated against the ground truth depth. For this, the mean and the standard deviation error on X and Z axes are computed for all objects sharing the same ground truth depth $= 10m, 20m, \ldots, 90m$. Here, the error is computed as the absolute difference between the estimated position and the ground truth. The overall result is presented in Figure 4.8, showing the mean and the standard deviation error in terms of object's depth. As illustrated in the figure, the errors are smaller for close objects than for the far ones. The reason of this variance is that the projection of objects on the image plane is influenced by their distances from the camera. Specifically, the appearance of far objects is small on the image plane, where a deviation

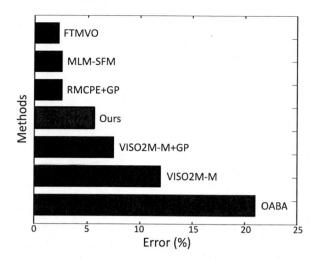

Figure 4.9: Comparative evaluation of the camera odometry estimation on the Kitti dataset. Apart from the algorithm described in this section, following approaches are considered: SFM [27], RMCPE+GP [23], VISO2M-M+GP [28], VISO2-M [27], OABA [10].

of a few pixels has a big impact in the 3D space. In contrast to this, near objects occupy an important region in the image plane, where the deviation is less likely due to high resolution. In addition, small deviation does not affect the localisation in the 3D space.

The result presented above validates the capability of the 3D trajectory extraction method in localising objects in the 3D space. Although neither the intrinsic parameters of the camera nor the depths of objects are available, the method obtained reasonable results.

In addition to object trajectory estimation, the calculation of the camera position (camera odometry) is also evaluated. Consequently, the odometry set proposed by the Kitti benchmark [11] consisting of 11 stereo sequences recorded from a moving camera is employed. The camera is mounted on a car driving in different environments (e.g., city, highway, etc.). Only the left images are considered in this evaluation and the resulting output of the method is the relative pose (translation and rotation) of the camera compared with its initial position. Figure 4.9 shows the ranking of the method described in this section in comparison to some state-of-the-art techniques using monocular cameras. In addition, Figure 4.10 illustrates two examples of camera odometry obtained by the proposed method.

Furthermore, the overall error in terms of translation (position) and

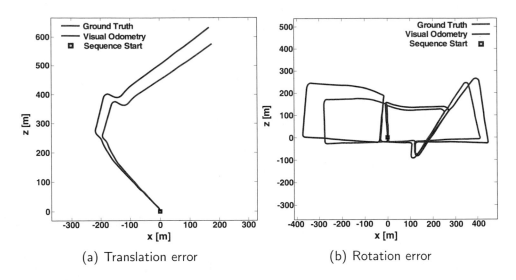

(a) Translation error   (b) Rotation error

Figure 4.10: Examples of the camera pose estimation in comparison to ground truth.

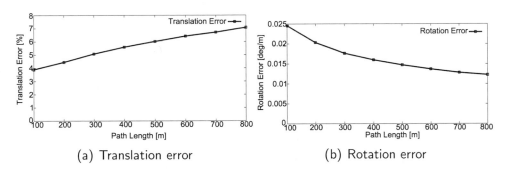

(a) Translation error   (b) Rotation error

Figure 4.11: Translation and rotation errors in terms of path length.

rotation is presented in Figure 4.11. The error is computed as the average percentage error of all sequences in terms of the travelled path. Specifically, while Figure 4.11(a) shows that the translation error accumulates over time, Figure 4.11(b) proves that rotation is not affected in cases of longer paths.

4.3 Conclusion and Future Trends

Analysis of moving objects is crucial for the semantic interpretation of video data. This chapter deals with the topic of moving objects in video, in particular, the automatic extraction of 2D and 3D object trajectories in video data. While Section 4.1 deals with aspects of object tracking in 2D and polar video, Section 4.2 addresses the problem of 3D object trajectory extraction from 2D video. Both sections refer to author's own contributions which have already been published partly in [2, 3, 6, 7].

Section 4.1 summarises an original method for unknown object tracking in output images from 360-degree cameras called Modified Training-Learning-Detection (MTLD) [6, 7]. It is based on recently introduced Training-Learning- Detection (TLD) algorithm [15]. Unlike TLD, MTLD is capable of detecting the unknown objects of interest in 360-degree images.

For the semantic analysis of activities and events in videos, it is important to capture the spatio-temporal relation among objects in the 3D space. In Section 4.2, an original methodology that extracts 3D trajectories of objects from 2D videos, captured from a monocular moving camera, is summarised [3, 2]. Compared to existing methods that rely on restrictive assumptions, the described algorithm can extract 3D trajectories with much less restriction by adopting new example-based techniques which compensate the lack of information. Here, the focal length of the camera based on similar candidates is estimated and used to compute depths of detected objects. Contrary to other 3D trajectory extraction techniques, the original method is able to process video data taken from a stable camera as well as a non-calibrated moving camera without restrictions. For this, the Reversible Jump Markov Chain Monte Carlo (RJ-MCMC) particle filtering has been modified to be more suitable for camera odometry without relying on geometrical feature points.

While this chapter describes mostly techniques for the extraction of 2D and 3D object trajectories, their interpretation supporting the semantic video analysis will play the most important role in the future. An example for this is shown in Section 4.2.2. However, in the near future more complicated activity patterns by studying objects trajectories will be recognised. For this purpose, discriminative features, especially CNN-based, are planned to be extracted from those trajectories. Considering an object activity, its detection can be combined with the tracking process towards building a feedback mechanism. Here, the intention is that the output of each process is used as a cue of the other one.

References

[1] Z. Boukhers, , Y. Wang, K. Shirahama, K. Uehara, and M. Grze-gorzek. Convoy Detection in Crowded Surveillance Videos. In M. Chetouani, J. Cohn, and A. Salah, editors, *International Workshop on Human Behavior Understanding at ACM Multimedia*, pages 137–147, Amsterdam, Netherlands, October 2016. Springer.

[2] Z. Boukhers, K. Shirahama, and M. Grzegorzek. Example-based 3D Trajectory Extraction of Objects from 2D Videos. *IEEE Transactions on Circuits and Systems for Video Technology*, 2017.

[3] Z. Boukhers, K. Shirahama, F. Li, and M. Grzegorzek. Extracting 3D Trajectories of Objects from 2D Videos Using Particle Filter. In *International Conference on Multimedia Retrieval*, Shanghai, China, June 2015.

[4] C. H. Chen, Y. Yao, D. Page, B. Abidi, A. Koschan, and M. Abidi. Heterogeneous fusion of omnidirectional and ptz cameras for multiple object tracking. *IEEE Transactions on Circuits and Systems for Video Technology*, 18(8):1052–1063, 2008.

[5] Wongun Choi, C. Pantofaru, and S. Savarese. A general framework for tracking multiple people from a moving camera. *IEEE Trans. Pattern Anal. Mach. Intell.*, 35(7):1577–1591, 2013.

[6] Ahmad Delforouzi, Seyed Amir Hossein Tabatabaei, Kimiaki Shirahama, and Marcin Grzegorzek. Polar object tracking in 360-degree camera images. In *International Symposium on Multimedia*, pages 347–352. IEEE, 2016.

[7] Ahmad Delforouzi, Seyed Amir Hossein Tabatabaei, Kimiaki Shirahama, and Marcin Grzegorzek. Unknown object tracking in 360-degree camera images. In *23rd International Conference on Pattern Recognition*, pages 1799–1804. IEEE, 2016.

[8] Martin Ester, Hans-Peter Kriegel, Jörg Sander, and Xiaowei Xu. A density-based algorithm for discovering clusters in large spatial databases with noise. In *Proc. of KDD 1996*, pages 226–231, 1996.

[9] Pedro F. Felzenszwalb, Ross B. Girshick, David McAllester, and Deva Ramanan. Object detection with discriminatively trained part-based

models. *IEEE Trans. Pattern Anal. Mach. Intell.*, 32(9):1627–1645, 2010.

[10] Duncan P. Frost, Olaf Khler, and David W. Murray. Object-aware bundle adjustment for correcting monocular scale drift. In *Robotics and Automation (ICRA), IEEE International Conference on*, pages 4770–4776, 2012.

[11] Andreas Geiger, Philip Lenz, and Raquel Urtasun. Are we ready for autonomous driving? the kitti vision benchmark suite. In *Computer Vision and Pattern Recognition (CVPR), IEEE Conference on*, pages 3354–3361, 2012.

[12] Z. He, X. Li, X. You, D. Tao, and Y. Y. Tang. Connected component model for multi-object tracking. *IEEE Transactions on image processing*, 25(8):3698–3711, 2016.

[13] Hoyoung Jeung, Heng Tao Shen, and Xiaofang Zhou. Convoy queries in spatio-temporal databases. In *Proc. of ICDE 2008*, pages 1457–1459, 2008.

[14] Hoyoung Jeung, Man Lung Yiu, Xiaofang Zhou, Christian S Jensen, and Heng Tao Shen. Discovery of convoys in trajectory databases. *Proceedings of the VLDB Endowment*, 1(1):1068–1080, 2008.

[15] Z. Kalal, K. Mikolajczyk, and J. Matas. Tracking-learning-detection. *IEEE Transactions on Pattern Analysis and Machine Intelligence*, 34(7):1409–1422, july 2012.

[16] S. Karthikeyan, Thuyen Ngo, Miguel Eckstein, and B.S. Manjunath. Eye tracking assisted extraction of attentionally important objects from videos. In *IEEE Conference on Computer Vision and Pattern Recognition*, pages 3241–3250, 2015.

[17] Zia Khan, T. Balch, and F. Dellaert. MCMC-based particle filtering for tracking a variable number of interacting targets. *IEEE Trans. Pattern Anal. Mach. Intell.*, 27(11):1805–1819, 2005.

[18] B. Ma, H. Hu, J. Shen, Y. Liu, and L. Shao. Generalized pooling for robust object tracking. *IEEE Transactions on image processing*, 25(9):4199–4208, 2016.

[19] I. Markovic, F. Chaumette, and I. Petrovic. Moving object detection, tracking and following using an omnidirectional camera on a mobile robot. In *2014 IEEE International Conference on Robotics and Automation (ICRA)*, pages 5630–5635, 2014.

[20] A. Mazzu, P. Morerio, L. Marcenaro, and C. S. Regazzoni. A cognitive control-inspired approach to object tracking. *IEEE Transactions on image processing*, 25(6):2697–2711, 2016.

[21] A. Milan, S. Roth, and K. Schindler. Continuous energy minimization for multitarget tracking. *IEEE Transactions on Pattern Analysis and Machine Intelligence*, 36(1):58–72, 2014.

[22] A. Milan, K. Schindler, and S. Roth. Multi-target tracking by discrete-continuous energy minimization. *IEEE Transactions on Pattern Analysis and Machine Intelligence*, PP(99):1–1, 2015.

[23] Mohammad Hossein Mirabdollah and Bärbel Mertsching. On the second order statistics of essential matrix elements. In *Pattern Recognition, German Conference on*, pages 547–557, 2014.

[24] F. Rameau, D. Sidibe, C. Demonceaux, and D. Fofi. Tracking moving objects with a catadioptric sensor using particle filter. In *Computer Vision Workshops, 2007. ICCV Workshops 2007. IEEE 11th International Conference on*, pages 328–334, Nov 2011.

[25] G. Scotti, L. Marcenaro, C. Coelho, F. Selvaggi, and C. S. Regazzoni. A novel dual camera intelligent sensor for high definition 360 degrees surveillance. In *Intelligent Distributed Surveilliance Systems, IEE*, pages 26–30, 2004.

[26] J. Shao, C. C. Loy, and X. Wang. Scene-independent group profiling in crowd. In *IEEE Conference on Computer Vision and Pattern Recognition (CVPR)*, pages 2227–2234, 2014.

[27] Shiyu Song and Manmohan Chandraker. Robust scale estimation in real-time monocular sfm for autonomous driving. In *Computer Vision and Pattern Recognition (CVPR), IEEE Conference on*, pages 1566–1573, 2014.

[28] Shiyu Song and Manmohan Chandraker. Robust scale estimation in real-time monocular sfm for autonomous driving. In *Computer Vision*

and *Pattern Recognition (CVPR), IEEE Conference on*, pages 1566–1573, 2014.

[29] A. Vedaldi and B. Fulkerson. VLFeat: An open and portable library of computer vision algorithms. http://www.vlfeat.org/, 2008.

[30] L. Wen, Z. Lei, S. Lyu, S. Z. Li, and M. H. Yang. Exploiting hierarchical dense structures on hypergraphs for multi-object tracking. *IEEE Transactions on pattern analysis and machine intelligence*, 38(10):1983–1996, 2016.

[31] J. Xiao, R. Stolkin, and A. Leonardis. Single target tracking using adaptive clustered decision trees and dynamic multi-level appearance models. In *IEEE Conference on Computer Vision and Pattern Recognition*, pages 4978–4987, 2015.

[32] Z. H. Xiong, I. Cheng, W. Chen, A. Basu, and M. J. Zhang. Depth space partitioning for omni-stereo object tracking. *IET Computer Vision*, 6(2):153–163, 2012.

[33] X.Wang, E. Tueretken, Franc, o. Fleuret, and P. Fua. Tracking interacting objects using intertwined flows. *IEEE Transactions on pattern analysis and machine intelligence*, 38(11):2312–2326, 2016.

[34] S. Yi, X. Wang, C. Lu, and J. Jia. L0 regularized stationary time estimation for crowd group analysis. In *IEEE Conference on Computer Vision and Pattern Recognition (CVPR)*, pages 2219–2226, 2014.

[35] Y. Zhang, X. Chen, J. Li, C. Wang, and C. Xia. Semantic object segmentation via detection in weakly labeled video. In *IEEE Conference on Computer Vision and Pattern Recognition*, pages 3641–3649, 2015.

Part III

Human Data Interpretation

Chapter 5

Physical Activity Recognition

The World Health Organization (WHO) defines physical activity as any bodily movement produced by skeletal muscles that requires energy expenditure - including activities undertaken while working, playing, carrying out household chores, travelling, and engaging in recreational pursuits[1]. Insufficient physical activity is 1 of the 10 leading risk factors for death worldwide and a key risk factor for noncommunicable diseases (NCDs) such as cardiovascular diseases, cancer and diabetes. Regular moderate intensity physical activity - such as walking, cycling, or participating in sports - has significant benefits for health. For instance, it can reduce the risk of cardiovascular diseases, diabetes, colon and breast cancer, and depression. Moreover, adequate levels of physical activity will decrease the risk of a hip or vertebral fracture and help control weight. However, more than 80% of the world's adolescent population is insufficiently physically active.

In this chapter, selected algorithms for atomic activity recognition (Section 5.1) as well as gait recognition (Section 5.2) including the author's own scientific contributions are described. Moreover, conclusions are drawn and further possible research directions are mentioned in Section 5.3.

5.1 Atomic Activity Recognition

Activity recognition has been identified as a key component of building personal fitness advisers or assisting senior persons to live in their own

---

[1]http://www.who.int/topics/physical_activity

Figure 5.1: Wearable devices become more important for activity recognition since new sensor modalities are integrated into them. A smartphone is typically equipped with an accelerometer, gyroscope and magnetometer. Smartwatches have pulse-sensors and sensors for electrodermal activity [3] and some smartglasses offer electrooculography [1].

homes for a longer period of time [5]. Hence, the proliferation of wearable devices like smartphones, smartwatches and smartglasses is paving the way to perform activity recognition with the help of technology that people are already familiar with (see Figure 5.1). This is in stark contrast to systems that are monitoring people with the help of cameras. People are often worried about privacy issues when cameras are used and the installation of cameras comes with non negligible costs that are necessary to operate the system.

With the fast development of new wearable devices, we can also observe the increase in the number of built-in sensors. While several years ago wearable devices were mostly equipped with an accelerometer and a gyroscope, nowadays additional sensors like heart-rate, barometer, magnetometer, galvanic skin response or electrooculography are introduced. This opens new possibilities to track more details of the daily routine of a person, but it also introduces the necessity to investigate the applicability of each new sensor modality. One of the strategies for these investigations is to use the sensor data in a machine learning set-up, where sensor data must be firstly represented by meaningful features. However, defining which parts of the data are in fact meaningful or which representation might be appropriate for the activity recognition classifier is often a difficult task that requires specific domain knowledge or lots of experimentation.

For this reason, this chapter focuses on the evaluation of a feature learning approach [13] that automatically extracts features from the underlying sensor data. The approach described in this chapter is based on the Bag-of-Features technique, which summarises local characteristics of the data in a single common feature vector [91]. As local characteristics are parts of the raw sensor data, manual feature extraction or laborious preprocessing is not performed. Due to this strategy, new sensors can easily be integrated into the system. As one can see below, the fusion of multiple sensors is done in a simple and intuitive manner by concatenating extracted features from each sensor into one vector.

This section is structured as follows. In Section 5.1.1, a survey of most related approaches in the field of smart home architectures and activity recognition is presented. Section 5.1.2 explains the original approach for time-series classification. In Section 5.1.3, results achieved in various experiments regarding the detection and classification of activities are reported.

5.1.1 Survey of Related Approaches

Traditionally, the fields of smart home technology and activity recognition are highly overlapping. Smart homes provide the hardware to collect and process relevant data, while activity recognition approaches extract semantic meanings from the collected data by adopting machine learning methods. The following paragraphs are summarising the most important approaches in those areas.

Smart Home Technology

For more than two decades the research community has been developing different approaches that focus on the recognition of activities for in-home settings. The need for in-home experiments is motivated by the fact that people behave in a different manner when they feel observed and/or are not used to the experimental environment. This makes it hard to transfer results obtained in laboratory settings to more realistic scenarios or even commercial products. This paragraph summarises only the most relevant approaches in this area. More details have been analysed in various surveys published in the last years [7, 95, 6, 65].

One common theme of many studies is to utilise motion sensors that are fixed at some location in the house/apartment or at specific objects like microwaves or toilets. The biggest advantage of motion sensors is their cheap price and the simplicity of the data. The output is often a binary value that, e.g., represents the presence of a resident at a specific location [102] or indicates if a certain object was used [105, 69, 83, 56, 41, 89]. Participants of such studies also report that, even if motion sensors are placed at visible places, they forget or ignore their existence over time [102]. The PlaceLab living lab [47] is a 1000 sq. ft. apartment that is fully equipped with various sensors and computers. PlaceLab also offers the possibility to use cameras and microphones to annotate activities. Furthermore, additional sensors like accelerometers and gyroscopes can be attached to participants. The output data are transferred over a wireless network and synchronised with all other sensors. This laboratory was used in [69], in which they monitor a married couple over a time span of ten weeks. They compare the activity recognition accuracy for different sensor modalities and conclude that many activities can be detected only by knowing the location of the user, which is a strong argument for motion sensors.

In addition to the pure hardware set-up, researchers have also realised that an expandable architecture is the basis to built long-term usable smart home systems. An example is the Gator Tech Smart House [44]. While equipped with an impressive amount of smart devices, it also offers various services to the developer of such systems. Raw sensor data are abstracted into a physical layer so that developers can thus define services without having to understand the physical world [44]. The CARDEA-MuSA [39, 15] is an example for another framework with the ability to integrate and connect various sensors and use these advanced for health-monitoring.

An approach that targets especially user friendliness is described by the CASAS system [30]. The main components of the system are various motion sensors that the user can install on his own. Due to its architecture, the system can be extended by additional sensors and only a small, low-cost server is needed to perform activity recognition. At the time of publication the estimated costs for the whole system amount to $2765.

One common disadvantage among the different approaches is that additional sensors must be equipped within the house, even if the amount of work load differs among the presented works. This leads to an obstacle that many users are not willing to overcome.

Activity Recognition from Continuous Data

Architectures for smart homes mostly rely on binary data obtained from motion sensors or reed switches. However, the constantly increasing number of wearable devices has also brought a great deal of effort in working with real-valued sensor output, which are referred to as *continuous data* [27, 19, 62, 8, 97]. This is especially true since the variety of sensor modalities increases with every new wearable device generation. Sensors like accelerometers, gyroscopes or magnetometers are common for almost all devices. However, new devices also offer sensors like barometer, heart rate sensor, electrooculography (EOG), electromyography (EMG) or sensors for electrodermal activity (EDA). The main advancement in the last years is that new sensors have a strong focus on the tracking of biometric health data [61, 14, 74].

The framework described in Section 5.1.2 relies only on a few assumptions about the underlying sensor data. For this reason, it can easily deal with new sensor modalities, which is an important point for future research. This is often in contrast to related work that has to make certain assumptions or that suffers from other shortcomings [19]. For example, template matching methods measure the similarity of time sequences on the basis of Euclidean distance or Dynamic Time Warping [76, 68, 120]. If two time sequences are alike, they are considered as the same activity. However, it was found that these methods are easily corrupted by noise in the signal [66]. Generative activity recognition methods estimate the probability that a given time sequence is generated by assuming that the user performed a specific activity. Hidden Markov Models and their extensions [103, 121, 20] belong to the predominantly used techniques of this group. The advantage of these methods is that they take temporal dependencies among data points into account. However, a substantial amount of training data is essential to capture all the different variations of an activity [27]. The overwhelming amount of research focuses on feature-based approaches. These features should represent characteristics of the underlying time sequence and be representative for each activity. For example, statistical features summarise time sequences in terms of their mean value or variance, while parameters from the frequency domain can represent repetitive patterns of the signal [46, 52, 86, 40, 53, 96, 48, 84]. More sophisticated features describe characteristic events of an activity like the occurrence of specific eye-movements [18] or biomedical events, e.g., duration of inhalation/exhalation and heart beat intervals [85]. While such features might significantly improve the classification result, it often requires domain knowledge that only experts can provide.

Avoiding the creation of the above-mentioned hand-crafted features has become one of the main research issues in machine learning. Instead, feature learning, the task of automatically extracting meaningful features from data, is brought to the fore. A simple but effective version of feature learning is to count the occurrences of relevant pieces in the time signal. This so-called codebook approach has its origin in image classification [31, 49], where it analyses a large number of patches (small regions) in images and constructs a codebook consisting of characteristic patches called *codewords*. An image is then represented by a feature signifying the distribution of codewords.

Codebook-based methods have also been shown to be successful candidates for various areas of activity and emotion recognition [109, 80, 12, 91]. More advanced feature-learning methods stem from the field of deep learning and have also already been applied to human activity recognition [87, 75, 77, 88, 42]. However, one big disadvantage of deep learning architectures is a large number of hyper-parameters that require an extensive optimisation phase.

Due to its advantages, the codebook approach used for the classification of time-series is described in more detail in Section 5.1.2.

5.1.2 Codebook Approach for Classification

First of all, some important terms need to be clarified. Referring to time series, the whole dataset containing all the data available for training/testing a classifier is meant. A sequence, however, is only one part of the dataset, for example a window of 10 seconds. Finally, a subsequence is again one window within the sequence (see Figure 5.2). The goal of activity recognition is to predict the label (i.e., underlying activity) on a sequence level using a machine learning approach.

Figure 5.3 shows an overview of the method described in this section. It consists of three steps. Figure 5.3 (a) illustrates the codebook construction step that groups subsequences collected from the dataset into clusters of similar ones. A codebook is constructed as a set of codewords, where each codeword is the centre of a cluster. Figure 5.3 (b) outlines the second step, the codeword assignment, where a feature of a sequence is extracted by assigning each subsequence to the most similar codeword and counting the number of occurrences for each codeword. In other words, this feature

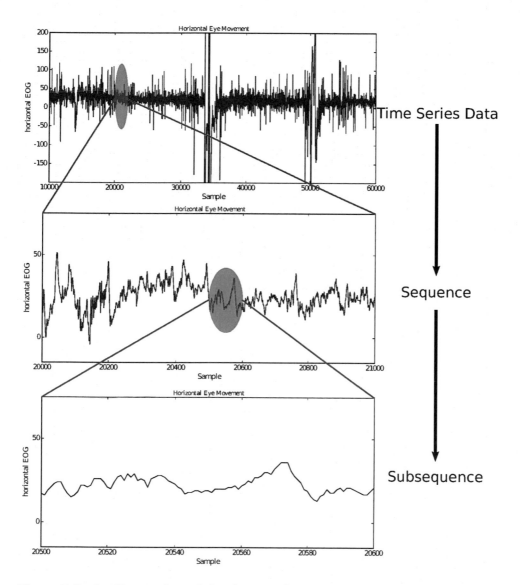

Figure 5.2: An illustration of the dataset decomposition into subsequences.

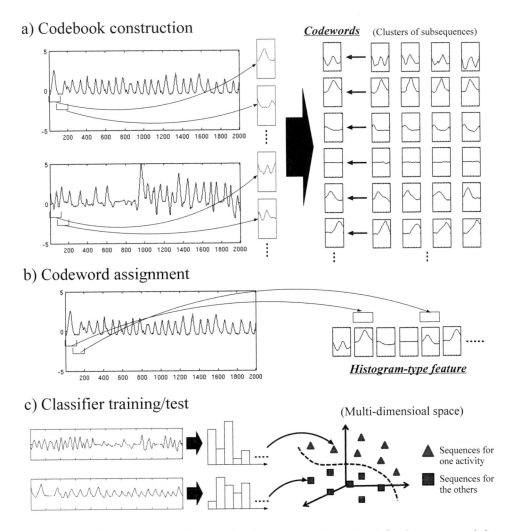

a) Codebook construction

Codewords (Clusters of subsequences)

b) Codeword assignment

Histogram-type feature

c) Classifier training/test

(Multi-dimensioal space)

▲ Sequences for one activity

■ Sequences for the others

Figure 5.3: An overview of the codebook-based method for human activity recognition.

is a histogram representing the frequency of each codeword within one sequence. The last step is the classifier training/testing based on the fact that sequences represented by such features can be considered as points in the multi-dimensional space, as shown in Figure 5.3 (c). As depicted by the dashed line in Figure 5.3 (c), a classifier draws a classification boundary to discriminate between training sequences annotated with a certain activity class and those annotated with the others. Based on this boundary, the classifier determines the activity class of a test sequence.

Codebook Construction: Since it is not possible to know beforehand which codewords are characteristic for a specific activity, it is necessary to learn them initially from the dataset and build a codebook. Constructing the codebook is a part of the training phase and is performed on unlabelled data. This is especially important since obtaining labelled data in activity recognition is still a task that requires lots of effort.

The first step in the codebook construction is to find suitable codewords. For this, subsequences of equal length are extracted from the training dataset. A subsequence is a sliding window of size w that is shifted from the beginning until the end of the dataset. In more detail, the window is placed at every l-th time point, whereby a small l causes a large overlap between neighbouring subsequences. While this "dense sampling" of subsequences seems redundant, it has been shown to lead to better results than "sparse sampling" with a small overlap [79]. Note that the window size w and the sliding size l are hyper-parameters and must be chosen appropriately. However, w can be chosen independently from the expected duration of the activities since the final classification is based on the histogram of codewords within a given time interval but not on the codewords itself.

The second step groups all extracted subsequences into N different clusters. In the implementation reported in [55], k-means clustering [43] is performed to find N clusters consisting of similar subsequences. The distance among two subsequence is measured as the Euclidean distance. Since k-means clustering depends on initial cluster centres that are randomly determined, it is conducted 10 times to select the best result that yields the minimum sum of Euclidean distances between subsequences and their assigned cluster centres. Based on the best clustering result, a codebook consisting of N codewords is obtained whereby each cluster centre equals one codeword. The optimal number of codewords N must be determined experimentally.

Codeword Assignment: To convert a sequence into a feature representation, a histogram that represents the distribution of the N codewords within a sequence is built. Subsequences, which are extracted in the same way to the codebook construction step, are assigned to the most similar codeword and its frequency is incremented. Finally, this histogram of codewords is normalised so that the sum of frequencies of all the N codewords is one. Note that while this "hard assignment" approach assigns a subsequence to a single codeword, researchers have developed a "soft assignment" approach that implements its flexible assignment to multiple codewords [104]. However, preliminary tests did not show a significant performance improvement of the soft assignment approach, despite its expensive computational cost. Thus, the hard assignment approach is used in the framework described in [55].

Classifier Training/Testing: A binary classifier is trained that distinguishes training sequences labelled with a target activity from other training sequences. The former and latter are called "positive sequences" and "negative sequences", respectively. To gain high discrimination power, a variety of characteristic subsequences need to be considered using hundreds of codewords (i.e., N is large). Because each sequence is represented with a high-dimensional feature, a Support Vector Machine (SVM) is used due to its effectiveness for high-dimensional data [106]. The SVM draws a classification boundary based on the "margin maximisation" principle so that the boundary is placed in the middle between positive and negative sequences, which makes the generalisation error independent of the number of dimensions [106]. Actually, the combination of the codebook approach and an SVM has been justified in many classification tasks of images/videos, which are represented by features with thousands of dimensions [49]. For a test sequence, the trained SVM outputs a score between 0 and 1 based on its distance to the classification boundary [25]. Finally, the recognition of C activities is conducted using C SVMs, each of which is built as a binary classifier for one activity. Then, the activity of a test sequence is determined as the one characterised by the highest SVM score.

The SVM implemented according to [55] uses the Radial Basis Function (RBF) kernel that has one parameter to control the complexity of a classification boundary. This parameter is set to the mean of squared Euclidean distances among training sequences, because it stably offers reasonable performances without conducting computationally expensive cross validation [119]. In addition, the SVM parameter to control the penalty of misclassification is empirically set to 2. This SVM parameter setting has been proven to be generally applicable to different activity recognition tasks [91], and is used throughout all the experiments.

Fusion of Multiple Features: Since different sensors capture different characteristics of an activity, the recognition performance can be improved by fusing features extracted from those sensor data. To realise this dynamic sensor selection, three fusion approaches are explored (see Figure 5.4).

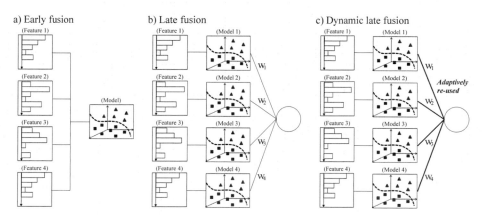

Figure 5.4: An illustration of the early, late and dynamic late fusion approaches.

Figure 5.4 (a) shows the early fusion approach [94] where codebook-based features extracted from different types of sensor data are combined into a single high-dimensional feature, based on which an SVM is constructed. Hence, a codebook is constructed for each single sensor and consequently, each sensor provides its own histogram-type feature.

Figure 5.4 (b) depicts the late fusion approach [94] where each type of feature is used to construct a separate SVM. For a test example x, the final recognition score $f(x)$ is obtained by linearly combining the score $f_i(x)$ produced by the SVM on the ith sensor data, that is, $f(x) = \sum_i w_i f_i(x)$ $(\sum_i w_i = 1, w_i \geq 0)$. Here, the weight w_i for the i-th sensor data is computed in the following way: Firstly, the training dataset is divided into two subsets with the same size and one of them is used for training SVMs on different types of sensor data, and the other one for testing these SVMs and computing their optimal weighted combination. In particular, a gradient-ascend approach is used to obtain the weights that maximise the recognition performance on the second subset. Afterwards, these weights are used to fuse SVMs using the whole training dataset. In other words, the weights obtained for SVMs trained on a half of training dataset are assumed to be applicable to more accurate SVMs trained on the whole dataset.

However, the early fusion approach needs to build an SVM for each of all the possible sensor combinations. And every time the user activates or deactivates sensors, a different SVM has to be loaded. In addition, the late fusion approach requires an expensive computational cost, because weights have to be computed for all possible sensor combinations. To overcome this, a "dynamic late fusion" approach shown in Figure 5.4 (c) can also be used [55]. Here, weights are computed only for the combination of all sensors, and adaptively re-used depending on sensor selection. Specifically, weights for not-selected sensors are set to zero, and weights for the selected sensors are normalised so that their summation is one.

5.1.3   Experiments and Results

A detailed evaluation of the codebook approach applied for physical activity recognition using the codebook approach described in Section 5.1.2 has been reported in [55]. This section describes the experimental setup and summarises the performance evaluation.

As reported in [55], the hardware configuration used for the experimental evaluation of the method described in Section 5.1.2 is depicted in Figure 5.5. First, as depicted in Figure 5.5 (a), a user takes three mobile devices, Google NEXUS 5X (smartphone), Microsoft Band 2 [2] (smartwatch) and JINS MEME [1] (smartglasses), which are used to capture the body, hand, and head movements, respectively. From these devices, the following eight types of sensor data are obtained:

1. Smartphone's accelerometer (*sp-acc*): This sensor delivers a three-dimensional sequence that indicates acceleration forces (including gravity forces) acting on the smartphone's x, y and z axes.

2. Smartphone's gyroscope (*sp-gyro*): This sensor delivers a three-dimensional sequence that presents angular velocities on the x, y and z axes.

3. Smartphone's gravity (*sp-grav*): This sensor delivers a three-dimensional sequence that represents gravity forces on the x, y and z axes. This is useful for capturing transitions of the smartphone's orientations over time.

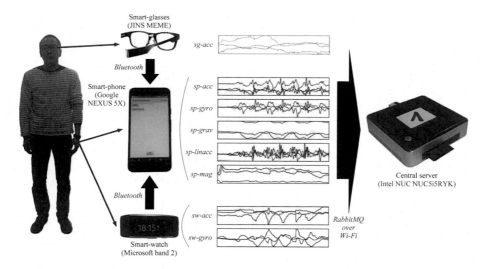

Figure 5.5: An overview of the activity recognition system.

4. Smartphone's linear accelerometer (*sp-linacc*): This sensor delivers a three-dimensional sequence that indicates acceleration forces on the x, y and z axes, where gravity forces are excluded.

5. Smartphone's magnetometer (*sp-mag*): This sensor delivers a three-dimensional sequence that describes intensities of the earth's magnetic field along the x, y and z axes. Such intensities are useful for determining the smartphone's orientation.

6. Smartwatch's accelerometer (*sw-acc*): Similar to *sp-acc*, this sensor delivers a three-dimensional sequence of acceleration forces applied to x, y and z axes of a smartwatch

7. Smartwatch's gyroscope (*sw-gyro*): Similar to *sp-gyro*, this sensor delivers a three-dimensional sequence of angular velocities on the x, y and z axes.

8. Smartglasses' accelerometer (*sg-acc*): This sensor delivers a three-dimensional sequence of acceleration forces on the smartglasses' x, y and z axes.

Sampling rates of *sp-acc*, *sp-gyro*, *sp-grav* and *sp-linacc* are 200Hz, the sampling rate of *sp-mag* is 50Hz, those of *sw-acc* and *sw-gyro* are 67Hz, and that of *sg-acc* is 20Hz. By following the general framework shown in Figure 5.5, *sw-acc*, *sw-gyro* and *sg-acc* are firstly sent to the smartphone via Bluetooth connection, and then all the sensor data are transferred to the central server through RabbitMQ [4] on Wi-Fi connection. The server (the activity recognition method is executed on) is established on Intel NUC NUC5i5RYK (CPU: Core i5-5250U 1.6GHz, RAM: 16GB, HDD: 450GB, OS: Debian 4.8.4-1).

One codebook is constructed from each type of sensor data, that is, a set of three-dimensional sequences. In order to capture correlations among three dimensions, codewords are extracted by performing clustering on "three-dimensional subsequences". Specifically, a subsequence collected by a window of size w is represented as a $3w$-dimensional vector, where the first w, the subsequent w and the last w dimensions represent values on the x, y and z axes, respectively. It should be noted that this subsequence representation can be used in the subsequent codebook construction, codeword assignment and classifier training/test processes with no modification. Regarding the hyper-parameters, codebooks for *sp-acc*, *sp-gyro*, *sp-grav* and *sp-linacc* are constructed using the window size $w = 128$ and the sliding size $l = 8$, codebooks for *sp-mag*, *sw-acc* and *sw-gyro* are constructed with $w = 64$ and $l = 4$, and the codebook for *sg-acc* is built with $w = 32$ and $l = 1$. Although these values are chosen based on preliminary experiments, one criteria is that a sufficient number of subsequences can be collected from a sequence of five seconds, which is the unit to build recognition models (see below). More concretely, more than 100 subsequences are collected from *sp-acc*, *sp-gyro*, *sp-grav* and *sp-linacc* sequences, more than 45 subsequences are collected from a *sp-mag* sequences, and more than 60 subsequences are located in *sw-acc*, *sw-gyro* and *sg-acc* sequences. With this, the resulting feature of a sequence appropriately represents the distribution of subsequences. The number of codewords N is experimentally set to 1024 for all types of sensor data. Except the above-mentioned tuning of hyper-parameters w, l and N, no extra tuning or pre/post-processing has been done. An overview over all sensor parameters can be found in Table 5.1.

Following 11 activities have been targeted: 1. lying, 2. sitting, 3. standing, 4. walking, 5. bending, 6. getting up, 7. lying down, 8. putting a hand back, 9. sitting down, 10. standing up, and 11. stretching a hand. We prepare a training dataset which contains the eight types of sensor data for 145 activity executions of one user. For each of the 11 activities, the dataset includes more than 10 executions each of which lasts five seconds and signifies a different style (e.g., the user lies on his stomach, on his back, on his side, changes lying styles, etc.). This enables to cover

	sp-acc, sp-gyro sp-grav, sp-linacc	sp-mag	sw-acc, sw-gyro	sg-acc
Sampling Rate (Hz)	200	50	67	20
Window Size w	128	64	64	32
Sliding Size l	8	4	4	1

Table 5.1: Parameters of sensors used for physical activity recognition.

a variation of the same activity and carry out semantically meaningful recognition. In addition, the codebook-based recognition method does not require the exact boundaries of an activity. Instead, the method only requires the activity to be "included" in five seconds, so that the resulting feature encompasses subsequences corresponding to the moment of this activity.

For each of the 11 activities, an SVM is constructed using the training dataset. Four activities (lying, sitting, standing and walking) are regarded as *static*, and the remaining seven as *dynamic*. This is based on the fact that static activities indicate states of the user while dynamic activities represent short-time movements occurring in different states. In other words, dynamic activities occur while doing different static activities. For instance, the user can stretch his hand while standing or sitting. Thus, it is not reasonable that an SVM for a static activity is constructed by regarding executions for all the other activities as negative examples, because these executions may include moments of the static activity. Hence, negative examples for the static activity are collected as executions for the other "static" activities, since each static activity execution only includes one state of the user. For a dynamic activity, negative examples are collected as executions for all the other static and dynamic activities, as they do not contain any moment of the dynamic activity. Positive examples are obtained as executions of an activity regardless of whether it is static or dynamic. Using such positive and negative examples, SVMs are built for all 11 activities.

The performance of these SVMs is examined on a test dataset consisting of 124 executions (test examples), which are performed by the same user to the training dataset in a different day. Two evaluation measures are used. The first is an accuracy representing the rate of correct predictions over 124 test examples. Considering concurrent occurrences of static and dynamic activities, the prediction for a test example of a static (or dynamic) activity is determined as the one for which the highest SVM score is observed among four static (or seven dynamic) activities. This is because the accuracy computation mixing static and dynamic activities underestimates the recognition performance. Let us assume that a test example where the user stretches his hand while standing is labelled as stretching a hand. For this test example, the SVM for stretching a hand should output a high score, but a higher score may be produced by the model for standing because the user is actually standing. Thus, the separation between static and dynamic activities is necessary for meaningful evaluation.

However, the deterministic evaluation based on accuracies may be too rigid. Thus, an Average Precision (AP) [73] as the second evaluation measure is used. The AP does not require any deterministic decision on a test example, but considers the difference between SVM scores assigned to test examples for a target activity and the ones for the other test examples. Specifically, test examples are ranked based on SVM scores for the target activity. Then, the AP is calculated as the average of precisions each of which is computed at the position of a test example for the target activity. In other words, the AP approximates the area under the recall-precision curve created based on SVM scores. A larger AP means a better result where more test examples for the target activity are ranked at higher positions. Because of this ranking-based statistical computation, the separation between static and dynamic activities is not considered for the AP computation. For evaluation of a static activity, some test examples for dynamic activities may have higher SVM scores than the ones for the static activity. But a good method assigns high SVM scores to test examples for the static activity and ranks them at higher positions compared to the ranking produced by another method. In this way, APs are useful for relative performance comparison among methods. Finally, the Mean of APs (MAP) over all 11 activities is used as an overall evaluation measure.

Overall Performance Evaluation

Overall, the system using the early fusion approach achieves an accuracy of 87.1% where evaluations for static and dynamic activities are separated as described before. Figure 5.6 (a) and (b) show the confusion matrix for static activities and the one for dynamic activities. In each matrix, rows and

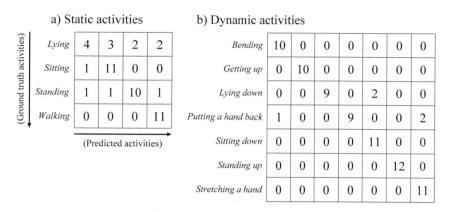

a) Static activities

(Ground truth activities)

Lying	4	3	2	2
Sitting	1	11	0	0
Standing	1	1	10	1
Walking	0	0	0	11

(Predicted activities)

b) Dynamic activities

Bending	10	0	0	0	0	0	0
Getting up	0	10	0	0	0	0	0
Lying down	0	0	9	0	2	0	0
Putting a hand back	1	0	0	9	0	0	2
Sitting down	0	0	0	0	11	0	0
Standing up	0	0	0	0	0	12	0
Stretching a hand	0	0	0	0	0	0	11

Figure 5.6: The confusion matrix for static and dynamic activities.

columns correspond to ground truth and predicted activities, respectively. As shown in Figure 5.6 (a), the most problematic activity is lying because it is easily confused with the other activities depending on the user's postures. One possible solution is to capture the orientation of the smartglasses by equipping a gravity or magnetometer sensor in them. Except lying, the other activities are recognised quite accurately. Especially, in several misrecognition cases, the system's outputs are reasonable or even correct. For example, as depicted in Figure 5.6 (b), the system predicts the activity "putting hand back" for two executions annotated with the ground truth activity "stretching hand", and these predictions are evaluated as incorrect. However, after the user stretched his hand, he actually put it back during the five-seconds executions and forgot the annotation. In such a situation, the system can perform detailed recognition which identifies activities that the user was not aware of. Figure 5.7 displays APs and MAP of the system over all 11 activities. Although APs vary depending on activities, the methodology achieves a very high MAP value 88.8%.

5.2   Gait Recognition

Gait is a walking style and can be considered as a biometric feature to identify people. Unlike other biometric modalities such as fingerprints, DNA, palm print, hand geometry, face and iris recognition which require the physical contact and cooperation of human with the system, gait can be collected at distance without any interaction with the system. More-

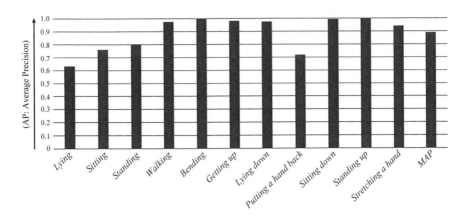

Figure 5.7: Average Precisions (APs) and Mean of APs (MAP).

over, it can be performed at low resolution in non-invasive and hidden manners, which is unobtrusive. It is extremely useful in many applications such as visual surveillance and service robots interacting with humans in daily life. However, gait also has some limitations. It can be affected due to injuries, different types of walking surface, wearing clothes and etc. Although gait is not as powerful as other biometric modalities, the characteristics to recognise individuals at a distance make it irreplaceable in many applications such as visual surveillance.

This section is structured as follows. First, a survey of related approaches in the area of gait recognition is given in Section 5.2.1. Subsequently, a method for spatiotemporal representation of gait is introduced in Section 5.2.2. Finally, experiments are described and results are presented in Section 5.2.3.

5.2.1 Survey or Related Approaches

In literature, gait recognition techniques can be divided into two broad categories: (1) model-based and (2) model-free approaches. Model-based approaches describe the structure of the human body and its motion for person identification. They track the different body parts and joint positions over time, using an underlying mathematical structure. The structural model [64, 92, 24, 70] considers the stick figures, ellipse fitting and interlinked pendulum to construct a model, using the prior knowledge of human body shape. The motion models [17, 114, 32, 110, 16] extract the motion information from human body parts such as joint angle trajectories, rotation patterns of hip and thigh. Yam et al. [114] used a temporal template matching technique on the gait cycle to extract the angles of thigh and lower leg rotation. They developed a gait signature using the phase-weighted magnitudes of the lower order Fourier components of these rotations. The authors in [32] proposed a gait feature by exploiting the angular motion of the hip and thigh using the Fourier series. Wang et al. [110] proposed a structural and motion-based model to refine the feature extraction for gait recognition, using a condensation framework. They modelled the human body using fourteen rigid parts connected to each other at join locations and the joint angle trajectories are computed on these location to recognise the individual's gait. In [92], a 3D voxel model is derived from silhouette images and proposed for gait recognition. Voxel models is constructed using ellipsoids fitting technique into four different components of lower limbs. The features derived from the ellipsoids are modelled using a Fourier representation. Lee et al. [64] modelled the human silhouette using seven different ellipses, representing the various human body regions. They considered several statistical measurements on these regions over time such as: mean, standard deviation, location of its centroid, magnitude and phase of these moment based regions for gait and gender classification. Recent studies [115, 78, 17] have shown that model-based approaches can, to some extent, deal with rotation and occlusion problems, but they are computationally expensive and sensitive to the quality of video data. Therefore, they are not suitable for real-world and real-time applications.

Alternatively, the model-free approaches do not model the structure of human motion and normally operate on the sequence of segmented silhouettes of the human body region. They either construct a template image from the extracted silhouettes in a gait sequence [72, 10, 26, 11, 118, 107, 99, 113] or use the temporal information of human motion in person identification [67, 9, 21, 29, 57, 115, 60]. Perhaps, the simplest model-free technique using a template image from the segmented silhouettes is proposed in [72]. They extract the human body silhouettes using background modelling and average them over a gait cycle, known as Gait Energy Image (GEI). Later, this representation is classified using the Bayesian classifier. Several improvements in [72], such as Gait Entropy Image (GEnI) [11], AEI [118], Chrono-Gait Image (CGI) [107] and Frame Difference Energy Image (FDEI) [26] have also been proposed. Many researchers [67, 115, 60, 21] exploited the human motion information for gait recognition. They built the shape of motion using optical flow field, which are investigated to recognise the individuals. Bashir et al. [9] proposed a histogram based gait representation using the motion intensity and its direction information from optical flow field. The authors of [21] computed the spatio-temporal cuboids of optical flow from the video sequences and fed to Convolutional Neural Network (CNN) to obtain a high level gait representation. Lam et al. [60] proposed the computation of optical flow fields on segmented silhouettes and formulated in a representation known as Gait Flow Image (GFI) for person identification. Some researchers [117, 38] have also computed the several features such as height, width, centroid position from the segmented silhouette/contour of human's body region on the gait cycle, to approximate the gait patterns.

In comparison with model-based approaches, the model-free approaches are low in computation and have demonstrated more convincing results on benchmark gait databases. However, the silhouette-based gait recognition techniques are highly dependent on the accurate segmentation of the human body region from the background, which is still a challenging problem. An inaccurate segmentation of the human body region will not only disrupt the estimation of a gait cycle but also degrade the recognition accuracy [117, 45]. Numerous techniques (such as [93, 45]) have also exploited the depth images from Microsoft Kinect to accurately segment the human body region from the background, however, the biggest restriction is the field-of-view, which is very limited (1-4 meters) [51]. A simple but effective gait recognition technique using the the spatio-temporal characteristics of human motion is described in the subsequent section. It exploits the distinctive motion information of individual's gait, using dense trajectories. Moreover, it neither requires the estimation of gait cycle nor the segmentation of the human body region. The experimental results on various benchmark gait databases confirm its effectiveness.

5.2.2 Spatiotemporal Representation of Gait

Numerous feature extraction techniques have been proposed and exploited in computer vision for image and video representation: SIFT (Scale Invariant Feature Transform), SURF (Speeded-Up Robust Feature) and trajectory are a few to mention. Recently, dense trajectories have demonstrated excellent results in image classification and action recognition [108, 81]. The motivation in using the dense trajectories for gait recognition is that they encode the local motion patterns and can be easily computed from the video sequences. A sample of dense points is selected from each frame and tracked in successive frames based on displacement information using optical flow field. Each point $p_t = (x_t, y_t)$ at frame t is tracked in frame $t + 1$ from a dense optical flow field, using median filtering. In a given trajectory, the shape of displacement vectors is: $S = \Delta P_t, ..., \Delta P_{t+L-1}$, where L is the length of the trajectory shape and $\Delta P_t = P_{t+1} - P_t$. The vector S is then normalised by the sum of the magnitude of the displacement vectors. That is,

$$S' = \frac{(\Delta P_t, ..., \Delta P_{t+L-1})}{\sum_{j=t}^{t+L-1} ||\Delta P_j||} \quad , \tag{5.1}$$

where S' represents the shape of trajectory. Wang et al. [108] also proposed the encoding of Histogram of Oriented Gradient (HOG) and Histogram of Optical Flow (HOF). Moreover, the relative motion information between the pixels along the horizontal and vertical axis is also computed by taking the derivative along the respective components of HOF, and their information is encoded in MBH_x (Motion Boundary Histogram) and MBH_y, respectively. In addition, the derivative along the horizontal and vertical components of HOF is computed to encode the relative motion information between the pixels along the respective axis, known as MBH_x and MBH_y, respectively. The orientation information of each of the above mentioned local descriptors are quantised into histograms and normalised with the $L2$-norm, separately. Several combinations of these local descriptors are evaluated on TUM GAID gait database [45] to recognise their effectiveness in person identification and the results are illustrated in Figure 5.8. The empirical results demonstrate that HOG in combination with MBH outperform the rest. Since HOG capture the static appearance of a person and MBH highlight the information about the changes in optical flow field (i.e., motion boundaries), combining the person appearance and local motion characteristics greatly improves the results of the identification.

Once the local descriptors are extracted, they are used to construct a signature to characterise an image or video sequence (i.e., feature encoding). The encoding process converts the local descriptors into a fixed length vector. This process is normally accomplished by the vector quantisation of local descriptors and building a histogram of visual words (also known as bag-of-visual-words). However, inspired by the recent success of the Fisher Vector (FV) encoding [90], the local descriptors are transformed into high-level representation using FV encoding. It comprises the description of local descriptors by its deviation from the generative model

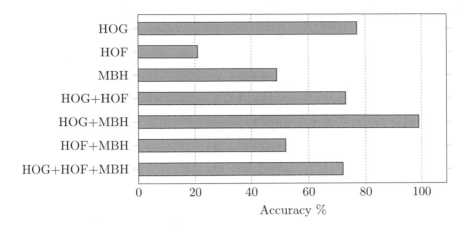

Figure 5.8: Performance of various motion descriptors for gait recognition on the TUM GAID [45] gait database.

(i.e., GMM), which is computed using the gradient of its log-likelihood with respect to the model parameters.

FV is derived from Fisher kernel [90] which combines the characteristics of both discriminative and generic approaches, using a kernel from the generative model of the data. The process of FV encoding begins by learning a GMM. For a given feature set $X = \{x_t \mid t = 1, ..., T\}$, it can be mapped into a vector using the probability density function $p(X \mid \theta)$

$$F_X = \frac{1}{T} \nabla_\theta \log p(X|\theta) \quad , \tag{5.2}$$

where F_X represents the FV and ∇_θ is the gradient of the log-likelihood function describing the contribution of parameters in the generation process. Let x_t be a D-dimensional local descriptor and $q_t(i)$ be the soft assignment of t-th descriptor to the i-th mixture. Moreover, let us assume that the covariance matrix $\sum_i$ is diagonal and can be represented as σ_i. The gradient vector with respect to the mean μ_i and the covariance σ_i can be formulated as

$$u_i = \frac{1}{T\sqrt{w_i}} \sum_{t=1}^{T} q_t(i) \frac{x_t - \mu_i}{\sigma_i} \quad , \tag{5.3}$$

$$v_i = \frac{1}{T\sqrt{2w_i}} \sum_{t=1}^{T} q_t(i) \left[\frac{(x_t - \mu_i)^2}{\sigma_i^2} - 1 \right] \quad , \tag{5.4}$$

134

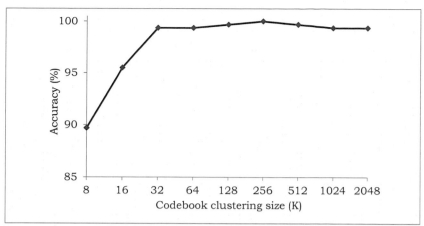

Figure 5.9: Influence of the codebook clustering size on the accuracy in gait recognition for the TUM GAID dataset.

where u_i and v_i are $D-$dimensional gradient vectors with respect to the mean μ_i and the covariance σ_i known as the first and the second order differences of descriptor points to the i-th cluster centre, respectively. The final representation of FV for the feature set X is obtained by concatenating all the u_i and the v_i for $i = 1, ..., K$ clusters. That is,

$$f = [u_1^\top, v_1^\top, u_2^\top, v_2^\top, ..., u_K^\top, v_K^\top]^\top \quad . \tag{5.5}$$

The total size of f is $2KD$. All the local descriptors (i.e., HOG, MBHx and MBHy) are encoded separately.

5.2.3   Experiments and Results

To build a codebook with GMM, one million local descriptors are randomly selected from each descriptor. The influence of various mixture components ranging from 2^3 to 2^{11} is evaluated in feature encoding for gait representation. Figure 5.9 illustrates the influence of various Gaussian components on the TUM GAID database [45]. The empirical results demonstrate that excellent results can be obtained using mixture number 2^8. The recognition accuracy either remains constant or even decreases, when the cluster size goes beyond 2^8. Perhaps a possible reason for the decrease in accuracy is the large size of the encoded vector. Since, FV scales linearly with the size of codebook, therefore, this large size may effect the recognition accuracy.

To classify the high dimensional encoded features, a Linear Support Vector Machine (SVM) is used which has been considered a powerful classification tool in many applications. In the comparison of SVM, the other similarity based classifiers such K-Nearest Neighbour and probability based classifiers like Naive Bayes do not perform well on high dimensional features [50]. SVM first maps the training samples into a high dimensional space and then generates a hyperplane between the different classes of objects using the principle of maximising the margin. Because of this principle, the generalisation error of the SVM is theoretically independent from the number of feature dimensions. Specifically, the implementation of SVM in the LIBLINEAR library [36] is exploited which has demonstrated excellent classification results on large sparse datasets. For each database, a 10-fold cross validation is performed to validate the model with the selection of meta-parameters, prior to it the actual model is trained on the full training database.

The technique is evaluated on the most well known four large benchmark gait databases to show its effectiveness. These databases include: TUM GAID [45], NLPR [112], CASIA-B [116], and CASIA-C [99].

TUM GAID Gait Database

The TUM GAID is one of the biggest gait databases, captured using Microsoft Kinect in an outdoor environment of Munich, Germany. The database comprises the walk sequences of 305 subjects, in total 3370 video sequences. Three different variations of walk, normal walk (N), walk with a back-pack (B) and walk with coating shoes (S) are recorded for each subject. Figure 5.10 displays few sample images from the TUM GAID gait database. The same distribution of the database described in [45], is exploited for gallery and probe set. The performance of the technique in comparison with state-of-the-art methods is outlined in Table 5.2. The recognition results demonstrate the superiority of the original technique in all experiments.

NLPR Gait Database

The NLPR gait database contains the gait sequences of 20 subjects, recorded in the outdoor environment. Each subject has four gait sequences, captured with three different viewing angles. The technique is evaluated on the sequences, recorded in lateral view. Figure 5.11 illustrates some sample images from the NLPR gait database in lateral view. In the experimental setup, first three gait sequences of each subject are used as a gallery set and the remaining fourth one is used in the probe set.

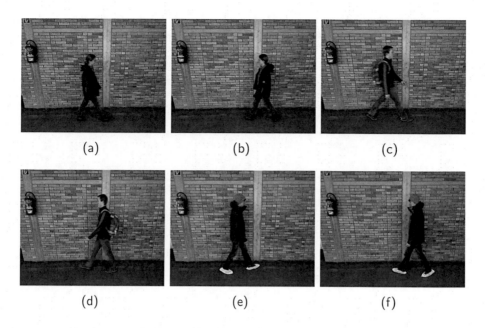

Figure 5.10: Example images from the TUM GAID gait database. (a-b): normal walk, (c-d): walk with a backpack, and (e-f): walk with coating shoes.

Table 5.2: Comparison of recognition results (%) on the TUM GAID gait database for diverse methods. Each column N, B, S corresponds to a different experiment and the average is computed as sum of the weighted mean scores.

Method	N	B	S	Weighted Average
GEI [45]	99.4	27.1	56.2	61.2
GEV [45]	94.2	13.9	87.7	65.5
SEIM [113]	99.0	18.4	96.1	71.3
GVI [113]	99.0	47.7	94.5	80.4
SVIM [113]	98.4	64.2	91.6	84.9
DGHEI [45]	99.0	40.3	96.1	78.5
CNN-SVM [21]	99.7	97.1	97.1	98.3
CNN-NN128 [21]	99.7	98.1	95.8	98.1
H2M [23]	99.4	100.0	98.1	99.4
DCS [23]	99.7	99.0	99.0	99.4
Proposed	**99.7**	**100.0**	**99.7**	**99.9**

(a)	(b)

Figure 5.11: Example images from the NLPR gait database: (a) left to right walk and (b) right to left walk in a lateral view.

The recognition results in comparison with state-of-the-art methods are described in Table 5.3. The experimental results reveal that the original

Table 5.3: Comparison of recognition results on the NLPR gait database for diverse methods.

Method	Recognition Accuracy
Wavelet descriptors [71]	82.5
PSC [59]	97.50
NN [63]	87.5
2D polar-plane [28]	92.5
Gait+Face+Distance [37]	90.0
PSA [111]	88.8
Curves+NN [98]	89.3
STC+PCA [112]	82.5
WBP [58]	100.0
HSD [57]	100.0
Proposed Method	**100.0**

technique achieves the highest recognition results.

CASIA-B Gait Database

The CASIA-B gait database contains the walk sequences of 124 subjects. The gait sequences are recorded in a well controlled laboratory environment, using 11 different viewing angles. Three different variations of walk, namely: normal walk (nm), walk with a backpack (bg) and walk with

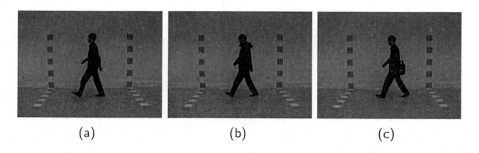

(a)   (b)   (c)

Figure 5.12: Example images from the CASIA-B database: (a) normal walk, (b) walk with coat and (c) walk with bag in a lateral view.

coating shoes (cl) are recorded for each subject. The proposed method is evaluated on the sequences, recorded in lateral view. Figure 5.12 demonstrates the various variations of walking styles in the database. In the experimental setup, the first four gait sequences of nm for each subject are used as a gallery set and the remaining two sequences of nm, bg and cl are used in the probe set, separately. The obtained recognition results in comparison with the state-of-the-art methods are presented in Table 5.4. The experimental results demonstrate that the original method outperforms other state-of-the-art algorithms in most of the experiments and achieves the highest average recognition rate of 96.2%.

CASIA-C Gait Database

The CASIA-C gait database comprises walk sequences of 153 subjects. The video sequences were captured at night using a low resolution thermal camera. The database contains four different variations of walk, namely: normal walk (fn), slow walk (fs), fast walk (fq), and walk with a backpack (fb). Figure 5.12 demonstrates the few variations of walk in the database. The technique is evaluated on the database to show its effectiveness for low resolution video and with different walk variations. The first three sequences of fn are used in a gallery set and the remaining fourth sequence of fn and two sequences of fs, fq, and fb are used in the probe set, separately. The recognition results in compression with the state-of-the-art methods are presented in Table 5.5. The proposed method achieves the best average recognition rate of 99.8%.

Table 5.4: Comparison of recognition results on the CASIA-B gait database for diverse methods in lateral view. Each column of nm, bg and cl corresponds to a different experiment and the average is computed as the mean score of all the experiments.

Experiment	nm	bg	cl	Average
TM [10]	97.6	52.0	32.7	60.8
GEI [107]	91.6	31.7	24.0	49.1
CGI [107]	88.0	43.7	43.0	58.2
AEI+2DLPP [118]	98.4	91.9	72.2	87.5
Baseline method [116]	97.6	52.0	32.2	60.8
RF+FSS+CDA [35]	100.0	50.0	33.1	61.0
HSD [57]	94.5	62.9	58.1	71.8
M_j+ACDA [10]	100.0	91.0	80.0	90.3
PFM [22]	100.0	100.0	85.5	95.2
SDL [117]	98.4	93.5	**90.3**	94.1
Proposed Method	**100.0**	**100.0**	88.7	**96.2**

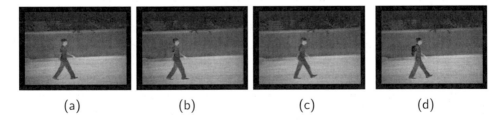

(a) (b) (c) (d)

Figure 5.13: Example images from CASIA-C database: (a) normal walk, (b) slow walk, (c) fast walk and (d) walk with bag.

Table 5.5: Performance evaluation on the CASIA-C database. Each column of fn, fs, fq and fb corresponds to a different experiment and the average is computed as the mean score of all experiments. The best results are given in bold.

Methods	fn	fs	fq	fb	Average
AEI+2DLPP [118]	88.9	89.2	90.2	79.7	87.0
WBP [58]	99.0	86.4	89.6	80.7	88.9
NDDP [101]	97.0	83.0	83.0	17.0	70.0
HSD [57]	97.0	86.0	89.0	65.0	84.2
Wavelet packet [33]	93.0	83.0	85.0	21.0	70.5
Pseudo shape [100]	98.4	91.3	93.7	24.7	77.03
Gait curves [34]	91.0	65.4	69.9	25.5	62.9
HTI [99]	94.0	85.0	88.0	51.0	79.5
SDL [117]	95.4	91.2	92.5	81.7	90.2
PFM [22]	100.0	98.7	100.0	99.3	99.5
Proposed	**100.0**	99.4	**100.0**	**99.7**	**99.8**

5.3   Conclusion and Future Trends

This chapter deals with the topic of physical activity recognition. In Section 5.1, the original methodology for atomic activity recognition automatically classifying data recorded by sensors (e.g., accelerometer) embedded in wearables (smartglasses, smartwatch, smartphone) is described. Section 5.2 presents an original algorithm for gait recognition and experimentally compares it to related state-of-the-art approaches.

Atomic Activity Recognition: The algorithm presented in Section 5.1 is based on the so called codebook approach adopted to deal with time series. It automatically classifies data recorded by sensors (e.g., accelerometer) embedded in wearables (smartglasses, smartwatch, smartphone) in real-time. The current version of the methodology deals with the recognition of the so called atomic activities. These are fine-grained movements of the human body (e.g., stretching hand, sitting down, standing up, etc.). The effectiveness of the approach has been validated on a real-world dataset consisting of eight types of sensor data obtained from a smartphone, smartwatch and smartglasses.

   In the future, a much larger training dataset needs to be collected in order to not only improve the recognition performance but also increase the number of activities to be recognised. However, when such large-scale training data are used, the currently applied non-linear SVMs may have problems in terms of computational costs and memory consumption. This is because a non-linear SVM needs to compute kernel values (similarities) of a test example to training examples selected as support vectors (in the worst case all training examples become support vectors). Thus, a linear SVM is planned to be used because its classification can be done just by taking the product between the feature vector of a test example and the optimised weight vector. Furthermore, the linear SVM will run on an extended version of codebook-based feature, like Fisher vector representation or Vector of Locally Aggregated Descriptors (VLAD) [82]. This represents an example with a very high-dimensional feature, with which the linear SVM can attain a high discrimination power. Finally, it will be also explored how to identify high-level activities (e.g., cooking, cleaning a room and dressing) by combining recognition results of low-level activities that our current system targets. To further improve the methodology, context information like location and time of the day will also be used, since these are often important properties when trying to distinguish among various similar activities [54].

Gait Recognition: This chapter also deals with another aspect of physical activity recognition, the gait analysis described in Section 5.2. Gait is a biometric feature that offers human identification at a distance and without physical interaction with any imaging device. Moreover, it performs well even in low-resolution imagery which makes it ideal for use in numerous human identification applications, such as: access control, visual surveillance and monitoring systems. Most existing gait-based person recognition algorithms either construct a human body model based on various skeletal data characteristics such as joints positioning and their orientation, or they use gait features, e.g., stride length, gait patterns and other shape templates. Such approaches extract the human-body silhouettes, contours, or skeleton from the images, and therefore their performance highly depends upon the accurate segmentation of a human body region, which is still a challenging problem. The original gait recognition method described in Section 5.2 exploits the spatiotemporal motion characteristics of an individual without the need of silhouette extraction and other related features. It computes a set of spatiotemporal features from the gait video sequences and uses them to generate a codebook. Fisher vector is used to encode the motion descriptors which are classified using linear Support Vector Machine (SVM). The performance of the proposed algorithm has been evaluated on five widely used datasets, including indoor (CMU-MoBo, NLPR, CASIA-C) and outdoor (CASIA-B, TUM GAID) gait databases. It achieved excellent results on all databases and outperformed the related state-of-the-art algorithms.

References

[1] Jins meme: The world's first wearable eyewear that lets you see yourself. https://jins-meme.com/en/. Accessed: 2017-03-15.

[2] Microsoft band. https://www.microsoft.com/microsoft-band. Accessed: 2017-03-15.

[3] Monitor stress, seizures, activity, sleep. https://www.empatica.com/. Accessed: 2017-03-15.

[4] RabbitMQ - messaging that just works. https://www.rabbitmq.com/. Accessed: 2017-03-13.

[5] Gregory D Abowd, Aaron F Bobick, Irfan A Essa, Elizabeth D Mynatt, and Wendy A Rogers. The aware home: A living laboratory for technologies for successful aging. In *Proceedings of the AAAI-02 Workshop Automation as Caregiver*, pages 1–7, 2002.

[6] A. Al-Fuqaha, M. Guizani, M. Mohammadi, M. Aledhari, and M. Ayyash. Internet of things: A survey on enabling technologies, protocols, and applications. *IEEE Communications Surveys Tutorials*, 17(4):2347–2376, Fourth Quarter 2015.

[7] Mohsen Amiribesheli, Asma Benmansour, and Abdelhamid Bouchachia. A review of smart homes in healthcare. *Journal of Ambient Intelligence and Humanized Computing*, 6(4):495–517, 2015.

[8] Ling Bao and Stephen S. Intille. *Activity Recognition from User-Annotated Acceleration Data*, pages 1–17. Springer Berlin Heidelberg, Berlin, Heidelberg, 2004.

[9] K. Bashir et al. Gait representation using flow fields. In *BMVC*, pages 1–11, 2009.

[10] K. Bashir, T. Xiang, and S. Gong. Feature selection for gait recognition without subject cooperation. In *BMVC*, pages 1–10, 2008.

[11] K. Bashir, T. Xiang, and S. Gong. Gait recognition without subject cooperation. *Pattern Recognition Letters*, 31(13):2052–2060, 2010.

[12] M. G. Baydogan, G. Runger, and E. Tuv. A bag-of-features framework to classify time series. *IEEE Transactions on Pattern Analysis and Machine Intelligence*, 35(11):2796–2802, November 2013.

144

[13] Yoshua Bengio, Aaron Courville, and Pascal Vincent. Representation learning: A review and new perspectives. *IEEE Transaction on Pattern Analysis and Machine Intelligence*, 35(8):1798–1828, 2013.

[14] M. Berchtold, M. Budde, D. Gordon, H. R. Schmidtke, and M. Beigl. Actiserv: Activity recognition service for mobile phones. In *Proceedings of the 2010 ACM International Symposium on Wearable Computers*, ISWC '10, pages 1–8, October 2010.

[15] V. Bianchi, F. Grossi, I. De Munari, and P. Ciampolini. Musa: A multisensor wearable device for aal. In *2011 Federated Conference on Computer Science and Information Systems (FedCSIS)*, pages 375–380, September 2011.

[16] Aaron F Bobick and Amos Y Johnson. Gait recognition using static, activity-specific parameters. In *Proceedings of the IEEE Computer Society Conference on Computer Vision and Pattern Recognition*, volume 1, pages I–I. IEEE, 2001.

[17] I. Bouchrika and M.S. Nixon. Model-based feature extraction for gait analysis and recognition. In *International Conference on Computer Vision/Computer Graphics Collaboration Techniques and Applications*, pages 150–160. Springer, 2007.

[18] A. Bulling, J. A. Ward, H. Gellersen, and G. Troster. Eye movement analysis for activity recognition using electrooculography. *IEEE Transactions on Pattern Analysis and Machine Intelligence*, 33(4):741–753, April 2011.

[19] Andreas Bulling, Ulf Blanke, and Bernt Schiele. A tutorial on human activity recognition using body-worn inertial sensors. *ACM Computing Surveys*, 46(3):33:1–33:33, January 2014.

[20] Andreas Bulling, Jamie A. Ward, Hans Gellersen, and Gerhard Tröster. Robust recognition of reading activity in transit using wearable electrooculography. In *Proceedings of the Sixth International Conference on Pervasive Computing*, PERVASIVE'08, pages 19–37, 2008.

[21] F.M. Castro et al. Automatic learning of gait signatures for people identification. *arXiv preprint arXiv:1603.01006*, 2016.

[22] F.M. Castro et al. Fisher motion descriptor for multiview gait recognition. 31(01):1756002, 2017.

[23] F.M. Castro, M.J. Marín-Jiménez, and N. Guil. Multimodal features fusion for gait, gender and shoes recognition. *Machine Vision and Applications*, pages 1–16, 2016.

[24] Y. Chai et al. A novel human gait recognition method by segmenting and extracting the region variance feature. In *18th International Conference onPattern Recognition*, volume 4, pages 425–428. IEEE, 2006.

[25] C.-C. Chang and C.-J. Lin. Libsvm: A library for support vector machines. *ACM Transactions on Intelligent Systems and Technology*, 2(3):27:1–27:27, 2011.

[26] C. Chen et al. Frame difference energy image for gait recognition with incomplete silhouettes. *Pattern Recognition Letters*, 30(11):977–984, 2009.

[27] L. Chen, J. Hoey, C. D. Nugent, D. J. Cook, and Z. Yu. Sensor-based activity recognition. *IEEE Transactions on Systems, Man, and Cybernetics, Part C (Applications and Reviews)*, 42(6):790–808, November 2012.

[28] Shi Chen and Youxing Gao. An invariant appearance model for gait recognition. In *2007 IEEE International Conference on Multimedia and Expo*, pages 1375–1378. IEEE, 2007.

[29] Sruti Das Choudhury and Tardi Tjahjadi. Silhouette-based gait recognition using procrustes shape analysis and elliptic fourier descriptors. *Pattern Recognition*, 45(9):3414–3426, 2012.

[30] D. J. Cook, A. S. Crandall, B. L. Thomas, and N. C. Krishnan. Casas: A smart home in a box. *Computer*, 46(7):62–69, July 2013.

[31] Gabriella Csurka, Christopher Dance, Lixin Fan, Jutta Willamowski, and Cédric Bray. Visual categorization with bags of keypoints. In *Proceedings of the Workshop on Statistical Learning in Computer Vision*, number 1-22, pages 1–2, 2004.

[32] David Cunado, Mark S Nixon, and John N Carter. Automatic extraction and description of human gait models for recognition purposes. *Computer Vision and Image Understanding*, 90(1):1–41, 2003.

[33] F. Dadashi et al. Gait recognition using wavelet packet silhouette representation and transductive support vector machines. In *2nd International Congress on Image and Signal Processing*, pages 1–5. IEEE, 2009.

[34] Brian DeCann and Arun Ross. Gait curves for human recognition, backpack detection, and silhouette correction in a nighttime environment. In *SPIE Defense, Security, and Sensing*, pages 76670Q–76670Q. International Society for Optics and Photonics, 2010.

[35] Yohan Dupuis, Xavier Savatier, and Pascal Vasseur. Feature subset selection applied to model-free gait recognition. *Image and vision computing*, 31(8):580–591, 2013.

[36] Rong-En Fan, Kai-Wei Chang, Cho-Jui Hsieh, Xiang-Rui Wang, and Chih-Jen Lin. Liblinear: A library for large linear classification. *Journal of machine learning research*, 9(Aug):1871–1874, 2008.

[37] Xin Geng, Liang Wang, Ming Li, Qiang Wu, and Kate Smith-Miles. Distance-driven fusion of gait and face for human identification in video. *Proc Image Vis Comput*, 2007.

[38] Michela Goffredo, John N Carter, and Mark S Nixon. Front-view gait recognition. In *2nd IEEE International Conference on Biometrics: Theory, Applications and Systems*, pages 1–6. IEEE, 2008.

[39] F. Grossi, V. Bianchi, G. Matrella, I. De Munari, and P. Ciampolini. An assistive home automation and monitoring system. In *2008 Digest of Technical Papers - International Conference on Consumer Electronics*, pages 1–2, January 2008.

[40] T. Gu, L. Wang, Z. Wu, X. Tao, and J. Lu. A pattern mining approach to sensor-based human activity recognition. *IEEE Transactions on Knowledge and Data Engineering*, 23(9):1359–1372, September 2011.

[41] S. Hagler, D. Austin, T. L. Hayes, J. Kaye, and M. Pavel. Unobtrusive and ubiquitous in-home monitoring: A methodology for

continuous assessment of gait velocity in elders. *IEEE Transactions on Biomedical Engineering*, 57(4):813–820, April 2010.

[42] Nils Y. Hammerla, Shane Halloran, and Thomas Plötz. Deep, convolutional, and recurrent models for human activity recognition using wearables. In *Proceedings of the 25th International Joint Conference on Artificial Intelligence*, IJCAI '16, pages 1533–1540, July 2016.

[43] J. Han, M. Kamber, and J. Pei. *Data Mining: Concepts and Techniques*. Morgan Kaufmann, third edition, 2011.

[44] S. Helal, W. Mann, H. El-Zabadani, J. King, Y. Kaddoura, and E. Jansen. The gator tech smart house: a programmable pervasive space. *Computer*, 38(3):50–60, March 2005.

[45] M. Hofmann, S. Bachmann, and G. Rigoll. 2.5D gait biometrics using the depth gradient histogram energy image. In *IEEE Fifth International Conference on Biometrics: Theory, Applications and Systems*, pages 399–403. IEEE, 2012.

[46] Jin-Hyuk Hong, Julian Ramos, and Anind K. Dey. Understanding physiological responses to stressors during physical activity. In *Proceedings of the 2012 ACM Conference on Ubiquitous Computing*, UbiComp '12, pages 270–279, 2012.

[47] Stephen S. Intille, Kent Larson, Emmanuel Munguia Tapia, Jennifer S. Beaudin, Pallavi Kaushik, Jason Nawyn, and Randy Rockinson. Using a live-in laboratory for ubiquitous computing research. In *Proceedings of the Forth International Conference on Pervasive Computing*, PERVASIVE'06, pages 349–365, 2006.

[48] Luciana C Jatoba, Ulrich Grossmann, Chistophe Kunze, Jorg Ottenbacher, and Wilhelm Stork. Context-aware mobile health monitoring: Evaluation of different pattern recognition methods for classification of physical activity. In *Proceedings of the 30th Annual International Conference of the IEEE Engineering in Medicine and Biology Society*, EMBS '08, pages 5250–5253, 2008.

[49] Y. G. Jiang, J. Yang, C. W. Ngo, and A. G. Hauptmann. Representations of keypoint-based semantic concept detection: A comprehensive study. *IEEE Transactions on Multimedia*, 12(1):42–53, January 2010.

[50] Muhammad Hassan Khan, Jullien Helsper, Zeyd Boukhers, and Marcin Grzegorzek. Automatic recognition of movement patterns in the vojta-therapy using rgb-d data. In *IEEE International Conference on Image Processing (ICIP)*, pages 1235–1239. IEEE, 2016.

[51] Muhammad Hassan Khan, Kimiaki Shirahama, Muhammad Shahid Farid, and Marcin Grzegorzek. Multiple human detection in depth images. pages 1–6, 2016.

[52] J. Kim and E. Andr. Emotion recognition based on physiological changes in music listening. *IEEE Transactions on Pattern Analysis and Machine Intelligence*, 30(12):2067–2083, December 2008.

[53] S. Koelstra, C. Muhl, M. Soleymani, J. S. Lee, A. Yazdani, T. Ebrahimi, T. Pun, A. Nijholt, and I. Patras. Deap: A database for emotion analysis ;using physiological signals. *IEEE Transactions on Affective Computing*, 3(1):18–31, January 2012.

[54] Kimberle Koile, Konrad Tollmar, David Demirdjian, Howard Shrobe, and Trevor Darrell. Activity zones for context-aware computing. In *Proceedings of the Fifth International Conference on Ubiquitous Computing (UbiComp 2003)*, pages 90–106, 2003.

[55] L. Köping, K. Shirahama, and M. Grzegorzek. A General Framework for Sensor-based Human Activity Recognition. *Computers in Biology and Medicine*, 2017.

[56] Narayanan C. Krishnan and Diane J. Cook. Activity recognition on streaming sensor data. *Pervasive and Mobile Computing*, 10, Part B:138 – 154, 2014.

[57] W. Kusakunniran. Attribute-based learning for gait recognition using spatio-temporal interest points. *Image and Vision Computing*, 32(12):1117–1126, 2014.

[58] Worapan Kusakunniran, Qiang Wu, Hongdong Li, and Jian Zhang. Automatic gait recognition using weighted binary pattern on video. In *6th IEEE International Conference on Advanced Video and Signal Based Surveillance*, pages 49–54. Springer, 2009.

[59] Worapan Kusakunniran, Qiang Wu, Jian Zhang, and Hongdong Li. Pairwise shape configuration-based psa for gait recognition under

small viewing angle change. In *8th IEEE International Conference on Advanced Video and Signal-Based Surveillance (AVSS)*, pages 17–22. IEEE, 2011.

[60] Toby HW Lam, King Hong Cheung, and James NK Liu. Gait flow image: A silhouette-based gait representation for human identification. *Pattern recognition*, 44(4):973–987, 2011.

[61] N. D. Lane, E. Miluzzo, H. Lu, D. Peebles, T. Choudhury, and A. T. Campbell. A survey of mobile phone sensing. *IEEE Communications Magazine*, 48(9):140–150, September 2010.

[62] O. D. Lara and M. A. Labrador. A survey on human activity recognition using wearable sensors. *IEEE Communications Surveys Tutorials*, 15(3):1192–1209, Third Quarter 2013.

[63] Heesung Lee, Sungjun Hong, and Euntai Kim. An efficient gait recognition based on a selective neural network ensemble. *International Journal of Imaging Systems and Technology*, 18(4):237–241, 2008.

[64] Lily Lee and W Eric L Grimson. Gait analysis for recognition and classification. In *Proceedings of the Fifth IEEE International Conference on Automatic Face and Gesture Recognition*, pages 155–162. IEEE, 2002.

[65] Ruijiao Li, Bowen Lu, and Klaus D. McDonald-Maier. Cognitive assisted living ambient system: a survey. *Digital Communications and Networks*, 1(4):229 – 252, 2015.

[66] Jessica Lin and Yuan Li. Finding structural similarity in time series data using bag-of-patterns representation. In *Proceedings of the 21st International Conference on Scientific and Statistical Database Management*, SSDBM 2009, pages 461–477, 2009.

[67] J. Little and J. Boyd. Recognizing people by their gait: the shape of motion. *Videre: Journal of Computer Vision Research*, 1(2):1–32, 1998.

[68] Jiayang Liu, Lin Zhong, Jehan Wickramasuriya, and Venu Vasudevan. uwave: Accelerometer-based personalized gesture recognition and its applications. *Pervasive Mobile Computing*, 5(6):657–675, December 2009.

[69] Beth Logan, Jennifer Healey, Matthai Philipose, Emmanuel Munguia Tapia, and Stephen Intille. A long-term evaluation of sensing modalities for activity recognition. In *Proceedings of the 9th International Conference on Ubiquitous Computing*, UbiComp '07, September 2007.

[70] Haiping Lu, Konstantinos N Plataniotis, and Anastasios N Venetsanopoulos. A full-body layered deformable model for automatic model-based gait recognition. *EURASIP Journal on Advances in Signal Processing*, 2008:62, 2008.

[71] Jiwen Lu, Erhu Zhang, and Cuining Jing. Gait recognition using wavelet descriptors and independent component analysis. In *International Symposium on Neural Networks*, pages 232–237. Springer, 2006.

[72] J. Man and B. Bhanu. Individual recognition using gait energy image. *IEEE transactions on pattern analysis and machine intelligence*, 28(2):316–322, 2006.

[73] Christopher D. Manning, Prabhakar Raghavan, and Hinrich Schütze. *Introduction to Information Retrieval*. Cambridge University Press, New York, NY, USA, 2008.

[74] Andrea Mannini and Angelo Maria Sabatini. Machine learning methods for classifying human physical activity from on-body accelerometers. *Sensors*, 10(2):1154–1175, 2010.

[75] H. P. Martinez, Y. Bengio, and G. N. Yannakakis. Learning deep physiological models of affect. *IEEE Computational Intelligence Magazine*, 8(2):20–33, May 2013.

[76] David McGlynn and Michael G. Madden. An ensemble dynamic time warping classifier with application to activity recognition. In Max Bramer, Miltos Petridis, and Adrian Hopgood, editors, *Research and Development in Intelligent Systems XXVII*, pages 339–352. Springer London, London, 2011.

[77] Francisco J. O. Morales and Daniel Roggen. Deep convolutional feature transfer across mobile activity recognition domains, sensor

modalities and locations. In *Proceedings of the 2016 ACM International Symposium on Wearable Computers*, ISWC '16, pages 92–99, 2016.

[78] M. Nixon et al. Model-based gait recognition. 2009.

[79] Eric Nowak, Frédéric Jurie, and Bill Triggs. Sampling strategies for bag-of-features image classification. In Aleš Leonardis, Horst Bischof, and Axel Pinz, editors, *Proceedings of the 9th European Conference on Computer Vision (ECCV 2006), Part IV*, 2006.

[80] P. Ordonez, T. Armstrong, T. Oates, and J. Fackler. Using modified multivariate bag-of-words models to classify physiological data. In *Proceedings of the 2011 IEEE 11th International Conference on Data Mining Workshops*, pages 534–539, December 2011.

[81] X. Peng, L. Wang, X. Wang, and Y. Qiao. Bag of visual words and fusion methods for action recognition: Comprehensive study and good practice. *Computer Vision and Image Understanding*, 150:109 – 125, 2016.

[82] Xiaojiang Peng, Limin Wang, Xingxing Wang, and Yu Qiao. Bag of visual words and fusion methods for action recognition. *Computer Vision and Image Understanding*, 150(C):109–125, 2016.

[83] M. Philipose, K. P. Fishkin, M. Perkowitz, D. J. Patterson, D. Fox, H. Kautz, and D. Hahnel. Inferring activities from interactions with objects. *IEEE Pervasive Computing*, 3(4):50–57, October 2004.

[84] Angkoon Phinyomark, Pornchai Phukpattaranont, and Chusak Limsakul. Feature reduction and selection for emg signal classification. *Expert Systems with Applications*, 39(8):7420 – 7431, 2012.

[85] R. W. Picard, E. Vyzas, and J. Healey. Toward machine emotional intelligence: analysis of affective physiological state. *IEEE Transactions on Pattern Analysis and Machine Intelligence*, 23(10):1175–1191, October 2001.

[86] K. Plarre, A. Raij, S. M. Hossain, A. A. Ali, M. Nakajima, M. Al'absi, E. Ertin, T. Kamarck, S. Kumar, M. Scott, D. Siewiorek, A. Smailagic, and L. E. Wittmers. Continuous inference of psychological stress from sensory measurements collected in the natural

environment. In *Proceedings of the 10th ACM/IEEE International Conference on Information Processing in Sensor Networks*, pages 97–108, April 2011.

[87] Thomas Plötz, Nils Y. Hammerla, and Patrick Olivier. Feature learning for activity recognition in ubiquitous computing. In *Proceedings of the 22th International Joint Conference on Artificial Intelligence*, IJCAI'11, pages 1729–1734, 2011.

[88] Valentin Radu, Nicholas D. Lane, Sourav Bhattacharya, Cecilia Mascolo, Mahesh K. Marina, and Fahim Kawsar. Towards multimodal deep learning for activity recognition on mobile devices. In *Proceedings of the 2016 ACM International Joint Conference on Pervasive and Ubiquitous Computing: Adjunct*, UbiComp '16, pages 185–188, 2016.

[89] P. Rashidi, D. J. Cook, L. B. Holder, and M. Schmitter-Edgecombe. Discovering activities to recognize and track in a smart environment. *IEEE Transactions on Knowledge and Data Engineering*, 23(4):527–539, April 2011.

[90] J. Sánchez et al. Image classification with the fisher vector: Theory and practice. *International journal of computer vision*, 105(3):222–245, 2013.

[91] Kimiaki Shirahama, Lukas Köping, and Marcin Grzegorzek. Codebook approach for sensor-based human activity recognition. In *Proceedings of the 2016 ACM International Joint Conference on Pervasive and Ubiquitous Computing: Adjunct*, UbiComp '16, pages 197–200, 2016.

[92] Sabesan Sivapalan, Daniel Chen, Simon Denman, Sridha Sridharan, and Clinton Fookes. 3d ellipsoid fitting for multi-view gait recognition. In *8th IEEE International Conference on Advanced Video and Signal-Based Surveillance (AVSS)*, pages 355–360. IEEE, 2011.

[93] Sabesan Sivapalan, Daniel Chen, Simon Denman, Sridha Sridharan, and Clinton Fookes. Gait energy volumes and frontal gait recognition using depth images. In *International Joint Conference on Biometrics*, pages 1–6. IEEE, 2011.

[94] Cees G. M. Snoek, Marcel Worring, and Arnold W. M. Smeulders. Early versus late fusion in semantic video analysis. In *Proceedings of the 13th Annual ACM International Conference on Multimedia*, MM '05, pages 399–402, 2005.

[95] Sam Solaimani, Wally Keijzer-Broers, and Harry Bouwman. What we do - and don't - know about the smart home: An analysis of the smart home literature. *Indoor and Built Environment*, 24(3):370–383, 2015.

[96] M. Soleymani, J. Lichtenauer, T. Pun, and M. Pantic. A multimodal database for affect recognition and implicit tagging. *IEEE Transactions on Affective Computing*, 3(1):42–55, January 2012.

[97] T. G. Stavropoulos, G. Meditskos, S. Andreadis, and I. Kompatsiaris. Real-time health monitoring and contextualised alerts using wearables. In *2015 International Conference on Interactive Mobile Communication Technologies and Learning (IMCL)*, pages 358–363, November 2015.

[98] Han Su and Fenggang Huang. Gait recognition using principal curves and neural networks. In *International Symposium on Neural Networks*, pages 238–243. Springer, 2006.

[99] D. Tan et al. Efficient night gait recognition based on template matching. In *18th International Conference on Pattern Recognition*, volume 3, pages 1000–1003, 2006.

[100] D. Tan, K. Huang, S. Yu, and T. Tan. Recognizing night walkers based on one pseudoshape representation of gait. In *IEEE Conference on Computer Vision and Pattern Recognition*, pages 1–8. IEEE, 2007.

[101] D. Tan, S. Yu, K. Huang, and T. Tan. Walker recognition without gait cycle estimation. In *International Conference on Biometrics*, pages 222–231. Springer, 2007.

[102] Emmanuel Munguia Tapia, Stephen S. Intille, and Kent Larson. Activity recognition in the home using simple and ubiquitous sensors. In Alois Ferscha and Friedemann Mattern, editors, *Proceedings of the Second International Conference on Pervasive Computing*, PERVASIVE'04, pages 158–175. 2004.

[103] D. Trabelsi, S. Mohammed, F. Chamroukhi, L. Oukhellou, and Y. Amirat. An unsupervised approach for automatic activity recognition based on hidden markov model regression. *IEEE Transactions on Automation Science and Engineering*, 10(3):829–835, July 2013.

[104] Jan C. van Gemert, Cor J. Veenman, Arnold W. M. Smeulders, and Jan-Mark Geusebroek. Visual word ambiguity. *IEEE Transactions on Pattern Analysis and Machine Intelligence*, 32(7):1271–1283, 2010.

[105] Tim van Kasteren, Athanasios Noulas, Gwenn Englebienne, and Ben Kröse. Accurate activity recognition in a home setting. In *Proceedings of the 10th International Conference on Ubiquitous Computing*, UbiComp '08, 2008.

[106] V.N. Vapnik. *Statistical Learning Theory*. Wiley-Interscience, 1998.

[107] C. Wang et al. Human identification using temporal information preserving gait template. *IEEE transactions on pattern analysis and machine intelligence*, 34(11):2164–2176, 2012.

[108] H. Wang and C. Schmid. Action recognition with improved trajectories. In *Proceedings of the IEEE International Conference on Computer Vision*, pages 3551–3558. IEEE, 2013.

[109] Jin Wang, Ping Liu, Mary F.H. She, Saeid Nahavandi, and Abbas Kouzani. Bag-of-words representation for biomedical time series classification. *Biomedical Signal Processing and Control*, 8(6):634 – 644, 2013.

[110] L. Wang, H. Ning, T. Tan, and W. Hu. Fusion of static and dynamic body biometrics for gait recognition. *IEEE Transactions on circuits and systems for video technology*, 14(2):149–158, 2004.

[111] Liang Wang, Tieniu Tan, Weiming Hu, and Huazhong Ning. Automatic gait recognition based on statistical shape analysis. *IEEE transactions on image processing*, 12(9):1120–1131, 2003.

[112] Liang Wang, Tieniu Tan, Huazhong Ning, and Weiming Hu. Silhouette analysis-based gait recognition for human identification. *IEEE transactions on pattern analysis and machine intelligence*, 25(12):1505–1518, 2003.

[113] T. Whytock, A. Belyaev, and N.M. Robertson. Dynamic distance-based shape features for gait recognition. *Journal of Mathematical Imaging and Vision*, 50(3):314–326, 2014.

[114] ChewYean Yam, Mark S Nixon, and John N Carter. Gait recognition by walking and running: a model-based approach. In *5th Asian Conference on Computer Vision*, 2002.

[115] Y. Yang, D. Tu, and G. Li. Gait recognition using flow histogram energy image. In *22nd International Conference on Pattern Recognition*, pages 444–449. IEEE, 2014.

[116] S. Yu et al. A framework for evaluating the effect of view angle, clothing and carrying condition on gait recognition. In *18th International Conference on Pattern Recognition*, volume 4, pages 441–444. IEEE, 2006.

[117] W. Zeng, C. Wang, and F. Yang. Silhouette-based gait recognition via deterministic learning. *Pattern recognition*, 47(11):3568–3584, 2014.

[118] Erhu Zhang, Yongwei Zhao, and Wei Xiong. Active energy image plus 2dlpp for gait recognition. *Signal Processing*, 90(7):2295–2302, 2010.

[119] J. Zhang, M. Marszalek, S. Lazebnik, and C. Schmid. Local features and kernels for classification of texture and object categories: A comprehensive study. *International Journal of Computer Vision*, 73(2):213–238, 2007.

[120] Feng Zhou and Fernando Torre. Canonical time warping for alignment of human behavior. In Y. Bengio, D. Schuurmans, J. D. Lafferty, C. K. I. Williams, and A. Culotta, editors, *Advances in Neural Information Processing Systems 22*, pages 2286–2294. 2009.

[121] C. Zhu and W. Sheng. Human daily activity recognition in robot-assisted living using multi-sensor fusion. In *2009 IEEE International Conference on Robotics and Automation*, pages 2154–2159, May 2009.

Chapter 6

Cognitive Activity Recognition

The following chapter discusses the state-of-the-art works and presents the author's scientific contribution to the area of cognitive activity recognition. Section 6.1 gives the definition of cognition, and discusses cognitive activity relation to health especially in context of the human ageing. As the brain activity is the crucial source of information about cognitive abilities of a person, Section 6.2 provides information on appropriate sensors. Section 6.3 presents an overview of the renowned methods and approaches utilising a variety of sensor data in order to properly recognise cognitive activities. In Section 6.4, the author introduces the electrooculography-based approach using the eye-movement information for the activity recognition. Section 6.5 shows the possible application of the presented method and validates the obtained results, while in Section 6.6 the final conclusions and future plans are drawn.

6.1 Definition, Taxonomy, Impact on Health

Cognition is defined as a mental process of acquiring knowledge and understanding through our thoughts, experience and the information received from five senses – including such aspects as: reasoning, awareness, perception, knowledge, intuition or judgement. Each human being is characterised by a set of cognitive skills that are needed for a person to be able to talk, think, read, recall things from memory, analyse images and sounds or draw association between numerous pieces of information. The decline of cognitive skills and abilities is usually a part of the ageing process and related death of brain cells, or a result of an illness/disease and injuries that affect the brain such as Alzheimer's disease, multiple sclerosis or stroke[1]. Within the population of elderly people it can be observed that a number of them never show any symptoms of an age-related loss of cognitive skills and abilities, however a greater number of older seniors experience a decline in cognitive functions. In order to maintain the cognitive skills, reduce the risk of dementia or keep the mind sharp, various types of mental exercises stimulating the brain can be performed, which are equally important for the brain to stay active and alive as the physical exercises are important to keep the body fit. Such cognitive activities regarding conscious part of the cognition involve every day activities i.e. social interaction, engaging in meaningful conversation, slightly changing daily routines, or performing other mind-challenging activities such as drawing, reading, playing music, photography or watching television/video.

6.2   Sensing the Brain Activity

Sensing the brain activity is crucial to the cognitive activity recognition as the cognition processes are taking place in the human brain. The devices and sensors allowing to observe the brain activity were designed for medical purposes, thus in most cases they are stationary devices utilising relatively invasive methods of acquiring the information. For these reasons, electrooculography (EOG) is the most promising technique for mobile application.

6.2.1   Electroencephalography

Electroencephalography (EEG) is a diagnostic method allowing to monitor and record an electrical activity of the brain. A number of (non)invasive electrodes placed around the scalp measure the voltage fluctuation resulting from ionic current within the neurons of the brain. This gives the possibility to record spontaneous electrical activity of the brain within a given time interval. EEG is known to be noisy and can be easily obstructed by a muscle movement, which leads to the complex and time consuming signal processing.

---

[1]http://www.who.int/mediacentre/factsheets/fs396/en/

6.2.2 Electrooculography

Electrooculography (EOG) is a technique used to track the eye-movement based on the measurement of the standing-potential between the cornea and retina (between front and back of an eye). This method utilises several electrodes placed around the eyes to measure the potential difference between the electrodes when the eye moves from the centre position towards one of the electrodes. This technique of tracking eye movements with a lightweight, unobtrusive electrooculography (EOG) system [1] seems to be suitable for day-long data collection.

6.2.3 Functional Magnetic Resonance Imaging

Functional Magnetic Resonance Imaging (fMRI) is a functional neuroimaging method using MRI (Magnetic Resonance Imaging) to measure brain activity based on the correlation between cerebral blood flow changes and the neuronal activation – blood flow is increasing in an area of the brain that is currently in use. The measurements are frequently corrupted by noise coming from various sources, and the technique itself is using blood-oxygen-level dependent contrast which is administered to the patients – which discriminates against this approach in the daily use.

6.2.4 Functional Near-InfraRed Spectroscopy

Functional Near-Infrared Spectroscopy (fNIRS) is a functional neuroimaging method relying on the the principle of neurovascular coupling known as Blood-Oxygenation-Level-Dependant response, which is also the core of fMRI technique. The fNIRS method involves the quantification of chromophore concentration resolved from the measurement of near-infrared light attenuation and temporal or phase changes. This approach is known for low spacial resolution, ability to record only brain surface and inaccurate activation localization.

6.3 Survey of Related Methods

Eye movement analysis has been attracting researchers investigating visual behaviours for a long time. The early studies, focusing on recognising objects perceived by human observers, use Markov processes in order to model the visual fixations [8]. The obtained fixations were sequenced into character strings, and then the edit distance was applied to quantify the similarity between eye movement sequences. In [7], the authors investigated the sequences of temporal fixations using discrete time Markov chains to discover fixation clusters that can point out features attracting observer's attention. Such information can be especially helpful during a training process. This was utilised by a method proposed in [5], where the information about dynamics of saccadic eye movements is used to evaluate the results of student's training on assessing tomography images. The automated eye movement analysis proposed in [18] along with sequence matching and HMM-based methods allow to interpret eye movements with a high accuracy and in a significantly short computation time. Recently, the research community has become interested in human activity recognition, utilising a variety of sensors available in devices of every day use like smartphones, smartwatches or fitness wristbands. However, eye-trackers and the information about eye movements, that are strongly correlated with cognitive aspects, have rarely been used to track our daily-life activities. In [12, 11], the authors proposed a method using the information on blinking frequency, eye movement and head motion as a combined feature for *j48* decision tree to distinguish activities like reading, talking and walking. Eye movement data obtained with EOG were utilised by a method proposed in [14] to estimate the number of words a user reads, using a simple valley detection algorithm to detect line breaks on the horizontal signal component of EOG. A more advanced method for recognising not only reading activity but also copying a text, taking hand-written notes, watching television or browsing the web, was proposed in [3]. The authors developed a large set of hand-crafted features describing eye movement data by capturing fundamental eye movement characteristics and dynamics. Those features are string representations of saccade, fixation and blink features, that are ranked and evaluated using minimum-Redundancy-Maximum-Relevance (mRMR) feature selection [17] and a Support Vector Machine (SVM) classifier.

The method proposed in [2] for interfacing with a speller utilised a thresholding algorithm to detect different saccadic eye movements. The authors defined five different thresholds to distinguish near and far saccadic movements, fixations and near saccadic movements for horizontal (EOG_H) and vertical (EOG_V) components of EOG data and blinks. Then the classification is performed by comparing extracted peaks obtained from EOG_H and EOG_V with the thresholds. In [10], the authors proposed a simple approach to reading activity recognition based on the observation, that reading text creates characteristic patterns on EOG_H depicting the smooth pursuit of text and rapid transition from right to left while switching the lines (repetitive large negative peaks). The peaks are found by applying minimum and maximum peak separation thresholds to the derivatives of a preprocessed EOG_H signal. The authors stated that the number of peaks indicates the number of lines the user read, while the distance between them reflects the time the user needed to read one line of text. A method for recognising reading tasks based on autoregressive features extracted from EOG data was proposed in [6]. The authors decided to utilise four different autoregressive models, widely used for extracting features from biomedical signals, based on the assumption that data at any point are closely related to few preceding data points. With this approach, they could extract several features from raw EOG signals, which were passed to a recurrent Elman neural network to automatically detect the reading activity. In [15], the authors presented a method to extract EOG features using Linear Predictive Coding (LPC) model applied to spectral entropies of EOG signals, where parameters were converted to LPC cepstral coefficients to obtain a more reliable and robust feature.

6.4 Electrooculography-Based Approach

In this section an electrooculography-based approach to cognitive activity recognition is presented. Similarly to the codebook approach described in Section 5.1.2, this method consists of three major steps: the codebook construction, codeword assignment and the classifier training and test. Based on the obtained results, a simple analysis of codewords is proposed in order to extract parts of EOG sequences the characteristic to a particular class of cognitive activity.

6.4.1 Cognitive Activity Recognition Method

Prior the fist step of the method, a data preprocessing is performed as raw data obtained with an EOG system is known to contain a large amount of noise introduced by muscle movements associated with facial mimicry. For this reason, several different noise reduction and approximation algorithms were investigated. As a result, the *moving average* produced the best results, increasing the accuracy of activity recognition.

The codebook construction is the first step where subsequences are sampled from sequences of EOG data and grouped into clusters based on their similarity using k-means clustering [9]. The codebook is then constructed as a set of codewords, which are obtained as cluster centres. Since EOG data tend to show some characteristics periodically (see Figure 6.1 a, b), an alternative representation of subsequences in a frequency domain is used. Thus, as an alternative to a subsequence consisting of time points of the raw EOG sequence, its vector representation consisting of Fast Fourier (FFT) coefficients is applied to obtain a different type of information about the subsequence. A codebook for this FFT-based representation can be obtained using aforementioned k-means clustering with no modification. The second step is the codeword assignment where the feature is extracted from a sequence by assigning each subsequence to the most similar codeword based on the Euclidean distance between them. The feature obtained in this way is a histogram reflecting the frequency of each codeword. The last step is the classifier training and test where obtained features are considered as points in the multidimensional space. Thus, a classifier can be trained to discriminate between training sequences annotated with a certain activity class and the others, drawing the boundary between, e.g., "reading" and other activities. Given this boundary, the classifier can predict the activity class of a test sequence. For this reason, the proposed method uses the Support Vector Machine (SVM) as it is known to be effective for high-dimensional data [19]. An important part of using the SVM is its parameter setting. The method described in this chapter uses Radial Basis Function (RBF) kernel as it takes one parameter γ controlling the complexity of a classification. Another SVM parameter C controls the penalty of mis-classification. To obtain the best possible results, C and γ are set by performing grid search using cross-validation [4]. This approach for setting SVM parameters is used throughout all the experiments.

6.4.2   Investigating Codewords

The steps described above focus on obtaining effective features in order to accurately assign a sequence to the appropriate activity class. Such histogram-type features represent the distribution of individual codewords within a sequence. However, deeper understanding of which codewords are characteristic for particular activity classes still requires investigation. For this reason, simple statistical analysis involving probability and entropy calculation is employed.

By definition, an entropy is an expected, average value of information contained in each event. Also, the information is defined as the negative logarithm of the probability distribution of possible events. Assuming a codeword c, its entropy over n activity classes can be denoted as follows:

$$H(c) = \sum_{i=1}^{n} P_i(c) \cdot I_i(c) = - \sum_{i=1}^{n} P_i(c) \cdot log_2 P_i(c) \quad , \qquad (6.1)$$

where $P_i(c)$ is the probability that the codeword c is included in sequences for an activity $i \in 1 \ldots n$. If the probability is distributed equally between n activities, the entropy is high indicating the uncertainty and so the chosen codeword is not so characteristic. However, if the probability of a codeword is higher for one activity than the others, the value of entropy tends to zero and thus the codeword can be perceived as characteristic to the activity. Based on this, the desired codewords should be described with high probability and low entropy values.

6.5   Application and Validation

This section presents the experimental results of the codebook-based method (see Chapter 5.1.2) regarding the cognitive activity recognition task. At the beginning, a brief description of the dataset is provided with a short description of the implementation. Then, different representations of subsequences are discussed along with various combinations of feature vectors and their influence on the recognition accuracy. Afterwards, an analysis of codewords is performed describing their connection to certain activity classes.

6.5.1   Collecting a Dataset

The dataset used throughout all the experiments is obtained with the smart eye-ware called JINS-MEME [1] (see Figure 5.1) with integrated EOG-based eye-tracker, accelerometer and gyroscope. EOG data consisting of four data vectors (EOG_L, EOG_R, EOG_H, EOG_V) and additional data from the three-axis accelerometer (ACC_X, ACC_Y, ACC_Z) were collected with JINS-MEME glasses, since the preliminary experiments showed that the results obtained using only EOG signals are not good enough to effectively distinguish between several cognitive activities. The EOG_L (or EOG_R) data represent differences between the electric potential field of the pole at left (NL) (or right (NR)) nose pad and the reference one of the pole at the bridging part (BR) [13]. The EOG_H is defined as a difference between the electric potential field of the left nose pad NL and the one of the pole at the right nose pad (NR), while EOG_V is an average of EOG_L and EOG_R.

Data collection was performed in a controlled environment. One hundred adults participated in experimental sessions, in which their eye and head movements were recorded while performing the following three daily activities: (1) reading a printed page of text in a participant's native language, (2) drinking mineral water, and (3) watching a video. After each activity recording, participants took a short break to calm their eyes. Around 30 seconds long EOG and accelerometer sequences were recorded for each of these activities. Since these sequences were obtained with a high sampling rate of 100Hz, it is considered that they contain sufficient information to build an effective classifier. Figure 6.1 presents the EOG and accelerometer sequences collected during the reading activity. The

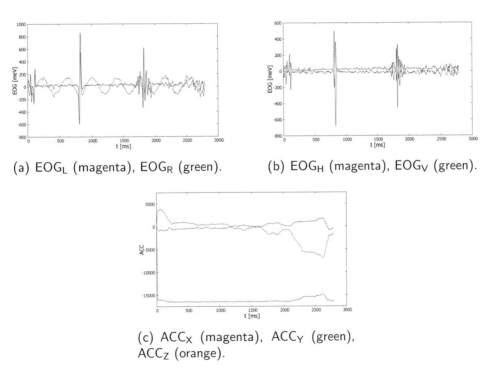

(a) EOG$_L$ (magenta), EOG$_R$ (green).   (b) EOG$_H$ (magenta), EOG$_V$ (green).

(c) ACC$_X$ (magenta), ACC$_Y$ (green),
ACC$_Z$ (orange).

Figure 6.1: Examples of EOG and accelerometer sequences obtained for the reading activity.

EOG and accelerometer data were collected by a Bluetooth-based data

streaming application of the smartglasses [1]. To sum up, the dataset consists of 100 data samples for each of the 3 activity classes, and each data sample consists of 7 sequences - 4 EOG and 3 accelerometer vectors.

6.5.2   Implementation Details

During the experiments a codebook is constructed using subsequences from all the 300 sequences from each type of sensor (i.e., 100 sequences $\times$ 3 activities). The performance is evaluated using cross validation, where, first, a half of the sequences is used for training and another half for testing. Then, the second half is used for training and the first one for testing. The cognitive activity recognition performance is measured as the accuracy, expressed as a percentage of how many sequences are correctly classified.

The method uses three main parameters describing the size of sliding window w, the sliding size s, and the number of codewords N. The parameter s allows to control the sampling rate. Assuming that a higher sampling rate could lead to a better performance [16], s is set to 8 through all the experiments. The values of parameters w and N are investigated by taking combinations of values defined by $w \in \{8, 16, 32, 64, 128\}$ and $N \in \{8, 16, 32, 64, 128, 256, 512\}$, to avoid under- or over-estimating recognition accuracies. Finally, using N, the obtained subsequences are clustered to construct a codebook for each of the following seven features: EOG_L, EOG_R, EOG_H, EOG_V, ACC_X, ACC_Y and ACC_Z. Early fusion is performed to combine these features into a single high-dimensional feature.

6.5.3   Results for Cognitive Activity Recognition

Accuracies are calculated for 35 results, each of which is obtained by applying early fusion to individual features, extracted with one combination of w and N. Figure 6.2a depicts the accuracy distribution of these 35 results. The best accuracy result of 86.6% was obtained for $w = 128$ and $N = 64$. During the experiments it was also observed that the values of w higher than 128 may decrease the recognition accuracy. The reason for this can be considered as overfitting, where codewords that are very specific to training sequences are mistakenly regarded as useful for classifying test sequences. The accuracy distributions of activity recognition using the codebooks built with FFT coefficients are shown in Figure 6.2b, where the best result of 96.6% was obtained ($w = 128$, $N = 256$).

165

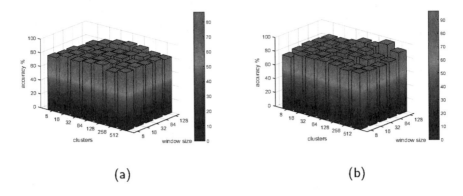

(a)   (b)

Figure 6.2: Accuracy distributions of cognitive activity recognition obtained with codebooks constructed on *raw subsequences* (a) and subsequences represented by FFT coefficients (b).

Despite of the satisfactory results obtained based on the FFT-based subsequence representation, investigations of data preprocessing approaches to additionally improve the accuracy were performed, especially since EOG data are sensitive to facial muscle movements. Several algorithms for noise removal and approximation methods were utilised, however in most cases no significant performance improvement was obtained. Nevertheless, using the moving average filter with the sliding window of size $w_{avg} = 8$ presented around 2-3% of performance improvement for both raw and FFT-based subsequence representations (88.5% for the former and 99.3% for the later, as shown in Figure 6.3). A feature built as a combination of the above-mentioned subsequence representations in both time and frequency domains was also investigated. However, there was no significant improvement in recognition accuracy.

6.5.4 Results for Codewords Investigation

Investigations to find out which codewords are characteristic for particular activity classes were also performed. Table 6.1 presents the exemplary results of the codeword investigation obtained for 9 of 64 codewords that were obtained with the proposed method using subsequences of preprocessed data ($w = 64$, $N = 128$). It can be observed that the data presented in Table 6.1 contain several features with high probabilities and low entropies in every activity class – desired situation as a low entropy indicates that the probability in one activity class is significantly higher

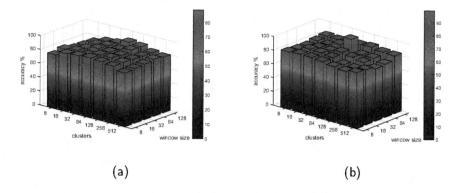

Figure 6.3: Accuracy distributions of cognitive activity recognition obtained with codebooks constructed on subsequences of *preprocessed data* (a) and subsequences represented by FFT coefficients (b).

than in the other classes. For example, the fourth codeword C_4 for the accelerometer sequence on z axis ACC_Z has very high probability for the drinking activity. This coincides with the fact that one very characteristic action is taken during drinking, that is tilting the head back while taking the sip of water. Also, there is no eye movements that could be linked with this activity class, thus codewords for EOG sequences have relatively low probability values. Features corresponding to eye movements are more likely to occur while describing the reading activity, where we are following a line of text and switching between those lines using our eyesight. These actions are captured, e.g., by codewords C_{10}, C_{31} and C_{62} for all four EOG sequences. The last activity class corresponding to watching television/video presents very little characteristics, only time to time showing some connection to eye movements – codeword C_{33} for EOG_H sequence. Nevertheless, this is justified as follows: Usually we are watching a video sitting on a couch which is placed in some distance to the screen. Thus, in most situations the whole surface of the screen is within a field of the eyes, so there is no reason to make large eye movement. These characteristic features are depicted in Figure 6.4.

6.6 Conclusion and Future Trends

In this chapter, related work and the author's own methodology for cognitive activity recognition based on data delivered by sensors embedded in

Table 6.1: Exemplary results of codeword investigation using probabilities and entropies.

Sequence		C_4	C_{10}	C_{19}	C_{21}	Probability C_{22}	C_{31}	C_{33}	C_{60}	C_{62}
Drinking	ACC_X	0.10	0.03	0.25	0.04	0.08	0.03	0.25	0.04	0.05
	ACC_Y	0.00	0.07	0.47	0.50	0.31	0.54	0.06	0.01	0.01
	ACC_Z	**0.99**	0.12	**0.99**	0.00	0.08	**0.99**	0.15	0.07	0.11
	EOG_L	0.14	0.03	0.05	0.02	0.17	0.02	0.06	0.05	0.00
	EOG_R	0.35	0.00	0.17	0.26	0.16	0.15	0.04	0.00	0.01
	EOG_H	0.01	0.03	0.09	0.02	0.00	0.18	0.00	0.02	0.02
	EOG_V	0.22	0.05	0.16	0.16	0.18	0.05	0.09	0.01	0.00
Reading	ACC_X	0.80	0.83	0.41	0.83	0.70	**0.96**	0.37	0.75	0.76
	ACC_Y	0.66	0.79	0.35	0.26	0.30	0.19	0.69	**0.96**	0.82
	ACC_Z	0.00	0.68	0.00	0.00	0.44	0.00	0.52	0.72	0.73
	EOG_L	0.56	**0.90**	0.78	0.85	0.00	**0.90**	0.78	0.89	**0.99**
	EOG_R	0.36	**0.92**	0.54	0.29	0.57	0.73	**0.90**	0.89	0.87
	EOG_H	**0.94**	**0.94**	0.87	**0.95**	0.00	0.66	0.00	**0.96**	**0.94**
	EOG_V	0.62	0.83	0.58	0.75	0.55	**0.94**	0.72	**0.95**	**0.93**
Watching video	ACC_X	0.09	0.13	0.33	0.11	0.21	0.00	0.37	0.20	0.17
	ACC_Y	0.32	0.13	0.17	0.23	0.38	0.26	0.23	0.02	0.15
	ACC_Z	0.00	0.19	0.00	**1.00**	0.46	0.00	0.32	0.19	0.15
	EOG_L	0.29	0.06	0.15	0.11	**0.82**	0.07	0.14	0.05	0.00
	EOG_R	0.28	0.07	0.27	0.44	0.26	0.10	0.05	0.09	0.10
	EOG_H	0.03	0.02	0.03	0.02	**1.00**	0.15	**1.00**	0.01	0.02
	EOG_V	0.15	0.10	0.25	0.07	0.25	0.00	0.18	0.02	0.06

Sequence	C_4	C_{10}	C_{19}	C_{21}	Entropy C_{22}	C_{31}	C_{33}	C_{60}	C_{62}
ACC_X	0.90	0.77	1.55	0.78	1.12	**0.00**	1.56	0.97	0.97
ACC_Y	0.96	0.92	1.47	1.49	1.57	1.44	1.11	**0.25**	0.73
ACC_Z	**0.00**	1.20	**0.00**	**0.00**	1.33	**0.00**	1.42	1.07	1.08
EOG_L	1.38	**0.53**	0.91	0.69	**0.00**	**0.54**	0.95	0.57	**0.08**
EOG_R	1.57	**0.00**	1.42	1.54	1.39	1.08	**0.55**	0.51	0.60
EOG_H	**0.35**	**0.38**	0.64	**0.31**	**0.00**	1.25	**0.00**	**0.27**	**0.35**
EOG_V	1.32	0.78	1.38	1.02	1.42	**0.34**	1.10	**0.30**	**0.38**

wearables (e.g., smartglasses) are described. The definition and health-related aspects of cognitive activity are summarised in Section 6.1. Section 6.2 provides important information on sensor modalities that are used for sensing the brain activity. A survey of related approaches is given in Section 6.3. The original electrooculography-based method for cognitive activity recognition based on the codebook approach used also for physical activity recognition (see Chapter 5) is explained in Section 6.4. The application of the methodology to recognition between three activities along with the corresponding experiments and results are described in Section 6.5.

The experimental results show that the codebook approach can be successfully utilised for the cognitive activity recognition task. Applied to EOG and accelerometer data, the proposed method achieved high accuracy results, predicting proper activity classes in 99.3% of cases without using prior knowledge or heuristics. Moreover, the entropy-based investigation of codewords appeared to be an easy-to-use analytical tool to gain knowledge about subsequences characteristic to a particular class of activities. These can be used to build a knowledge database on cognitive activities as there is not much known about characteristics of particular cognitive activity classes and they are still under investigation.

In the future, the number of cognitive activity classes will be significantly increased. Moreover, the methodology for cognitive activity recognition will be integrated into the general framework for holistic health monitoring. Other modules of the framework will continuously assess the physical and social activities as well as the emotional state of the users. In this way, predictive investigations on human health and condition will be possible.

References

[1] JINS MEME: The world's first wearable eyewear that lets you see yourself. https://jins-meme.com/en/. Accessed: 2017-03-08.

[2] N. Barbara and T. A. Camilleri. Interfacing with a speller using eog glasses. In *Proceedings of the 2016 IEEE International Conference on Systems, Man, and Cybernetics (SMC)*, pages 1069–1074, October 2016.

[3] A. Bulling, J. A. Ward, H. Gellersen, and G. Troster. Eye movement analysis for activity recognition using electrooculography. *IEEE Transactions on Pattern Analysis and Machine Intelligence*, 33(4):741–753, April 2011.

[4] Chih-Chung Chang and Chih-Jen Lin. LIBSVM: A library for support vector machines. *ACM Transactions on Intelligent Systems and Technology*, 2(3):1–27, May 2011.

[5] L. Dempere-Marco, Xiao-Peng Hu, S. L. S. MacDonald, S. M. Ellis, D. M. Hansell, and Guang-Zhong Yang. The use of visual search for knowledge gathering in image decision support. *IEEE Transactions on Medical Imaging*, 21(7):741–754, July 2002.

[6] S. D'Souza and S. Natarajan. Recognition of eog based reading task using ar features. In *International Conference on Circuits, Communication, Control and Computing*, pages 113–117, November 2014.

[7] Mohamed Elhelw, Marios Nicolaou, Adrian Chung, Guang-Zhong Yang, and M. Stella Atkins. A gaze-based study for investigating the perception of visual realism in simulated scenes. *ACM Transactions on Applied Perception*, 5(1):3:1–3:20, January 2008.

[8] S. S. Hacisalihzade, L. W. Stark, and J. S. Allen. Visual perception and sequences of eye movement fixations: a stochastic modeling approach. *IEEE Transactions on Systems, Man, and Cybernetics*, 22(3):474–481, May 1992.

[9] J. Han, M. Kamber, and J. Pei. *Data Mining: Concepts and Techniques*. Morgan Kaufmann, 2011.

[10] K. Huda, M. S. Hossain, and M. Ahmad. Recognition of reading activity from the saccadic samples of electrooculography data. In *In Proceedings of the 2015 International Conference on Electrical Electronic Engineering (ICEEE)*, pages 73–76, November 2015.

[11] Shoya Ishimaru, Kai Kunze, Koichi Kise, Jens Weppner, Andreas Dengel, Paul Lukowicz, and Andreas Bulling. In the blink of an eye: Combining head motion and eye blink frequency for activity recognition with google glass. In *Proceedings of the 5th Augmented Human International Conference*, pages 1–4, New York, NY, USA, 2014. ACM.

[12] Shoya Ishimaru, Kai Kunze, Katsuma Tanaka, Yuji Uema, Koichi Kise, and Masahiko Inami. Smart eyewear for interaction and activity recognition. In *Proceedings of the 33rd Annual ACM Conference Extended Abstracts on Human Factors in Computing Systems*, pages 307–310, New York, NY, USA, 2015. ACM.

[13] S. Kanoh, S. Ichi-nohe, S. Shioya, K. Inoue, and R. Kawashima. Development of an eyewear to measure eye and body movements. In *2015 37th Annual International Conference of the IEEE Engineering in Medicine and Biology Society (EMBC)*, pages 2267–2270, August 2015.

[14] Kai Kunze, Masai Katsutoshi, Yuji Uema, and Masahiko Inami. How much do you read?: Counting the number of words a user reads using electrooculography. In *Proceedings of the 6th Augmented Human International Conference*, pages 125–128, New York, NY, USA, 2015. ACM.

[15] Z. Lv, X. Wu, and M. Li. A research on eog feature parameters extraction based on linear predictive coding model. In *Proceedings of the Third International Conference on Bioinformatics and Biomedical Engineering*, pages 1–4, June 2009.

[16] E. Nowak, F. Jurie, and B. Triggs. Sampling strategies for bag-of-features image classification. In *Proceedings of the 9th European Conference on Computer Vision*, pages 490–503, 2006.

[17] Hanchuan Peng, Fuhui Long, and C. Ding. Feature selection based on mutual information criteria of max-dependency, max-relevance, and min-redundancy. *IEEE Transactions on Pattern Analysis and Machine Intelligence*, 27(8):1226–1238, August 2005.

[18] Dario D. Salvucci and John R. Anderson. Automated eye-movement protocol analysis. *Human-Compututer Interaction*, 16(1):39–86, March 2001.

[19] V. N. Vapnik. *Statistical Learning Theory*. Wiley-Interscience, 1998.

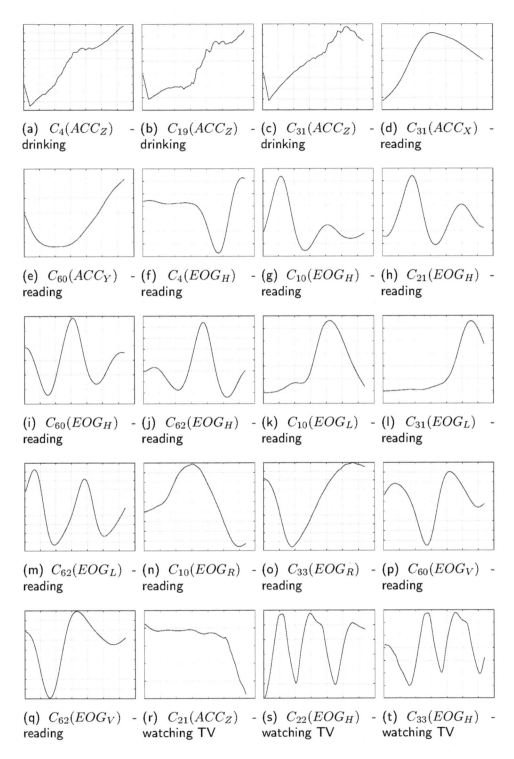

(a) $C_4(ACC_Z)$ - (b) $C_{19}(ACC_Z)$ - (c) $C_{31}(ACC_Z)$ - (d) $C_{31}(ACC_X)$ -
drinking   drinking   drinking   reading

(e) $C_{60}(ACC_Y)$ - (f) $C_4(EOG_H)$ - (g) $C_{10}(EOG_H)$ - (h) $C_{21}(EOG_H)$ -
reading   reading   reading   reading

(i) $C_{60}(EOG_H)$ - (j) $C_{62}(EOG_H)$ - (k) $C_{10}(EOG_L)$ - (l) $C_{31}(EOG_L)$ -
reading   reading   reading   reading

(m) $C_{62}(EOG_L)$ - (n) $C_{10}(EOG_R)$ - (o) $C_{33}(EOG_R)$ - (p) $C_{60}(EOG_V)$ -
reading   reading   reading   reading

(q) $C_{62}(EOG_V)$ - (r) $C_{21}(ACC_Z)$ - (s) $C_{22}(EOG_H)$ - (t) $C_{33}(EOG_H)$ -
reading   watching TV   watching TV   watching TV

Figure 6.4: Plots of characteristic codewords for particular activities mentioned in Table 6.1.

Chapter 7

Emotion Recognition

This chapter overviews state-of-the-art approaches and summarises the author's scientific contribution to the area of automated human emotion recognition. Section 7.1 describes fundamental concepts of emotion recognition including main emotion models, requirements for sensor selection as well as most related contests organised in this field (e.g., The Audio/Visual Emotion Challenge and Workshop[1]) providing ground truth datasets and frameworks for quantitative performance comparison. Section 7.2 surveys existing emotion recognition approaches that use multimodal data (e.g. video, audio, physiological). Finally, Section 7.3 closes the chapter by explaining several methods for emotion recognition that are based exclusively on human's physiological data. The author's contributions to emotion recognition can mainly be assigned to the last section of this chapter.

7.1 Automatic Recognition of Emotions

Over the last few years, a lot of progress has been achieved in various fields of pattern recognition, such as speech recognition or object recognition in images and videos, and led to the development and/or improvement of many real-life applications (e.g. driver-less cars, intelligent assistants on smartphones, etc.). The emergence of increasingly powerful processors and hardware - leading to the rise of promising classification approaches such as solutions based on Neural Networks - coupled to an existing demand for the development of such kind of technologies are some of the main reasons behind those advances.

---

[1]http://sspnet.eu/avec2016

The field of emotion recognition did not benefit as much from those technological and theoretical advances regarding pattern recognition, despite the existence of potential applications related to medical data understanding and psychological disorder detection, or to the development of emotion-sensitive intelligent systems. This lack of progress compared to other research fields can be attributed to different factors, like the difficulty to acquire emotion-related data to apply the common supervised learning approaches for pattern recognition and the scarcity of the datasets (especially for non-video data). The most important obstacle, however, is the lack of a rigorous scientific definition of what exactly emotions are, since the accepted literal definition ("complex state of feeling") is too vague and the perception of emotions can vary from one person to another.

7.1.1 Definition and Taxonomy of Emotions

So what does defining an emotion in a scientific way entail? Several different theoretical approaches have been proposed in the past to provide a way to rationally define this complex and - from a psychological point of view - not well understood phenomenon.

The most simple framework was proposed in 1980 by R. Plutchik [49], who introduced the idea of discrete emotional categories, claiming that some basic emotions universally recognisable by humans (no matter which cultural background they have) form distinct categories, and trigger universal facial expressions and behavioural reactions among the individuals feeling them. Plutchik's proposed model revolves around 8 basic emotions: joy, trust, fear, surprise, sadness, disgust, anger, anticipation. All of them can be organised in a wheel (see Figure 7.1), with each emotion having two others which are closely related to it (e.g. joy closely related to trust and anticipation) and one opposite (e.g., joy opposite of sadness). Every basic emotion can also vary in intensity to form different emotional states (e.g. ecstasy being the intense version of joy, while serenity being the mild one). The notion of a dyad was also introduced in Plutchik's work, to name the possible associations of the basic emotions to form new and more complex emotions. All pairs of basic emotions can be combined to form a dyad, except two opposite ones (e.g., joy can be combined with any other, except sadness, see Figure 7.2).

Plutchik's theory was carried on and perfected by P. Ekman in 1992 [18], who proposed a restricted panel of basic emotions revolving around only 6 emotional states: happiness, disgust, sadness, anger, fear and surprise. To

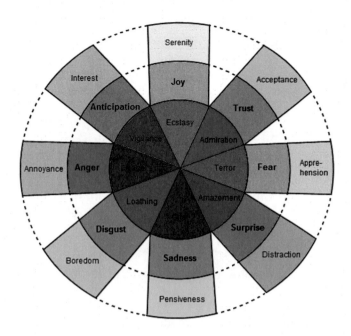

Figure 7.1: Plutchik's wheel of emotions, featuring the 8 basic emotions and their variations in intensity.

justify his choice, P. Ekman carried out a cross-cultural experiment which consisted of asking subjects from 21 different countries from all continents to identify the emotion associated with the expression displayed on black-and-white pictures of faces from the Pictures of Facial Affect (POFA) dataset. The study showed that people from a large majority of countries (and sometimes from all of them) agreed on the identification of those 6 basic emotions, no matter with which degree of intensity they were depicted in the pictures [20].

The framework of Plutchik and Ekman proposing basic emotions has, however, been criticised by a part of the research community for over-simplifying the definition of emotions, and not being enough to tackle the problem of the identification of more complex emotional phenomena. Several dimensional approaches - all proposing a finer definition of emotions by decomposing them along several different dimensions - were also made, each proposing their own axes of decomposition:

The Circumplex model developed by J. Russell in 1980 [52]: J. Russell claimed that emotions could be decomposed following two axes. The first axis, called arousal, is used to measure the level of physical

175

	Joy	Trust	Fear	Surprise	Sadness	Disgust	Anger	Anticipation
Joy		Love	Guilt	Delight		Morbidness	Pride	Optimism
Trust	Love		Submission	Curiosity	Sentimentality		Dominance	Fatalism
Fear	Guilt	Submission		Alarm	Despair	Shame		Anxiety
Surprise	Delight	Curiosity	Alarm		Dissapointment	Revulsion	Outrage	
Sadness		Sentimentality	Despair	Dissapointment		Remorse	Envy	Pessimism
Disgust	Morbidness		Shame	Revulsion	Remorse		Contempt	Cynism
Anger	Pride	Dominance		Outrage	Envy	Contempt		Aggression
Anticipation	Optimism	Fatalism	Anxiety		Pessimism	Cynism	Aggression	

Figure 7.2: Plutchik's dyads.

response of the subject when in a specific emotional state, while the second, called valence, characterises the level of attractiveness or positivity of this emotional state. Unlike the basic emotion theory, this definition has the advantage of being able to model the transitions between different emotional states of a subject (see Figure 7.3).

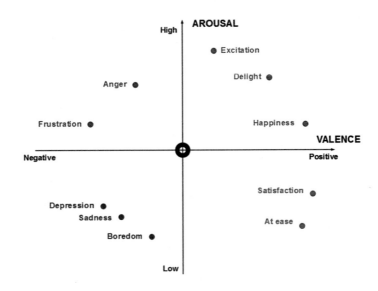

Figure 7.3: The Circumplex model.

The Pleasure-Arousal-Dominance (PAD) model, proposed in 1980 by A. Mehrabian [44], extends the Circumplex model by adding a third axis called dominance, with pleasure and arousal replacing valence and arousal respectively. The dominance axis can be used to classify emotions in a more fine way in this model, by adding an information on how dominant/controlling or submissive/controlled the subject feels in his or her current emotional state. For instance, 2 emotions with negative pleasure and positive valence such as fear and anger can be distinguished by being at the opposite of the dominance spectrum (see Figure 7.4).

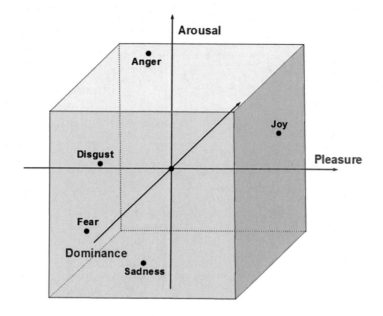

Figure 7.4: The PAD model.

The Positive Activation and Negative Activation (PANA) model, proposed by Watson and Tellegan in 1985 [17], decomposes emotion along 2 axes: one measuring the level of positive activation (active/elated/excited against drowsy/dull/sluggish), the other of negative activation (calm/relaxed/at rest against fearful/distressed/nervous) [14]. The axes are assumed to be independent, e.g., a high level of positive activation is not necessarily incompatible with a high level of negative activation. The PANA model is often seen as a 45 degree rotation of the Circumplex model with a different decomposition (see Figure 7.5).

The Lövheim cube of emotions: H. Lövheim proposed an emotion classification approach different from the previous models [39], made by monitoring the levels of 3 different neurotransmitters: serotonin (usually linked to well-being and happiness), dopamine (involved

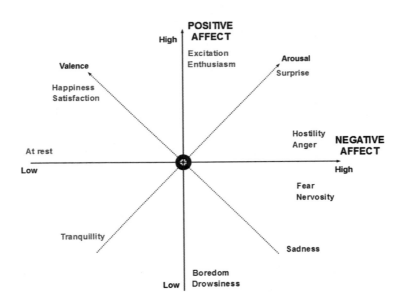

Figure 7.5: The PANA model

in reward-motivated behaviours) and noradrenaline (used to prepare the body for action), after observing that the combinations
of different levels of those neurotransmitters corresponded to particular emotions (see Figure 7.6). Compared to the other models,
this model has the advantage of proposing 3 axes of decomposition
which do not have to rely on subjective assessments to be measured.
Its main limitation however remains the difficulty to have access to
those levels of neurotransmitters in a way that is non-intrusive for
the subject, as the main current approaches rely either on blood or
urine analysis, or, for some of those, on the use of radioactively labelled substances injected in the subject's blood to get an imagery
of the distribution of the neurotransmitters in the subject's brain
(Positron Emission Tomography) [24].

If those approaches for the definition of emotions attempt to clarify ideas
from a theoretical point of view, they however do not necessarily solve
the problem of recognising the emotions of one subject with a high cer-
tainty in practice, the measure of the proposed alternative features (e.g.,
valence, arousal) remains still subjective for most of them. It should be
noted that even if the valence/arousal decomposition of emotions proposed by the Circumplex model, as well as the basic emotions approach
are mostly employed in current research works, none of those frameworks

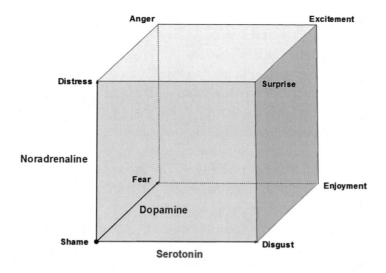

Figure 7.6: The Lövheim Cube of emotions.

have clearly established itself as the reference benchmark to define emotions in the research community. None of those approaches is perfect and each has its own drawbacks: while the discrete emotions theory might not be a good framework to work with complex emotions or to model transitions between different emotional states, the Circumplex model is also insufficient to clearly define certain emotions difficult to describe in terms of arousal/valence - such as surprise, which can be linked to both positive or negative levels of valence or to distinguish well different emotions with similar arousal/valence levels, such as fear and anger (both negative valence - positive arousal).

However, it can also be noted that from a machine learning point of view, the problem of formally conceptualising emotions intervenes mainly at the level of the emotion-related data acquisition, by making the labelling of the data difficult and potentially inaccurate. It is therefore still possible for machine learning researchers to carry out studies on emotion recognition despite this issue, by using alternative means to label the data during the experimental process with more confidence (e.g., real-time feedback from the experimental subjects, questionnaires, etc.), and make the assumption that the data is well labelled. This is the approach which has been the most commonly adopted for studies on the topic of emotion recognition, pending a clarification on the formal definition of emotions.

7.1.2 Existing Techniques for Emotion Recognition

An additional problem hindering significant progress in emotion recognition lies in the lack of consensus in the research community on the methodology to be used in studies. Few studies in this research field propose the same choice of emotions to recognise for instance, or agree on the way to acquire the emotion-related data. The choice of the sensors to use to obtain the data for the training set is indeed dependent on what particular emotions have to be recognised, as some sensor modalities might become more useful while others lose their relevance depending on the chosen classes. However, numerous studies have shown the importance of features describing the facial expression of the subjects, and therefore image and video-based modalities. But the latter are not the only ones.

Among the most common modalities used for emotion recognition, audio and physiological data can also be found, even if they are most of the time coupled with image or video data. Some studies make use of audio data only (e.g. detection of emotions in speeches) or physiological data only, but those remain marginal compared to the others. While some descriptors and techniques have shown to have a sensible impact on the performances of emotion recognition in the different research works performed over the past years, most of them are related to image or video data, which seems to confirm the important role of facial expressions for the communication of emotions highlighted by P. Ekman [19].

A proposal for a scientific definition of facial expressions has in particular imposed itself as the reference framework: the Facial Action Coding System (FACS) [46]. Based on the work of anatomist C. H. Hjortsjö who identified and described the mechanisms behind basic facial movements, it was proposed by P. Ekman and W. V. Friesen in 1978 to standardise and name the most common facial movements. 44 of them - called Action Units (AU) in the FACS - were listed in total (plus one neutral AU), each being designed by the name AUn with n between 0 and 44 (e.g., AU0 = neutral expression, AU1 = raise of inner brows, AU6 = raise of cheeks, etc.). Using the FACS, Ekman and Friesen claimed that a specific emotion can be identified by recognising a combination of different AU, e.g., happiness = AU6 + AU12 (cheeks raised + lip corners pulled), sadness = AU1 + AU4 + AU15 (inner brow raised + brow lowered + lip corners lowered), etc.

This idea of emotion recognition by the detection of certain facial expressions in single images raised the interest of the research community which proposed several image processing approaches and descriptors to detect the relevant AU. One in particular emerged as the state-of-the-art descriptor for AU detection: the Local Gabor Binary Patterns from Three Orthogonal Plans (LGBP-TOP). This simple video descriptor proposed by T. R. Almaev and M. F. Valstar in 2013 [56] has proven its effectiveness in problems of emotion recognition using video data of faces, by capturing spatio-temporal information regarding the evolution of textures on the faces with good efficiency. It relies on the use of Local Binary Patterns (LBP), a descriptor applied for characterising the texture of 1-channel images (e.g. grayscale images). The computation of LBP revolves around the following steps:

1. A 1-channel image of a given size is divided into cells of smaller size.

2. The value of each pixel in each cell is compared to its 8 neighbours. For each neighbour, 0 is attributed if its value is smaller than the one of the centre pixel, 1 otherwise. The 8 obtained resulting numbers form a 8-bit binary number, which is converted into a decimal (value between 0 and 255).

3. 256-bit histograms of decimal values obtained are computed among all cells.

4. Histograms of all cells are concatenated to form the LBP descriptor (vector of dimension $255\times$ number of cells).

Provided that an input video of the face of a subject is available, the following steps are performed in order to compute the LGBP-TOP descriptor:

1. A block of video frames (with a fixed number of successive frames) is defined. This 3D video volume has three axes: x and y (dimensions of the images) and t (time dimension).

2. All images of the block are turned into grayscale images (if input RGB images are used).

3. Specific pre-defined Gabor filters (filters characterised by the multiplication of a sinusoidal wave with a Gaussian) are applied to each frame of the video volume, to obtain a volume of Gabor Pictures (GP).

4. An altered version of LBP (with 59 histogram bins instead of 256) is computed for all frames (**(xy)** planes) of the block of GP and provides one histogram per frame. All frame histograms are then averaged to return a single averaged histogram.

5. Step 4 is repeated for all frames of the volume of GP along the two orthogonal planes to **(xy)** (i.e. **(xt)** and **(yt)** planes). Two more averaged histograms are obtained after this step.

6. The three averaged histograms obtained are then concatenated to provide the final LGBP-TOP descriptor (see Figure 7.7).

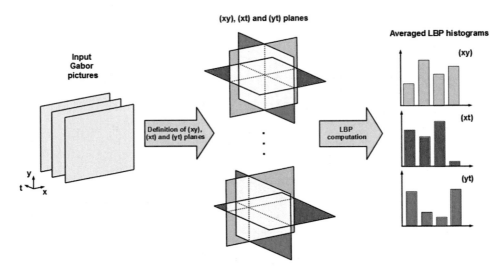

Figure 7.7: Computation of the LGBP-TOP descriptor.

LGBP-TOP descriptors have proven in particular to be pretty effective at the detection of AU when used as inputs of SVM classifiers. They bring an average improvement of 18% on the Cohn-Kanade dataset [55] and 14% on the MMI dataset [42] compared to the descriptors previously used for the recognition of 7 specific AU (2, 6, 7, 12, 20, 25, 45) [56], for an average recognition rate of 86%.

7.1.3 Emotion Recognition Challenges

Another difficulty - related to the two previous ones - which impedes the progress in the domain is the lack of a clarified framework for the different studies about emotion recognition, defining the type of data to be used or the emotions to be classified for the recognition problem. In order to address this issue, several proposals of Emotion Recognition Challenges have been made by researchers in the past few years; each of them providing a labelled dataset of selected emotions, most of the time with multimodal data comprising videos of the faces of the subjects, audio records, and sometimes physiological signals such as Electroencephalogram (EEG), Electrodermal Activity (EDA) (also known as Skin Conductance (SC)), Blood Volume Pulse (BVP), Electrooculography (EOG) or Electrocardiogram (ECG) to name some of the most common ones. Researchers participating in those challenges are then invited to propose either their best models or their best descriptors for emotion recognition, using one or several of the modalities of the dataset.

The existing challenges have mainly adopted either the Circumplex model or P. Ekman's framework of basic emotions for the definition of emotions. The recognition of the latter can be translated into a regression problem of arousal/valence in the first case, or a classification problem in the second case. The challenges with the highest impact in the field of emotion recognition for each of those approaches are:

- The Audio/Visual Emotion Challenge (AVEC) linked to the ACM Multimedia conference [43] and

- The Emotion Recognition in the Wild challenge (EmotiW) linked to the International Conference on Multimodal Interaction (ICMI) [4].

A more comprehensive description of each challenge and winning solutions is provided below.

AVEC Challenge

Since 2011, the AVEC challenge of the ACM Multimedia conference proposes a fixed framework and labelled dataset for researchers wanting to compare the performances of their approaches. The adopted model for emotion definition here is the Circumplex model, and participants are invited to propose a method able to continuously estimate in the most accurate way the arousal and valence levels of a subject. The dataset used is the Remote Collaborative and Affective Interactions dataset (RECOLA) [23] which contains data acquired from 27 French-speaking subjects asked to solve a collaborative task via video-conference in a natural and spontaneous way. For each subject, video data of the face, audio recordings and

ECG and EDA measurements are acquired. The labelling of the data is performed by 6 French-speaker assistants, asked to assess continuously the arousal and valence levels of each subject, for the 5 first minutes of the recordings (during which the interactions between the participants were the most interesting and potentially inducing emotions). The performance metric in this challenge is the Concordance Correlation Coefficient (CCC), used to measure the similarity between the ground truth arousal/valence time sequences and their estimations.

Some state-of-the-art features are also extracted from all modalities and then tested with a classifier to provide some baseline results. The following list shortly describes them (more details in [43]):

- From video data: appearance and geometric-based features LGBP-TOP and facial landmarks (on the eyes, eyebrows and the mouth) respectively;

- From audio data: several hand-crafted low-level features which have proven to give good recognition result for the modelling of emotion from speech, giving information about spectral, cepstral, prosodic and voice quality;

- From psychological features: hand-crafted features including the Hearth Rate (HR: speed of the heartbeat) and Heart Rate Variability (HRV: variations of time between heartbeats) from ECG, the Skin Conductance Level (SCL) and Skin Conductance Response (SCR) from EDA, and spectral and statistical descriptors from both ECG and EDA.

The initiators of the challenge performed a comparative study of the discriminative power of the different descriptors for both tasks of arousal and valence estimation, using Support-Vector Regression (SVR) and Neural Network (NN) models on each of the different features extracted from the raw data. Their results indicate that audio features seem to perform the best for arousal estimation, while video features are the most useful to estimate valence. Physiological modalities are performing quite well with ECG and EDA being the second best descriptor for arousal and valence estimations respectively.

It should be noted that the AVEC challenge also proposes a sub-challenge of depression recognition (binary classification problem) using the Distress Analysis Interview Corpus (DAIC) dataset [23]. Since depression often involves combinations of different basic emotions such as sadness, fear, anger, it will not be described in detail as it is seen as moving away from the topic of emotion recognition.For more details about this sub-challenge, refer to [43].

EmotiW Challenge

The EmotiW challenge, linked to the ICMI conference, proposes one main challenge for emotion recognition in videos (VReco) usually supplemented by a second sub-challenge on a related thematic area, whose topic changes depending on the challenge edition. Only the VReco challenge, more directly related to the subject of this chapter, will be described in the following.

The initiators of the EmotiW VReco challenge propose to work on a problem of emotion recognition of 7 different emotional classes based on P. Ekman's discrete emotion theory: anger, disgust, sadness, happiness, surprise, fear and neutral. The Acted Facial Expressions in the Wild dataset (AFEW) [5] is used. The latter contains videos of 428 different subjects (average age of 34.4 years) facing the camera, extracted from movies with their associated soundtracks (i.e., use of video and audio data). An algorithm parsing keywords from subtitles of the different movies is used in order to find relevant extracts. These are then manually labelled to obtain 1368 video samples in total, of length comprised between 300 and 5400ms, and extracted from 111 different movies. It can be noted that one of the main assets of the AFEW dataset is to provide images taken in a context which comes as close to reality as possible (e.g., in terms of illumination, possible influences of the background, etc.), as opposed to other datasets whose data is acquired in artificial and fixed experimental setups. The dataset is then divided into three parts: training, testing and validation.

Similarly to the AVEC challenge, some state-of-the-art descriptors are computed from both the audio and video data, and a comparative study of their effectiveness for emotion classification is performed. Once again, more details about those can be found in [4]:

- From video data: LGBP-TOP;

- From audio data: hand-crafted low-level-descriptors, related to the energy or spectre of the audio signals.

SVM classifiers with either linear or RBF kernels are then trained using video-based features only, audio-based features only, and both audio and video descriptors. The comparative study shows here the importance of the video-based descriptors, with the latter obtaining a classification accuracy of 33.15% on the validation set; higher than those obtained with audio only (26.10%) or even with both modalities fused (28.19%).

Other Challenges

Other existing main challenges related to emotion detection that can be evoked are the Facial Expression Recognition and Analysis challenge (FERA) [41] proposed by the European Social Signal Processing Network (SSPNet) which focuses on the detection of facial AU, and the INTER-SPEECH challenge [12] which targets the detection of emotion-related phenomena in speeches by the exclusive analysis of audio data (with different targets depending on the challenge edition, e.g. sincerity, social signals, autism, proficiency of the speaker in the spoken language, etc.). Considering that the objectives of those two challenges are not recognising emotions strictly speaking, they will not be described further in this chapter. More details about them can be found in the related papers [41] and [12] for FERA and INTERSPEECH, respectively.

7.2   Multimodal Emotion Recognition

In this section, a short overview of the current best techniques for the two most popular approaches for emotion recognition (arousal-valence estimation and basic emotion classification) is provided, featuring the winning solutions of the most recent editions of the AVEC and EmotiW challenges.

7.2.1   Arousal/Valence Estimation

The winning solution of the 2016 edition of the AVEC sub-challenge of emotion assessment was proposed by K. Somandepalli et al. [34] who came up with a method for continuous arousal and valence estimation using a coupled Support Vector Regression (SVR)/Kalman Filter (KF) approach, and all the available modalities as inputs (video, audio and physiological data of the RECOLA dataset [23]).

One particularity of this solution is its ability to detect moments when some sensor modalities are irrelevant, e.g., face not aligned with the camera causing video-based features to become inaccurate, or audio features computed when the subject is not speaking. This is done by computing two parameters at all times, a face status parameter $\in \{0, 1\}$ indicating whether the face of the subject is aligned with the camera (computed with the external C++ library dlib [36]]), and a voicing probability $\in [0, 1]$ indicating the probability that the subject is speaking (computed using the C++ Kaldi toolkit [16]). For either arousal or valence, 4 different Kalman filters are defined, one using audio and video data, one using video only, one using audio only and one last using physiological data only. Only the output of the relevant filter is considered, depending on the values of the Face Status and Voicing Probability (see Figure 7.8). It can also be noted

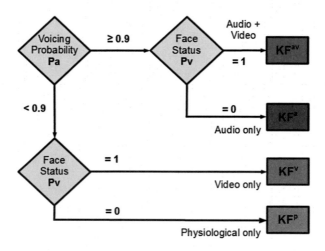

Figure 7.8: Conditional framework for the choice of Kalman filters.

that the KF estimating valence take the estimation of arousal as input in order to refine their own estimations.

In addition to the baseline features proposed in the AVEC framework (LGBP-TOP for video, hand-crafted low-level descriptors for audio, and HR, HRV, SCL, SCR for physiological signals), 2 additional descriptors (one audio, another physiological) are extracted:

- Teager Energy-based Mel-Frequency Cestrum Coefficients (TEM-FCC) [6], which are a variation of the Mel-Frequency Cestrum Coefficients (MFCC) often used in sound processing to characterise the short-term power of the input sound. The Teager energy operator [35] is applied to the magnitude of the discrete Fourier transform of the incoming signal before the computation of MFCC.

- Sparse Dictionary representation of EDA (SD-EDA) [54] is another signal processing method consisting of fitting the input EDA signal into a specific pre-determined shape in order to clean potential arte-facts. The final descriptor includes mean SCL, number of SRC and mean amplitude of SRC.

The method proposed then revolves around the 4 following main steps:

1. Extraction of video, audio and physiological features, and computation of face status and voicing probability.

2. First "noisy" estimation of both arousal and valence using the previously defined features and Support Vector Regression (SVR).

3. Determination of irrelevant modalities using face status and voicing probability.

4. Finer estimation of both arousal and valence using the noisy estimations of SVR and the Kalman Filter (KF) taking the relevant modalities as inputs.

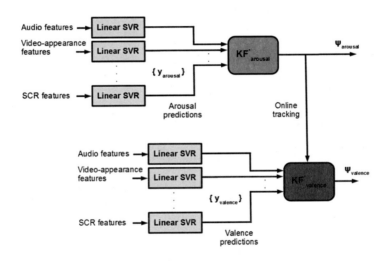

Figure 7.9: Arousal and valence estimation by SVR and KF.

The method manages to obtain an average CCC of 0.824 for arousal and 0.718 for valence on the validation set, and 0.703 for arousal and 0.681 for valence on the test set after a Leave-One-Out Cross Validation performed on the 9 subjects of both sets. It outperforms the baseline model using only the features presented in [43] by the initiators of the AVEC challenge (CCC of 0.793 and 0.659 on the validation set, and 0.682 and 0.638 on the testing set for arousal and valence respectively). The experimental results also show the important contributions of either the arousal prediction feedback for valence estimation, or the conditional framework for the choice of the KF. The system without one of those two components indeed performs lower on the validation set (CCC of 0.783 and 0.624 for arousal and valence without both, and 0.783 and 0.702 without the conditional KF choice).

7.2.2 Basic Emotion Recognition

The winning solution of the EmotiW 2016 contest was submitted by Y. Fan, X. Lu, D. Li, and Y. Liu [57] who proposed a system using a hybrid Deep Neural Network (DNN)/linear SVM classifier on video and audio data for the recognition of the 7 different emotions of the challenge (anger, disgust, sadness, happiness, surprise, fear and neutral). It is depicted in Figure 7.10.

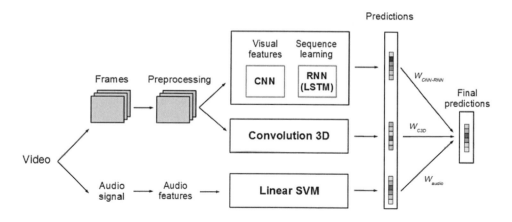

Figure 7.10: Hybrid DNN/SVM model for emotion classification using video and audio data.

The method revolves around the parallel processing of both video and audio data. Each modality is treated separately: the video data by two DNN simultaneously (a Convolutional Neural Network/Long-Short-Term Memory (CNN/LSTM) hybrid network, and a CNN performing 3D convolutions on a block of frames extracted from the input video (C3D)) and the audio data by an SVM with linear kernel. All three classifiers were trained separately, and the output class predictions were fused at the end by making a weighted sum of them, with weights determined by the performance of each classifier alone on the validation set (i.e. the higher the performance of the classifier, the bigger its associated weight).

In the following, details about the different parts of the proposed model are summarised.

Audio Processing: Low-level features (e.g., signal energy, MFCC, spectral shape related descriptors, etc.) are extracted using the openSMILE toolkit [22]. The features are then used to train a linear SVM for emotion classification.

Video Processing:

1. Data pre-processing: Faces in all frames of the video are extracted using Viola-Jones cascades [37], aligned applying a similarity transform based on facial points landmarks, and filtered using a CNN-based face detector to remove frames with no faces.

2. CNN-LSTM hybrid network: A transfer learning approach is employed to train the CNN. Its weights are initialised to those of the VGG16-Face CNN [45] (pre-trained on the Labelled Faces in the Wild [28] and YouTube Faces datasets [38]) up to the layer fc6 (32 layers in total). A fine-tuning of the weights using Stochastic Gradient Descent is then performed on the Facial Expression Recognition dataset (FER2013) [48]. The features computed by the previously trained CNN are used as inputs of a one-layered LSTM network with 128 LSTM cells, trained with a Stochastic Gradient Descent. Classification predictions are provided through a Softmax layer appended after the LSTM layer.

3. C3D network: Once again, a transfer learning approach is adopted to train this network. The C3D model pre-trained on the sport1m dataset [8] is used to initialise the weights, and fine-tuning is then performed on the AFEW dataset [5]. The network comprises 8 convolutional, 5 max-pooling and 2 fully-connected layers (see Figure 7.11). The size of the input video block (i.e. number of consecutive frames) is fixed to 16. A Softmax layer at the end of the network performs the classification.

The global multimodal model including CNN-LSTM, C3D (for video processing) and linear SVM (for audio processing) manages to achieve a

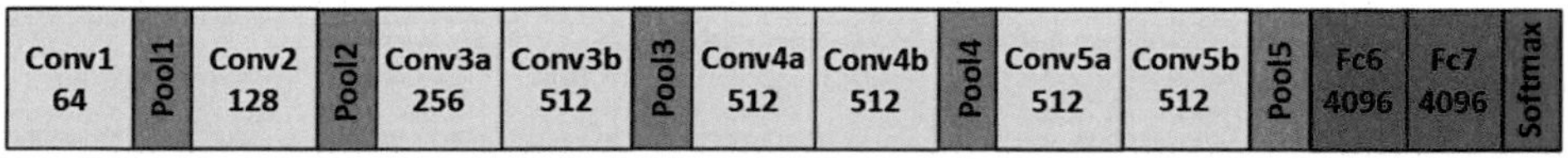

Conv1 64	Pool1	Conv2 128	Pool2	Conv3a 256	Conv3b 512	Pool3	Conv4a 512	Conv4b 512	Pool4	Conv5a 512	Conv5b 512	Pool5	Fc6 4096	Fc7 4096	Softmax

Figure 7.11: Architecture of the C3D network. The numbers designate the number of feature maps for convolutional layers, or the number of neurons for fully-connected layers.

59.02% accuracy on the test dataset of the EmotiW challenge for the recognition of the 7 emotions to classify (anger, disgust, sadness, happiness, surprise, fear and neutral). It greatly outperforms the proposed baseline method (40.47%) as well as the previous best solution submitted by the winner of the 2015 edition of the challenge (53.80%) [11], based on the detection of features related to facial AU.

	Anger	Disgust	Fear	Happiness	Neutral	Sadness	Surprise
Anger	74.70	0.00	4.82	3.61	13.25	1.20	2.41
Disgust	22.00	0.00	0.00	16.67	33.33	22.22	5.56
Fear	31.82	0.00	30.30	1.52	25.76	4.55	6.06
Happiness	8.15	0.00	0.74	74.81	13.33	2.22	0.74
Neutral	6.90	1.15	2.30	4.02	78.16	4.02	3.45
Sadness	22.54	0.00	8.45	4.23	23.35	35.21	4.23
Surprise	17.86	0.00	32.14	3.57	14.29	10.71	21.43

Figure 7.12: Confusion matrix of the CNN-LSTM/C3D/SVM hybrid model.

It can be noted by analysing the confusion matrix (see Figure 7.12, above) that the detection rate is not uniform among all emotions. Some emotions are detected easily (anger, happiness, and neutral), while others (disgust, fear, sadness, surprise) are often mistaken with each other or with the neutral emotion. Possible reasons for this phenomenon are the proximity of some emotions to each other (e.g., fear and surprise not being exclusive) or the possible unsuitability of the input modalities for the detection of a particular emotion (e.g., disgust not necessarily expressed on the face of the subject, often mistaken for neutral). Those experimental results act as a reminder of the importance of the definition of the emotions to recognise, and the choice of modalities to use.

7.3 Approaches Based on Physiological Data

The methods described in the previous section have shown a wide diversity in approaches to the emotion recognition problem, as well in classification performances obtained depending on the choice of emotions to recognise, modalities and classification models used. But all of them have in common the fact that they mainly rely on the video modality to obtain satisfying performances.

The acquisition of exploitable video data of the faces of the subjects is usually not an easy task though, or in some cases even impossible. In addition to the obstacles related to ethical issues and the intrusive nature of video-based sensors (e.g. agreement of the subject/system user usually necessary for the use of their images) also comes the technical problem of setting up cameras in a way they can capture images of the user's face at any moments. It can be noted that the same kind of privacy or technical related problems can occur concerning the collection of audio data. Furthermore, video modalities can have trouble to capture information regarding emotions involving a low amount of physical response (arousal), as most methods use them to capture movements on the subjects' faces.

For these reasons, an increasingly interest has recently been shown by a part of the research community in the topic of emotion recognition exclusively using physiological signals, also known as bio-signals. The latter, unlike other modalities, is fairly easy to acquire by using non-intrusive wearable sensors such as rings, wristbands or glasses. Physiological signals have been shown to be correlated to emotions in several previous research works. Some of them are listed here:

Electroencephalography (EEG) is the current reference method used to monitor the electrical activity of the brain. It is however commonly used to simply name the EEG signals instead. The latter are obtained by placing electrodes on the head of the subject which measure the voltage fluctuations caused by the activity of the brain. Previous studies have shown that EEG seems to be correlated with levels of arousal [10].

Electrodermal Activity (EDA) , also known as Skin Conductance or Galvanic Skin Response, designates the conductance of the skin, variations of which are caused by a change of state in the sweat glands of the skin. It can be noted that EDA signals usually have a typical shape, which features an alternance of two distinct phases:

a resting phase with the signals remaining relatively constant, and a very brief perturbation phase with some peaks observed in the level of EDA. The level of EDA during the resting phase is called Skin Conductance Level (SCL), while the peaks observed during the perturbation phase are referred to as Skin Conductance Response (SCR). EDA has been shown to increase linearly with the level of arousal of a subject [25].

Electrooculography (EOG) is the most relevant existing technique to measure the corneo-retinal standing potential between the front and the back of human eyes. EOG signals can be acquired by placing pairs of electrodes surrounding each eye in a top/bottom or left/right pattern. It is in particular used to track the movement of the eyes which cause variations of potential between the electrodes [3].

Electrocardiography (ECG) refers to the method of monitoring the electrical activity of the heart. ECG signals are obtained by placing electrodes on the subject's limbs and chest. They are indications showing that they correlate with emotions with negative valence [2].

Blood Volume Pulse (BVP) is the phasic change in blood volume that can be observed between each heartbeat. It is an indicator of the blood flow which can be used to calculate the HR, as well as inter-beat intervals [29].

It can be noted that due to the nature of the data provided by such sensors, the problem of emotion classification using physiological data only can be reformulated as a problem of 1D time signals classification (or regression if the valence/arousal model is used for the definition of emotions). From a pattern recognition point of view, the main difficulty of the problem lies in the choice of relevant features to extract from the input 1D time series for the emotion classification problem. From the manual crafting of simple features provided as inputs of a simple classification model (e.g., decision tree, SVM, etc.), to more elaborate solutions involving automatic feature crafting using DNN based approaches, the choice of the methodology to adopt remains pretty wide. The rest of this section will present several of those possible approaches through specific application examples of emotion recognition.

7.3.1 Stress Detection Using Hand-crafted Features

In this section, a simple method for a binary classification problem between stress and no-stress will be detailed to give a preview of how a very basic model can be built for a real-time emotion recognition problem using exclusively 1D physiological signals. It also shows an example of contribution in the field in terms of crafting manual features related to physiological signals.

Gouverneur et al. proposed in [47] a system for real-time stress detection, trained following a supervised learning approach, and relying on the use of the wristband Empatica E4 [1] to acquire data from the subject. The device used provides various behavioural and physiological signals such as EDA, Heart Rate, temperature and acceleration. The EDA and Heart Rate channels, sampled at a frequency of 4 Hz, were used in this study as they are the most relevant for the problem of stress detection. In order to enable the system to work in real-time, the common approach of a sliding time window of fixed length is employed. At all time steps, the sensor data comprised within the defined window is sent to the system to be processed. At the next time step, it then slides to include the newly acquired data points, and the process is repeated. In this project, the size of the time window is fixed to 8 seconds (i.e., 32 data points for each sensor channel with the adopted sampling frequency).

The acquisition of data to train a classification system is a paramount step of a supervised learning approach, but can turn out to be difficult when it comes to getting emotion-related data. Gouverneur et al. [47] followed an experimental setup consisting of four different stress-inducing experiments, each lasting for around 4 minutes and separated by 4-minute resting phases:

1. A simple stress induction test consisting of putting the subject's hand in icy water.

2. A phase where the subject is asked to perform some calculations consisting of subtracting a 2-digit number from a 4-digit number as quickly as possible.

3. A Troop test, where the subject is asked to give the correct colour of coloured words spelling the name of a different colour (e.g., when seeing the word "green" written in red, the correct answer to give is red) as quickly as possible.

194

4. A Trier social stress test (TSST), where the subject is asked to prepare a presentation in a limited amount of time, and then present it in front of a jury trained to show only neutral facial expression. In order to increase the level of stress, the interview is also filmed.

The data acquired during the resting phases and the experiments are respectively labelled as no-stress and stress from 5 different subjects. The original sensor records are then split into sequences of 60 seconds to obtain the different examples of the set. Data related to one subject was used to train the model, with the four others providing data for the testing set.

The Empatica E4 acquires EDA data via a pair of electrodes, whose contact with the skin can be shortly lost at some points, depending on the movements of the user. Those moments can be seen in the resulting data by the presence of some artefacts, taking the form of peaks of very high amplitude (see Figure 7.13). In order to remove them, a simple pre-processing step is applied, consisting of detecting points where the difference between its value and the one of its successor is above a pre-defined threshold. When such a point is detected, the next 20 values are removed, and a linear interpolation is used to fill the missing values.

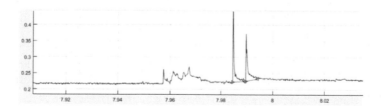

Figure 7.13: EDA signal (in red) and outlier values (in blue).

Several hand-crafted features are then computed on each of the 8-second time windows of pre-processed EDA and Heart Rate data. These are for the EDA signals: mean, standard deviation, variance, maximum value, mean amplitude, number of SCR peaks, mean rise time as well as the first 100 coefficients of the Fourier transform. For the Heart Rate signals features like the mean, standard deviation, variance, and maximum value were computed.

To extract the number of SRC peaks and mean rise times, additional computational steps are required. Information about SCL and SCR is obtained by computing tonic and phasic signals from the original EDA records. The tonic signal is obtained by computing the mean of the time window at each time step, and then subtracting it from the original record. The phasic signal is computed by subtracting the tonic signal from the original record (see Figure 7.14).

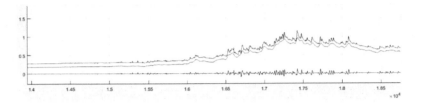

Figure 7.14: Original, tonic and phasic EDA signals (in red, yellow and purple respectively). The tonic signal is shifted downwards for more clarity.

Every SCR peak can be characterised by an onset (starting point), a top (peak) and an offset (ending point) (see Figure 7.15). Those three different points are identified by applying the following operations:

- An onset is detected if the value of the phasic signal at that point is non-negative, and the difference between it and the next one is greater than a predefined threshold.

- An offset is determined if the value of the phasic signal becomes negative again after an onset was detected.

- The peak is taken to be the maximum value between an onset and an offset.

Every pair of onset/offset detected in the time window raises the peak count by 1. The mean rise time is the average of all rise times in the window, computed by checking the time between the onset and the peak.

The different features defined previously are then used to train several classification models: naive Bayes, Decision Tree and Random Forests, SVM. Random Forests return the best stress classification results with an accuracy of 71% (67% for SVM, 63% for a single Decision Tree and 62% for an approach using naive Bayes).

7.3.2   Codebook Approach for Feature Generation

The previous section describes a very classical approach of supervised learning, relying on the definition of some hand-crafted features related to 1D

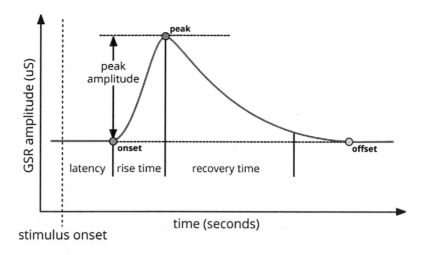

Figure 7.15: Onset, peak and offset of an EDA record.

physiological time signals which would be relevant for the classification problem. However, although this methodology has proven to be fairly effective, it also has its limitations.

Most of the time, the features chosen to be fed as inputs of the classification model are either very simple statistical values (e.g. mean, standard deviation, etc.) which compress the information contained in the original input data, or features which have a physical meaning from a human point of view (e.g., number of peaks in the EDA signal). In both cases it can be difficult to pick a set of features which would not lose too much information from the original signal, either because of the compression of the information, or because of the application of potentially non-accurate methods for the extraction of the more complex descriptors. In addition to this difficulty, there is no guarantee that the chosen set of features would give the best classification results compared to other possible features. This is especially the case in the context of physiological signal processing for emotion recognition, where the structure of the data is still fairly unknown and complex, and where no state-of-the-art hand-crafted features have been established as a standard yet (unlike in the image processing field, with LGBP-TOP for instance).

For these reasons, increasing interest in semi-automated and unsupervised feature crafting methods has been observed in the past years. Contrary to the manual hand-crafting of features, those approaches have the advantage of being able to find relevant descriptors which are neither obvious nor easy to interpret from a human point of view, and which would not have been found otherwise.

An example of a semi-supervised feature crafting method is provided by the codebook approach explained previously in Chapter 5.1.2. It can also extract patterns from 1D physiological signals relevant to the emotion recognition problem. The added value of this method (compared to the manual one) lies in the automatic selection of the patterns, the codewords in that case, to perform recognition in 1D time series, which is performed once the hyper-parameters (number of clusters, window size and sliding window step) are set. Making this task semi-automatic also allows the use of a much higher number of codewords than for manually defined ones.

In [33], an implementation of this codebook approach to generate features for an emotion recognition problem using physiological signals is proposed. The experiments were carried out on the dataset presented by Picard et al. in [50], which contains EDA, ECG, BVP and Respiration (i.e., measure of the chest cavity expansion generated by inhalation and exhalation) labelled data of 8 different emotions: anger, hate, grief, platonic love, romantic love, joy, reverence and neutral. The main steps of the approach published in [33] are depicted in Figure 7.16.

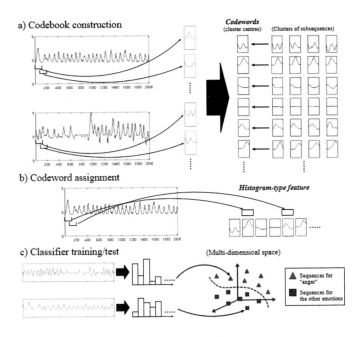

Figure 7.16: Codebook approach applied to physiological 1D signals for emotion classification.

A different codebook is generated on the 160 sequences of the dataset related to each sensor channel, for all four of them (EDA, ECG, BVP, Respiration). The normalised histograms generated from those four codebooks are then concatenated and fed as inputs of an SVM classifier. The adopted performance measure is the average accuracy obtained after one leave-one-out cross-validation consisting of 159 sequences for the training phase, and the remaining sequences for the testing phase. A grid-search is used to find the best values of the window size and number of codewords, while the sliding step of the window is set to a fixed value. In particular, 512 codewords are defined for each sensor modality, for a total of $4 \times 512 = 2048$ different patterns to recognise; a task which would have been very difficult to perform manually. The method obtains an average accuracy of 54.3%, and outperforms the method relying on the use of simple statistical hand-crafted features proposed in [50] (38.5% accuracy).

7.3.3 Deep Neural Networks for Feature Generation

Considering the good performances shown by semi-automatically crafted features compared to human-made ones, it could be interesting to go even further in the process of automatic generation of features. One type of model which is particularly suitable for this task are the Artificial Neural Networks (ANN), and especially deep variations of them (Deep Neural Networks, or DNN, which simply refer to ANN with at least more than 2 hidden layers).

ANN are increasingly popular pattern recognition models used for classification or regression tasks. They consist of networks of units, called neurons, which perform non-linear operations on their inputs. Each neuron is characterised by n inputs $(i_1, i_2, \ldots, i_n)$, n weights $(w_1, w_2, \ldots, w_n)$ each one being associated to one input, a non-linear function σ called activation function, and an additional parameter b called bias. One neuron performs a weighted summation of its inputs $S = \sum_{k=1}^{n} w_k \times i_k$. The result is then added to the bias, and fed as input of the activation function to output a value $o = \sigma(S + b)$ (see Figure 7.17). Artificial neurons are then organised in layers, with the outputs of the neurons in one layer being used as inputs of those of the next layer. The first, intermediate and last layers of an ANN are respectively called input, hidden and output layers. The training of an ANN consists of determining the best weights and biases of its neurons for a given classification or regression problem. It is usually performed by defining a loss function computing the error between the prediction of the network and the expected result. A gradient descent is then performed, using the backpropagation algorithm [30], to minimise this loss function by computing the derivative of the error with respect to each parameter, and updating the latter proportionally to the quantity obtained.

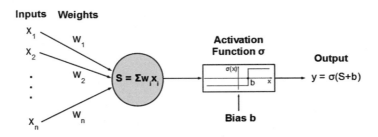

Figure 7.17: Artificial neuron.

Many different variations in ANN have been found and developed for the past years, all giving state-of-the-art results in many various domains such as object recognition in images and videos, automatic image captioning, speech processing. Here is a short description of the most popular ANN models:

Multi-Layer-Perceptron (MLP), named after the works of Rosenblatt who was the first to propose the mathematical model of artificial neurons [51]), is used to designate the simplest architecture of an ANN, with one input, one or several hidden and one output layer (see Figure 7.18).

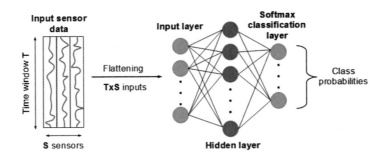

Figure 7.18: A Multi-Layer Perceptron for the processing of 1D time signals.

Convolutional Neural Networks (CNN) (see Figure 7.19) are a variation of ANN models created by LeCun in the late 80s [59]. CNN feature specific layers are called convolutional layers. In those layers, each neuron computes a convolutional product on a small part of the input image, delimited by a sliding window. The latter is then shifted over the whole image so the neuron can process it in its totality, and output a convoluted image called feature map. Convolutional layers are also often combined to pooling layers, which contain specific neurons whose role is to downsample the data fed as their input. CNN became extremely popular after Hinton et al. achieved an impressive improvement of nearly 11% accuracy compared to previous methods in the 2012 edition of the ImageNet Large-Scale Visual Recognition Challenge [9].

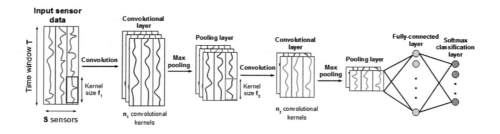

Figure 7.19: An example of Convolutional Neural Network with two pairs of convolutional and pooling layers for the processing of 1D time signals.

Recurrent Neural Networks (RNN) (see Figure 7.20) are ANN specifically designed to process data with time dependencies (e.g., successive frames of a video, time series, etc.). The neurons of this model can take their own output at time t as inputs at time $t + 1$. RNN have in particular proven to give state-of-the-art results in the field of speech recognition [7]. Variations of traditional RNN like Long-Short-Term-Memory networks (LSTM networks) are described in [21].

Autoencoders (see Figure 7.21) proposed by Hinton [26] are regular ANN similar to MLP with the specific restriction to have the same number of input and output neurons. They are trained to reproduce any input data they receive on their output layer, which is performed with a regular backpropagation using a suitable loss function. The

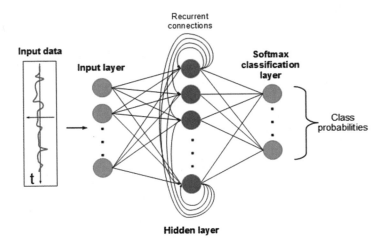

Figure 7.20: Recurrent Neural Network for 1D time signals processing.

main interest of autoencoders is that they can extract some features from any input data in a completely unsupervised way, without the need of any labelled data.

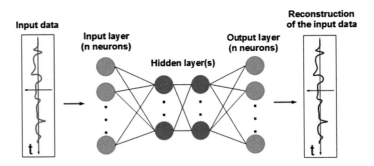

Figure 7.21: Autoencoder for the reconstruction of a 1D input signal.

Extensive analyses of those models were initiated in the field of image processing with CNN by LeCun Bengio and Hinton ([60], [58]) and Zeiler and Fergus [40], who showed that each neuron of the different hidden layer of an ANN acts as a specific feature extractor on the data given as its input (e.g., horizontal or vertical patterns in images). The first hidden layer can therefore be seen as a low-level descriptor extractor from the input data, while the deeper hidden layers compute higher-level features from those low-level descriptors.

However, the number of studies related to deep learning exclusively carried out on physiological signals remains small, mainly because of the scarcity of datasets featuring 1D bio-signals with emotional labels. Some CNN approaches adapted to 1D-signal processing have been tried though, like in the study from Bengio et al. [31] where EDA and BVP related features extracted by a CNN have shown to provide better results than hand-crafted descriptors for the classification of four emotions (relaxation, anxiety, fun, excitement) featured in the Mazeball dataset [27].

One possible solution to this obstacle related to the lack of 1D physiological data consists of using techniques belonging to the theory of transfer learning [53]. Transfer learning designates an ensemble of techniques whose aim is to transfer the knowledge acquired from a source domain to a target domain. In the case of ANN, it can be used to learn a specific feature representation on one dataset, and use this learned representation (i.e. learned weights and biases of the ANN) to make the training of the model easier on another dataset (transfer of parameters). Some theoretical works showed namely that the initialisation of the weights and biases of an ANN is a factor with a major impact on how well the training phase can unfold, as it can determine whether the optimisation process is stuck in non-optimal local minima or not [15]. However, it should be noted that if those transfer learning approaches have already been used several times for ANN trained to process image data (and in particular on DNN trained for object recognition on the ImageNet dataset [32] like the inception model developed by Google [13]), their use on 1D physiological data remains anectodic. In the future, the emergence of larger datasets featuring 1D bio-signals will hopefully help to bridge this gap.

7.4 Conclusion and Future Trends

In this chapter, the current state of the research in the field of emotion recognition is summarised. While the automatic recognition of emotions appears to be a task with promising outlets related to the design of human interactive systems, or to applications of medical data understanding, it is also not well understood and not very much explored, mainly because of the still relevant problem of defining emotions rigorously in a scientific way. Because of this uncertainty, no consensus has been found among the research community to define a common framework (which would set a dataset, the modalities to use or emotions to recognise) to make the comparison of the different studies carried out on this subject easier.

In spite of this obstacle, several attempts to define this framework have been made, and appeared under the form of challenges for emotion recognition. The different winning solutions of those challenges have confirmed the efficiency of several state-of-the-art descriptors or classification approaches for the recognition of emotions, mainly related to image and video modalities, such as the LGBP-TOP descriptor.

Even if images of facial expressions of the subjects have proven to be one of the most effective modalities for the detection of emotions, their acquisition is not always easy to set up in real life, because of ethical and technical issues. For those reasons, an increasing interest in approaches using non-intrusive sensor modalities to acquire data (e.g. wristband, glasses, rings, etc.) has been observed over the past years, in the wake of several studies which showed that some emotions and physiological signals are correlated. In particular, many traditional supervised learning approaches relying on the manual crafting of 1D time signal features to use as inputs of a classification model have been investigated. But the lack of understanding of the overall structure of the 1D emotional data, coupled with the absence of state-of-the-art features for this kind of modality have shifted the interest of the research community towards semi-automatic or automatic methods for feature crafting.

ANN are a family of methods for classification which is particularly suitable for this task of automatic extraction of features and patterns from any kind of input data. But the need for large datasets to train ANN properly, as well as the scarcity of 1D physiological data with emotional labels are an obstacle. The application of transfer learning methods to transfer the knowledge learned from one dataset to another one could be a solution to improve the results obtained by ANN for emotion recognition, and help to generalise the use of ANN to solve this problem using 1D time bio-signals exclusively.

References

[1] E4 wristband: https://www.empatica.com/e4-wristband. June 2016.

[2] P. Schaich J. Williams] A. Haag, S. Goronzy. Emotion recognition using bio-sensors: First step towards an automatic system. *Affective Dialogue Systems: Tutorial and Research Workshop*, 2004.

[3] H. Gellersen A. Bulling, J. A. Ward. Eye movement analysis for activity recognition using electrooculography. In *IEEE Transactions on Pattern Recognition*, 2011.

[4] J. Joshi J. Hoey T. Gedeon A. Dhall, R. Goecke. Emotiw 2016: Video and group-level emotion recognition challenges. 2016.

[5] S. Lucey T. Gedeon A. Dhall, R. Goecke. Collecting large, richly annotated facial-expression databases from movies. In *IEEE Multimedia*, 2012.

[6] V. Digalakis A. Georgogiannis. Speech emotion recognition using nonlinear teager energy based features in noisy environments. In *Proceedings of the 20th European Signal Processing Conference (EUSIPCO)*, pages 2045–2049, 2012.

[7] G. Hinton A. Graves, A. Mohamed. Speech recognition with deep recurrent neural networks. In Speech and Signal Processing, editors, *International Conference on Acoustics*, 2013.

[8] S. Shetty L. Leung R. Sukthankar L. Fei-Fei A. Karpathy, G. Toderici. Large-scale video classification with convolutional neural networks. In *Computer Vision and Pattern Recognition*, 2014.

[9] G. Hinton A. Krizhevsky, I. Sutskever. Imagenet classification with deep convolutional neural networks. In *Neural Information Processing Systems*, 2012.

[10] G. Channel J. C. Mota L. H. Viet-B. Sankur L. Akarun A. Caplier M. Rombaut A. Savran, K. Ciftci. Emotion detection in the loop from brain signals and facial images. In *Proceedings of ENTERFACE*, 2006.

[11] N. Ma Y. Chen A. Yao, J. Shao. Capturing au-aware facial features and their latent relations for emotion recognition in the wild. In *ACM International Conference on Multimodal Interaction*, 2015.

[12] A. Batliner J. Hirschberg J. K. Burgoon A. Baird A. Elkins Y. Zhang E. Coutinho K. Evanin B. Schuller, S. Steidl. The interspeech 2016 computational paralinguistics challenge: Deception, sincerity & native language. 2016.

[13] V. Vanhoucke A. Alemi C. Szegedy, S. Ioffe. Inception-v4, inception-resnet and the impact of residual connections on learning. In *Computer Vision and Pattern Recognition*, Feb. 2016.

[14] J. M. Talarico D. C. Rubin. A comparison of dimensional models of emotion: Evidence from emotions, prototypical events, autobiographical memories, and words. *Memory*, 17(8):802–808, Nov. 2009.

[15] B. Widrow D. Nguyen. Improving the learning speed of 2-layer neural networks by choosing initial values of the adaptive weights. *Neural Networks*, June 1990.

[16] G. Boulianne L. Burget O. Glembek N. Goel M. Hannemann P. Motlicek Y. Qian P. Schwartz J Silovsky G Stemmer K Vesely D. Powey, A. Ghoshal. The kaldi speech recognition toolkit. In *IEEE Workshop on Automatic Speech Recognition and Understanding*, 2011.

[17] A. Tellegen D. Watson. Toward a consensual structure of mood. *Psychological bulletin*, (1985).

[18] P. Ekman. An argument for basic emotions. *Cognition and Emotions*, 6:169–200, 1992.

[19] P. Ekman. Facial expression and emotion. *American Psychologist*, 1993.

[20] P. Ekman. Facial expressions. *Handbook of Cognition and Emotion*, pages 301–320, 1999.

[21] F. Cummins F. A. Gers, J. Schmidhuber. Learning to forget: Continual prediction with lstm. *Neural Computation*, 12(10):2451–2471, Oct. 2000.

[22] B. Schuller F. Eyben, M. Wllmer. Opensmile: the munich versatile and fast open-source audio feature extracto. In *18th ACM International Conference on Multimedia*, pages 1459–1462, Oct. 2010.

[23] J. Sauer D. Lalanne F. Ringeval, A. Sonderegger. Introducing the recola multimodal corpus of remote collaborative and affective interactions. In *Proceedings of EmoSPACE*, 2013.

[24] L. Farde. Quantitative analysis of d2 dopamine receptor binding in the human brain by pet. *Science*, 1986.

[25] T. Pun G. Chanel, K. Ansari-Asl. Valence-arousal evaluation using physiological signals in an emotion recall paradigm. In *Proceedings of the IEEE International Conference on Systems, Man and Cybernetics*, Oct. 2007.

[26] R. R. Salakhutdinov G. Hinton. Reducing the dimensionality of data with neural networks. *Science*, 313:504–507, Jul. 2006.

[27] A. Jhala G. N. Yannakakis, H. P. Martnez. Towards affective camera control in games. *User Modeling and User-Adapted Interaction*, 20(4):313–340, 2010.

[28] T. Berg E. Learned-Miller G.B. Huang, M. Ramesh. Labelled faces in the wild: a database for studying face recognition in unconstrained environments. In *Technical Report 07-49 of University of Massachusetts*, 2007.

[29] M. Pantic H. Gunes. Automatic, dimensional and continuous emotion recognition. *International Journal of Synthetic Emotions*, 1, 2010.

[30] S. Haykin H. Leung. The complex backpropagation algorithm. *IEEE Transactions on Signal Processing*, 39, Sept. 1991.

[31] G. N. Yannakakis H. P. Martinez, Y. Bengio. Learning deep physiological models of affect. *IEEE Computational Intelligence Magazine*, 20(4):20–33, 2010.

[32] R. Socher L. Li-K. Li F-F. Li J. Deng, W. Dong. Imagenet: a large-scale hierarchical image database. In *Computer Vision and Pattern Recognition*, June 2009.

[33] M. Grzegorzek K. Shirahama. Emotion recognition based on physiological sensor sata using codebook approach. In *Information Technologies in Medicine*, pages 27–36, 2016.

[34] M. Nasir B. M. Both S. Lee-S. S. Narayanan K. Somandepalli, R. Gupta. Online affect tracking with multimodal kalman filters. In *Proceedings of the 6th International Workshop on Audio/Visual Emotion Challenge*, Oct. 2016.

[35] J. F. Kaiser. On a simple algorithm to calculate the energy of a signal. *Acoustics, Speech and Signal Processing*, 1:381–384, 1990.

[36] D. E. King. Dlib-ml: a machine learning toolkit. *Journal of Machine Learning Research*, 10:1755–1758, 2009.

[37] Z. Yimin L. Jianguo, W. Tao. Iccv: Face detection using surf cascade. In *Computer Vision Workshop*, 2015.

[38] I. Maoz L. Wolf, T. Hassner. Face recognition in unconstrained videos with matched background similarity. In *Computer Vision and Pattern Recogntion*, 2011.

[39] H. Lövheim. A new three-dimensional model for emotions and monoanime neurotransmitters. *Med Hypothesis*, 78:341–348.

[40] R. Fergus M. D. Zeiler. Visualizing and understanding convolutional networks. In *Computer Vision and Pattern Recognition*, Nov. 2013.

[41] J. M. Girard G. McKneown M. Mehu L. Yin M Pantic J. F. Cohn M. F. Valstar, T. Almaev. Fera 2015 second facial expression recognition and analysis challenge. 2015.

[42] M. Pantic M. F. Valstar. Induced disgust, happiness and surprise: an addition to the mmi facial expression database. In *Proceedings of the International Conference of Language Resources and Evaluations*, pages 65–70, 2010.

[43] B. Schuller F. Ringeval D. Lalanne M. T. Torres S. Scherer G. Stratou R. Cowie M. Pantic M. Valstar, J. Gratch. Avec 2016 depression, mood and emotion recognition workshop and challenge. 2016.

[44] A. Mehrabian. Pleasure-arousal-dominance: a general framework for describing and measuring individual differences in temperament. *Current Psychology*, 33:405–421, 1980.

[45] A. Zisserman O. M. Parkhi, A. Vedaldi. Deep face recognition. In , *British Machine Vision Conference*, 2015.

[46] W. V. Friesen P. Ekman. The facial action coding system: a technique for the measurement of facial movement. *Consulting Psychologists Press*, 1978.

[47] L. Kping K. Shirahama P. Kleczek M. Grzergozek P. Gouverneur, J. Jaworek-Korjakowska. Classification of physiological data for emotion recognition. 2016.

[48] I. J. Goodfellow M. Mirza Y Bengio P. L. Carrier, A. Courville. Fer-2013 face database. In *Technical Report 1365 of University of Montreal*, 2013.

[49] R. Plutchik. The nature of emotions. *American Scientist*, 89:334, 2001.

[50] J. Healey R. W. Picard, E. Vyzas. Toward machine emotional intelligence: Analysis of affective physiological state. *IEEE Transaction on Pattern Analysis and Machine Intelligence*, 23:1175–1191, 2001.

[51] F. Rosenblatt. The perceptron: a probabilistic model for information storage and organization in the brain. *Psychological Review*, 65(6), 1958.

[52] J. Russel. A circumplex model of affect. *Journal of Personality and Social Psychology*, 39(6):1161–1178, 1980.

[53] Q. Yang S. J. Pan. A survey on transfer learning. *IEEE Transactions on Knowledge and data Engineering*, 22(10), Oct. 2010.

[54] L. I. Steins S. A. Cermak S. S. Narayanan T. Chaspari, A. Tsiartas. Sparse representation of electrodermal activity with knowledge-driven dictionaries. *IEEE Transactions on Biomedical Engineering*, 62(3):960–971, 2015.

[55] Y. Tian T. Kanade, J. F. Cohn. Comprehensive database for facial expression analysis. *Automatic Face and Gesture Recognition*, pages 46–53, 2000.

[56] M. F. Valstar T. T. Almaev. Local gabor binary patterns from three orthogonal planes for automatic facial expression recognition. In *Proceedings of the 2013 Humaine Association Conference on Affective Computing and Intelligent Interaction*, pages 356–361, Sept. 2011.

[57] D. Li Y. Liu Y. Fan, X. Lu. Video-based emotion recognition using cnn-rnn and c3d hybrid networks. In *ACM International Conference on Multimodal Interaction*, 2016.

[58] G. Hinton Y. LeCun, Y. Bengio. Deep learning. *Nature*, 521:436–444, May 2015.

[59] J. S. Denker D. Henderson R. E. Howard W. Hubbard L. D. Jackel Y. LeCun, B. Boser. Backpropagation applied to handwritten zip code recognition. *Neural Computation*, 1:541–551, 1989.

[60] Y. Bengio Y. LeCun. Convolutional networks for images, speech and time-series. *The Handbook of Brain Theory and Neural Networks*, 1995.

Part IV

Conclusion

Chapter 8

Summary and Future Vision

In this book, an overview of the most relevant scientific areas the author contributed to over the last three years is given. It shows the author's scientific evolution from topics related to the analysis of visual data towards aspects connected to algorithms dealing with data recorded by sensors integrated in devices worn by humans (wearables). The methodological basis in both cases usually remains the same. The structure of this book is explained by Figure 1.4 in Section 1.4.

This chapter starts with a summary of algorithms presented in Part II (Visual Scene Analysis, Section 8.1) and Part III (Human Data Interpretation, Section 8.2). Finally, the book closes with interdisciplinary considerations and future visions towards data-driven society in Section 8.3.

8.1   Visual Scene Analysis

In Part II selected aspects of Visual Scene Analysis (Large-Scale Multimedia Retrieval in Chapter 2, Shape-Based Object Recognition in Chapter 3, and Moving Object Analysis for Video Interpretation in Chapter 4) including the author's contributions to the field are presented. They are summarised in the following paragraphs.

Large-Scale Multimedia Retrieval (LSMR)   is the task where a large amount of multimedia data (e.g., image, video and audio) are analysed to efficiently find the ones relevant to a user-provided query. As described in many publications [16, 18, 20, 21], the most challenging issue is how to bridge the semantic gap which is the lack of coincidence between raw data

213

(i.e., pixel values or audio sample values) and semantic meanings that humans perceive from those data. In Chapter 2, a survey of traditional and state-of-the-art LSMR methods by mainly focusing on concept detection and event retrieval processes is given. Regarding the former, thanks to the preparation of large-scale datasets like ImageNet [7, 14] and the development of deep learning approaches (see Section 2.2.2), many concepts can be detected with acceptable accuracies. One open issue for concept detection is how to successfully extend deep learning approaches that have been successful for the image (i.e., spatial) domain to the video (i.e., temporal) domain. Although several methods use 3D convolutional neural networks [22] or Long Short Term Memory (LSTM) [19], there is still a significant room for improvement. Compared to concept detection, event retrieval needs much more research attention for both, the performance improvement and the method innovation.

Shape-Based Object Recognition: In Chapter 3, approaches for shape representation and matching, including original contributions, are described. With regard to shape representation, two shape descriptors are introduced in Section 3.2. The first one captures coarse-grained shape features with low computational complexity so that it can be fused with some rich descriptors [1, 2] to improve its description power. The second one models fine-grained shape properties. For shape matching, the algorithms are designed based on the type and structure of shape descriptors they use. Specifically, for the coarse-grained descriptor, shape matching is applied by calculating the distances between shape feature vectors. In order to improve the matching accuracy and flexibility of the coarse-grained descriptor, a supervised optimisation strategy is applied to control the discrimination power of each dimension in the feature space. For the fine-grained descriptor, shape matching is more complex since it contains rich feature structures. In addition to the inherent matching strategy, i.e., one-to-one interesting point matching, the idea of high-order graph matching is also considered to improve the matching accuracy of interesting points. For this, several potential functions are specifically designed. The experiments in Section 3.4 show the impressive robustness of the proposed methods in an object retrieval scenario.

Moving Object Analysis for Video Interpretation: Extracting and analysing object trajectories from videos is a basic problem in computer vision and has important applications in event understanding, robot localisation, video surveillance, etc. 2D and 3D trajectories of objects represent high-level semantic features, which can be used to automatically understand object activities in different kinds of videos [3]. In Chapter 4, selected methods for video interpretation based on the analysis of moving objects are described. Section 4.1 summarises an own method for unknown object tracking in output images from 360-degree cameras called Modified Training-Learning-Detection (MTLD) [5, 6]. It is based on the recently introduced Training-Learning- Detection (TLD) algorithm [9]. Unlike TLD, MTLD is capable of detecting the unknown objects of interest in 360-degree images. In Section 4.2, an own methodology that extracts 3D trajectories of objects from 2D videos, captured from a monocular moving camera, is summarised [3, 4]. Compared to existing methods that rely on restrictive assumptions, the described algorithm can extract 3D trajectories with much less restriction by adopting new example-based techniques which compensate the lack of information. Here, the focal length of the camera based on similar candidates is estimated and used to compute depths of detected objects. Contrary to other 3D trajectory extraction techniques, the author's own method is able to process video data taken from a stable camera as well as a non-calibrated moving camera without restrictions. For this, the Reversible Jump Markov Chain Monte Carlo (RJ-MCMC) particle filtering has been modified to be more suitable for camera odometry without relying on geometrical feature points. Finally, conclusions are drawn and further possible research directions are mentioned in Section 4.3.

8.2   Human Data Interpretation

In Part III selected aspects of Human Data Interpretation (Physical Activity Recognition in Chapter 5, Cognitive Activity Recognition in Chapter 6, and Emotion Recognition in Chapter 7) including the author's contributions to the field are presented. They are summarised in the following paragraphs.

Physical Activity Recognition: Chapter 5 starts with the description of an algorithm for atomic activity recognition in Section 5.1. It is based on the so called codebook approach adopted to deal with time series. It automatically classifies data recorded by sensors (e.g., accelerometer) embedded in wearables (smartglasses, smartwatch, smartphone) in real-time. The current version of the methodology deals with the recognition of the so called atomic activities. These are fine-grained movements of the human body (e.g., stretching hand, sitting down, standing up, etc.). The effectiveness of the approach has been validated on a real-world dataset consisting of eight types of sensor data obtained from a smartphone, smartwatch and smartglasses. Subsequently, an own gait recognition method is described in Section 5.2. It exploits the spatiotemporal motion characteristics of an individual without the need of silhouette extraction and other related features. It computes a set of spatiotemporal features from the gait video sequences and uses them to generate a codebook. Fisher vector is used to encode the motion descriptors which are classified using linear Support Vector Machine (SVM). The performance of the proposed algorithm has been evaluated on five widely used datasets, including indoor (CMU-MoBo, NLPR, CASIA-C) and outdoor (CASIA-B, TUM GAID) gait databases. It achieved excellent results on all databases and outperformed the related state-of-the-art algorithms. Finally, conclusions are drawn and further possible research directions are mentioned in Section 5.3.

Cognitive Activity Recognition: Chapter 6 discusses the state-of-the-art approaches and presents the author's scientific contribution to the area of cognitive activity recognition. Section 6.1 gives the definition of cognition, and discusses cognitive activity relation to health especially in context of human ageing. As the brain activity is the crucial source of information about cognitive abilities of a person, Section 6.2 provides information on appropriate sensors. Section 6.3 presents an overview of the renowned methods and approaches utilising a variety of sensor data in order to properly recognise cognitive activities. An original electrooculography-based method for cognitive activity recognition [11] based on the codebook approach used also for physical activity recognition (see Chapter 5) is explained in Section 6.4. The experimental results show that the codebook approach can be successfully utilised for the cognitive activity recognition task. Applied to EOG and accelerometer data, the proposed method achieved high accuracy results, predicting proper activity classes in 99.3% of cases without using prior knowledge or heuristics. Further, Section 6.5 shows the possible application of the presented method and validates the obtained results, while in Section 6.6 the final conclusions and future plans are drawn.

Emotion Recognition: While the automatic recognition of emotions appears to be a task with promising outlets related to the design of human interactive systems, or to applications of medical data understanding, it is also not well understood and not that much explored, mainly because of the still relevant problem of defining emotions rigorously in a scientific way. Because of this uncertainty, no consensus has been found among the research community to define a common framework (which would set a dataset, the modalities to use or emotions to recognise) to make the comparison of the different studies carried out on this subject easier. Chapter 7 overviews state-of-the-art approaches and summarises the author's scientific contribution to the area of automated human emotion recognition. Section 7.1 describes fundamental concepts of emotion recognition including main emotion models, requirements for sensor selection as well as most related contests organised in this field (e.g., The Audio/Visual Emotion Challenge and Workshop[1]) providing ground truth datasets and frameworks for quantitative performance comparison. Section 7.2 surveys existing emotion recognition approaches that use multimodal data (e.g., video, audio, physiological). Finally, Section 7.3 closes the chapter by explaining several methods for emotion recognition that are based exclusively on human's physiological data.

8.3   Data-Driven Society

The rapid development in the area of sensor technology has been responsible for a number of societal phenomena. For instance, the increased availability of imaging sensors integrated into digital video cameras has significantly stimulated the UGC (User Generated Content) movement beginning from 2005[2]. Another example is the groundbreaking innovation in wearable technology leading to a societal phenomenon called Quantified Self (QS), a community of people who use the capabilities of technical devices to gain a profound understanding of collected self-related data.

Machine learning algorithms benefit a lot from the availability of such huge volumes of digital data. For example, new technical solutions for challenges caused by the demographic change (ageing society) can be proposed in this way (see Figure 1.1), especially in the context of healthcare systems in industrialised countries (see Figure 1.3). Humans exist in a continuous feedback loop with the technology (example in Figure 1.2). The decision making process is often supported or even fully taken over

---

[1]http://sspnet.eu/avec2016
[2]A video-sharing platform www.youtube.com got launched in February 2005.

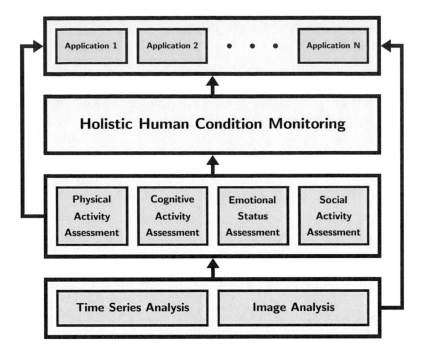

Figure 8.1: Holistic human condition monitoring using algorithms for time series and image analysis.

by machine learning algorithms. We live in a data-driven society and significantly contribute to this concept by voluntarily generating terabytes of data everyday. This societal transformation cannot be stopped anymore. Our objective should be to gain as much benefit as possible from this movement by limiting possible risks connected to it.

The author's vision in this area is to develop and investigate a generic platform for holistic human condition monitoring (see Figure 8.1). Based on the data delivered by sensors integrated in wearables (time series) and, if available, also images, the algorithms will continuously analyse humans' physical, cognitive, emotional and social states/activities. Integrated into a single module for holistic human condition monitoring, the software platform will perform long-term analysis of human data on a very large scale. Intelligent algorithms will automatically detect "interesting events" in these data. Both, real-time data analysis as well as cumulative assessments will be possible with the platform. The conceptualisation and development of these machine learning algorithms for the recognition of patterns in humans' physiological and behavioural data will happen on different levels of abstraction between the methodology and application. The codebook approach adopted to the time series analysis in [10, 11, 15, 17] will be an appropriate starting point for this. Later, still on the application agnostic level, new transfer learning strategies will be proposed. Transfer learning is necessary in such supervised pattern recognition settings, where collecting labelled training data for some of the considered classes is impossible. Such situations occur quite often in this context, since collecting physiological and behavioural data corresponding to certain extreme physical, cognitive, mental, and emotional states is ethically unacceptable or even practically impossible. Once the transfer learning strategy has been developed, instantiations of the generic pattern recognition framework for holistic human condition monitoring will be generated. Instantiations of the platform will realise different useful applications. The use cases addressed in the projects **Cognitive Village** [13] (see Section 1.2) as well as **My-AHA** [12] and **SenseVojta** [8] (see Section 1.3) are great examples for this.

References

[1] X. Bai and L.J. Latecki. Path similarity skeleton graph matching. *IEEE Transactions on Pattern Analysis and Machine Intelligence*, 30(7):1282–1292, 2008.

[2] S. Belongie, J. Malik, and J. Puzicha. Shape matching and object recognition using shape contexts. *PAMI*, 24(4):509–522, 2002.

[3] Z. Boukhers, K. Shirahama, and M. Grzegorzek. Example-based 3D Trajectory Extraction of Objects from 2D Videos. *IEEE Transactions on Circuits and Systems for Video Technology*, 2017.

[4] Z. Boukhers, K. Shirahama, F. Li, and M. Grzegorzek. Extracting 3D Trajectories of Objects from 2D Videos Using Particle Filter. In *International Conference on Multimedia Retrieval*, Shanghai, China, June 2015.

[5] Ahmad Delforouzi, Seyed Amir Hossein Tabatabaei, Kimiaki Shirahama, and Marcin Grzegorzek. Polar object tracking in 360-degree camera images. In *International Symposium on Multimedia*, pages 347–352. IEEE, 2016.

[6] Ahmad Delforouzi, Seyed Amir Hossein Tabatabaei, Kimiaki Shirahama, and Marcin Grzegorzek. Unknown object tracking in 360-degree camera images. In *23rd International Conference on Pattern Recognition*, pages 1799–1804. IEEE, 2016.

[7] J. Deng, W. Dong, R. Socher, L.-J. Li, K. Li, and F.-F. Li. ImageNet: A large-scale hierarchical image database. In *Proceedings of the 2009 IEEE Conference on Computer Vision and Pattern Recognition (CVPR 2009)*, pages 248–255, Washington, DC, USA, June 2009. IEEE Computer Society.

[8] Principal Investigator. *SenseVojta: Sensor-based Diagnosis, Therapy and Aftercare According to the Vojta Principle*. German Federal Ministry of Education and Research (BMBF), 12/2016 – 11/2019.

[9] Z. Kalal, K. Mikolajczyk, and J. Matas. Tracking-learning-detection. *IEEE Transactions on Pattern Analysis and Machine Intelligence*, 34(7):1409–1422, july 2012.

[10] L. Köping, K. Shirahama, and M. Grzegorzek. A General Framework for Sensor-based Human Activity Recognition. *Computers in Biology and Medicine*, 2017 (accepted for publication).

[11] P. Łagodzinski, K. Shirahama, and M. Grzegorzek. Codebook-based Electrooculography Data Analysis Towards Cognitive Activity Recognition. *Computers in Biology and Medicine*, 2017 (accepted for publication).

[12] Project. *My-AHA: My Active and Healthy Ageing*. Website: www.activeageing.unito.it, European Commission (Horizon 2020), 01/2016 – 12/2019.

[13] Project. *Cognitive Village: Adaptively Learning Technical Support System for Elderly*. Website: www.cognitive-village.de, German Federal Ministry of Education and Research (BMBF), 09/2015 – 08/2018.

[14] O. Russakovsky, J. Deng, H. Su, J. Krause, S. Satheesh, S. Ma, Z. Huang, A. Karpathy, A. Khosla, M. Bernstein, A. C. Berg, and F.-F. Li. ImageNet large scale visual recognition challenge. *International Journal of Computer Vision*, 115(3):211–252, December 2015.

[15] K. Shirahama and M. Grzegorzek. Emotion Recognition Based on Physiological Sensor Data Using Codebook Approach. In E. Pietka, P. Badura, J. Kawa, and W. Wieclawek, editors, *5th International Conference on Information Technologies in Biomedicine (ITIB 2016)*, pages 27–39, Kamien Slaski, Poland, June 2016. Springer.

[16] K. Shirahama and M. Grzegorzek. Towards Large-Scale Multimedia Retrieval Enriched by Knowledge about Human Interpretation - Retrospective Survey. *Multimedia Tools and Applications*, 75(1):297–331, January 2016.

[17] K. Shirahama, L. Köping, and M. Grzegorzek. Codebook Approach for Sensor-based Human Activity Recognition. In *ACM International Joint Conference on Pervasive and Ubiquitous Computing*, pages 197–200, Heidelberg, Germany, September 2016. ACM.

[18] A.W.M. Smeulders, M. Worring, S. Santini, A. Gupta, and R. Jain. Content-based image retrieval at the end of the early years. *IEEE Transactions on Pattern Analysis and Machine Intelligence*, 22(12):1349–1380, December 2000.

[19] N. Srivastava, E. Mansimov, and R. Salakhutdinov. Unsupervised learning of video representations using lstms. In *Proceedings of the 32Nd International Conference on International Conference on Machine Learning (ICML 2015)*, pages 843–852. JMLR.org, July 2015.

[20] S. Staab, A. Scherp, R. Arndt, R. Troncy, M. Grzegorzek, C. Saathoff, S. Schenk, and L. Hardman. Semantic Multimedia. In C. Baroglio, P. A. Bonatti, J. Maluszynski, M. Marchiori, A. Polleres, and S. Schaffert, editors, *Reasoning Web*, pages 125–170, San Servolo, Island, September 2008. Springer LNCS 5224.

[21] R. Tadeusiewicz. Intelligent web mining for semantically adequate images. In *Proceedings of the Fifth Atlantic Web Intelligence Conference (AWIC 2007)*, pages 3–10, Berlin, Heidelberg, June 2007. Springer Berlin Heidelberg.

[22] D. Tran, L. Bourdev, R. Fergus, L. Torresani, and M. Paluri. Learning spatiotemporal features with 3d convolutional networks. In *Proceedings of the 2015 IEEE International Conference on Computer Vision (ICCV 2015)*, pages 4489–4497, Washington, DC, USA, December 2015. IEEE Computer Society.

List of Figures

List of Tables